SO-BIA-738

UNAUTHORIZED METHODS

Transforming
Teaching
Series

Series Editor: James W. Fraser,
        Director of the Center for Innovation in
        Urban Education Northeastern University

Routledge's *Transforming Teaching* Series represents a commitment to support teachers in the practice of their profession. Each volume in this series will link critical educational theory to very specific examples of successful classroom practice and detailed descriptions of the kinds of curricular materials which are most useful in implementing theory in practice. Each volume will explore the political barriers and intellectual issues involved in implementing new forms of practice. While each volume and each editor will take a different approach, all of the volumes will be united in addressing primarily the concerns of teachers—and students in teacher education programs—and in combining the voices of thoughtful theorists and currently practicing classroom teachers.

Also published in the series:
Assessment for Equity and Inclusion: Embracing All Our Children
A. Lin Goodwin, editor

Teaching African American Literature: Theory and Practice
Marianna White Davis, Maryemma Graham, and Sharon Pineault-Burke, editors

Real Learning, Real Work: School-to-Work as High School Reform
Adria Steinberg

UNAUTHORIZED METHODS:
STRATEGIES FOR CRITICAL TEACHING

Joe L. Kincheloe and Shirley R. Steinberg,
Editors

Routledge

New York
London

Published in 1998 by

Routledge
29 West 35th Street
New York, NY 10001

Published in Great Britain in 1998 by

Routledge
11 New Fetter Lane
London EC4P 4EE

Copyright © 1998 by Routledge

Printed in the United States of America
Design: Debora Hilu

All rights reserved. No part of this book may be reprinted or reproduced or utilized in any form or by any electronic, mechanical, or other means, now known or hereafter invented, including photocopying and recording, or in any information storage or retrieval system without permission in writing from the publishers.

Library of Congress Cataloging-in-Publication Data
Unauthorized methods : strategies for critical teaching / editors. Joe
L. Kincheloe and Shirley R. Steinberg.
      p.   cm. — (Transforming teaching)
   Includes index.
   ISBN 0-415-91841-3 (hardcover). — ISBN 0-415-91842-1 (pbk.)
   1. Critical pedagogy. I. Kincheloe, Joe L.   II. Steinberg,
Shirley R., 1952–   . III. Series.
   LC196.U53 1998
   370.11'5—dc21   97-40803
                                                                    CIP

*Dedication to Nita Freire
with love and thanks for ten beloved years,
looking towards the future.*

*Dedicación a Nita Freire
con amor y agradecimiento por los dies años muy queridos,
que se extienden en el futuro.*

*Dedicação a Nita Freire
com amor e agradecimento pelos dez anos muito queridos,
que se prolongan no futuro.*

CONTENTS

CONTENTS

SERIES EDITOR'S FOREWORD
James W. Fraser

In *Unauthorized Methods: Strategies for Critical Teaching*, Joe L. Kincheloe and Shirley R. Steinberg have brought together a series of materials which make one simple point: that democracy, empowerment, and academic rigor can be realities in the curriculum of today's schools, but only if we make a fundamental shift in our ways of viewing both our students and the curriculum.

To some extent this volume provides teachers of the 1990s ways of making real what turn of the twentieth-century progressive educators called a "student-centered pedagogy." By moving the focus of energy from "covering the curriculum" or "raising the test scores" to the far more important issues of engaging the students' curiosity and enlisting them as cocreators of the knowledge that will be included in the school, the authors in this volume have provided the basis for a similar philosophy for the twenty-first century. By nurturing the imagination of their students and then inviting them to become fellow learners with the teachers, the authors of this volume move from a view of teaching that looks at discrete fragments of information that a student must master in order to make learning an important and lifelong process.

At the same time, these authors also transcend the limitations of what was "student-centered pedagogy," for they are talking about more than learning. They are ultimately talking about social change. As Joe Kincheloe and Shirley Steinberg note in their opening chapter, "When a critical teacher who doesn't share the culture, language, race or socioeconomic backgrounds of students enters the classroom, he or she becomes not an information provider but an explorer who works with students to create mutually understood texts." These new texts are much more than the content of the curriculum. Ultimately the texts Kincheloe and Steinberg and their collaborators are talking about are the models of new knowledge and a new society which may yet be multicultural and democratic and freedom loving. No wonder such pedagogies are "unauthorized methods." They challenge the status quo to its very foundations. And in doing this they offer the beginnings of a future which is better for all citizens.

I am grateful to each of the authors included in this volume for taking on the task of making these "unauthorized methods" so clear and so available to us. By engaging topics which cover the range of the curriculum of the schools—by including special education, bilingual education, literature and the arts, and also science and mathematics, and the use of technology—this volume casts its net widely and opens all parts of the curriculum to the possibility of being transformative. In doing this, these authors also add an important volume to Routledge's *Transforming Teaching* Series.

The *Transforming Teaching* Series is committed to including the voices of teachers, scholars, and others in the service of a rich, equitable, and inclusive schooling for all students. Rigorous theory must always be informed by practice, and indeed it is in the dialogue of theory and practice that both are refined. We will doom ourselves to anti-intellectual mediocrity if we fail to ask the most rigorous and critical theoretical questions about both current practices and the current society, and the kind of schooling which is ultimately needed for the development of an inclusive, multicultural democracy. But we will not build that new society if teachers do not have the practical tools in hand to do their work. Volumes like *Unauthorized Methods: Strategies for Critical Teaching* make an important contribution to meeting this need.

James W. Fraser
Transforming Teaching Series Editor
Director, Center for Innovation in Urban
Education, Northeastern University

I

LESSON PLANS FROM THE OUTER LIMITS:
Unauthorized Methods
Joe L. Kincheloe and Shirley R. Steinberg

Teachers have a difficult job. Faced with pressures from a variety of angles, teachers must struggle to maintain their motivation and their self-esteem. The fact that so many do is a miracle of sorts, testimony to their dedication and to their drive. We consider such dedicated and adept teachers heroic figures and do everything possible to show our appreciation and our respect for them when they teach our children or when they appear in our graduate classes. Having said this, however we, like generations of analysts before us, believe that teachers suffer because of problems in their professional training not only at colleges of education but at colleges of liberal arts and sciences as well. When teachers emerge from higher education—through no fault of their own—they are frequently unprepared to teach at a level commensurate with their potential. Colleges of liberal arts and sciences too often teach broad survey courses that encourage memorization of isolated facts, not systematic analysis of the field.

Such systematic analysis might involve studies of the genesis of the field, of the field as a discourse with examination of the tacit rules that shape it and determine its future, of the various schools of thought within the field and the etymologies of their disagreements, and of the ways that knowledge has been produced in the field including the strengths and weaknesses of research strategies. These explorations constitute only a few of the ways potential teachers might transcend the memorization ritual; throughout this book we will present many more. In our effort to get beyond traditional methods of teaching and educating teachers, we will present lesson "plans" that refuse to discount the intelligence of teachers. We assume that teachers should be scholars, that they should possess the freedom to make their own plans and that they should honor the responsibility to be knowledge producers who are capable of comfortably performing both secondary and primary research. Indeed, we call for a new rigor in teacher education and in elementary and secondary education. This book serves as a set of introductory, nontraditional ideas on how to provide teachers with ways of thinking, researching, and instructing that empower them to implement this new rigor.

While *Unauthorized Methods: Strategies for Critical Teaching* will provide teaching methods and lesson plans, please note that throughout our careers as teachers we have been uncomfortable with these terms. Often methods and lesson plans have implied specific blueprints for teachers that give a step-by-step checklist of what to do and how to do it. Many methods and lesson plan books delineate a particular path, a "right way" for teachers who are assumed to have little research ability or subject matter knowledge. Not only does such material insult teachers by "dumbing down" expectations (or as Donaldo Macedo would call it, "stupidification"), but they rarely take the effects of the social, economic, and political context into account. The concepts of oppression and power inequalities are missing, as racism, gender bias, and class bias become forbidden topics. Yet the new rigorous paradigm of teaching and teacher education that we imagine foregrounds the *interaction* among context, power, method, and subject matter. This vision is practical, achievable, and desirable in a democratic society. We will first discuss impediments to its achievement and then imagine the implications of this vision. Our vision is indeed unauthorized in its notions of critical teaching without prescribed, teacher-proof methods.

PARADIGMATIC RUMBLING

Major changes have occurred in academia over the last two decades. New ways of seeing and making sense of reality have emerged that challenge comfortable academic protocols, that set up the possibility of new ways of producing knowledge. We have written extensively about these changes elsewhere and will not recite the philosophical/theoretical aspects of them here (for such information see Kincheloe 1991, 1993, 1995; Kincheloe and Steinberg 1993, 1997). Succinctly put, a paradigmatic change of major proportions has taken place. A paradigm is a constellation of concepts, values, and techniques used by a scientific community or by a dominant culture to make sense of themselves and their world. As frameworks of understanding, paradigms guide the ways knowledge is produced. Until Thomas Kuhn described his notion of paradigmatic change in 1962, most scholars believed that scientific knowledge accumulated gradually

2

becoming more and more sophisticated and accurate. Kuhn and others undermined this view, maintaining that major conceptual change never comes as a result of a steady and orderly series of discoveries; on the contrary, conceptual change is abrupt, disconcerting, and traumatic. Einstein's early twentieth-century challenge to the dominant paradigm in physics exemplifies traumatic paradigmatic change. The universality of Newtonian physics collapsed as theories of relativity and quantum mechanics portrayed a far more complex physical universe. The world could never again be viewed in the same way.

Traditional methods of understanding the world no longer seem appropriate to many of us. The culture of modernist positivism that has tacitly shaped teaching and teacher education throughout most of the twentieth century no longer answers the compelling questions of our time. When we use the term *modernism* we are referring to the era of Western history beginning with the rise of science in the seventeenth and eighteenth centuries. Unable to cure the Black Plague that killed one-forth of Europe's population in the fourteenth century, Europeans sought new ways of making sense of the world. This impulse would lay the foundation of Western modernism and would express itself in the scientific method of René Descartes, Isaac Newton, and Francis Bacon. This scientific mode of reasoning, often termed *reductionism*, asserted that all aspects of complex phenomena can best be appreciated by reducing them to their constituent parts and then piecing these elements together according to causal laws (Mahoney and Lyddon 1988). A key aspect of modernist science has asserted that the same methods used to study the physical world should be used to study the social, psychological, and educational world. Serious problems emerge from such an assertion, as modernist researchers assume that students (like quartz crystals) are *objects* that will remain constant. Therefore, long-term generalizations can be made about children that disregard the ever-changing context in which they operate.

The label *positivism* was popularized by Auguste Comte, the nineteenth-century French philosopher, who argued that human thought had evolved through three stages: the theological stage (where truth was based on God's revelation); the metaphysical stage (where truth was based on abstract reasoning and argument); and the positivistic stage (where truth was based on scientifically produced knowledge). Comte sought to discredit the legitimacy of nonscientific thinking that did not take sense knowledge (knowledge obtained through the senses—empirical) into account (Kneller 1984; Smith 1983). He saw no difference between the ways knowledge should be produced in the

3

physical sciences and in the human sciences. From Comte's perspective we should study sociology the same way we study biology. Society, he argued, is nothing more than a body of neutral facts governed by immutable laws. Like biology, society is governed by natural laws. Accordingly, social actions would proceed with law-like predictability (Held 1980). In this context, education is also governed by unchanging laws; the role of the educator is to uncover them and then to act in accordance with them. For example, educational laws would include pronouncements on how students learn and how students should be taught. To the positivist educator there is only one *correct* way to teach and one *correct* body of subject matter. The context in which education takes place is irrelevant and the role of the teacher involves merely passing the correct subject matter to students using the correct pedagogical method.

The editors and authors of this book are united in their attempt to define counter-positivist instruction. Our lesson plans and methods are theoretically grounded on five differences from the old "authorized" paradigm:

1) Modernist positivism focuses on the parts (test scores, seating arrangements, different administrative strategies) in order to eventually understand the whole. *In the new paradigm this relationship is reversed*—the parts can only be understood in the context of the whole (the need to focus on our larger purposes as we learn methods of teaching);

2) Modernist positivism focuses on the identification of never-changing structures (knowledge as timeless truth, social laws, and a fixed core curriculum). *The new paradigm sees every structure as dynamic, constantly interacting with changing processes* (curriculum not as a fixed course of study but as a context-specific process changing with the evolving needs of society and individuals—the walk itself is just as important as the destination);

3) Modernist positivism claims that it produces an objective science untainted by human values (the curriculum is value-free, disinterested, merely the delineation of knowledge we have discovered). *The new paradigm makes no claim for objectivity*, as it celebrates human ways of knowing that are logical but also intuitive, emotional, and empathetic. Such an approach to knowledge production (epistemology) is often referred to as constructivism in that the world is "constructed" or brought forth in the process of knowing (learning becomes not as much an act of memorizing previously discovered information but an act of creating knowledge, of ordering our own experiences);

4) Modernist postivitism uses the architectural metaphor of a building to talk about knowledge—scientific information is characterized as the basic building block of matter (positivist science educators speak of DNA as the foundation that determines the structure of life, not just one of many aspects of living systems). *The new paradigm uses the concept of a network where all aspects are interconnected* (the science curriculum is never taught in isolation but in relation to networks of philosophical, political, economic, and theological knowledge—it is merely one part that influences and is influenced by the larger network of the universe);

5) Modernist positivism regards what it produces as the truth (the theory of evolution is true, the law of supply and demand in economics is true). *In the new paradigm no "fact" exists in a vacuum.* The characteristics of one entity are related to the characteristics of other entities. Because we can never understand and appreciate all of the possible relationships between parts, we never uncover the whole story. Thus, we offer only approximate explanations (the examples of teaching we offer in this book are not *truths* about teaching—they may indeed work for you in some situations, but in other contexts they may not work at all).

The new paradigm does not appeal to some people because of its complexity, its refusal to offer reductionistic answers to life's complex questions. The old paradigm is comforting to many because of its faith in traditional methods of science to explain the nature of the world and the "truth" about teaching. In the old paradigm meaning was lost as information was turned into factoids, bits and pieces of data removed from context. We learned to think in fragments removed from the context that gives our thoughts meaning through their connection to the larger good. School has little to do with such connections—rarely do we talk about human problems and the interconnectedness between them. We speak, for example, of adolescent suicide as a growing problem that needs to be addressed and we hold workshops to prepare teachers to identify those students who fit the "profile" of potential suicide victims. But that's where the process stops. Rarely do we connect the growth of adolescent suicide to the larger context of late-twentieth-century life with its economic problems and its loss of meaning. Viewed within this larger context, youth suicide can be understood at a new level of sophistication. Immediately the decontextualized inadequacy of the teacher workshops confronts us. Once we begin to contextualize youth suicide our ability to develop viable responses to it improves dramatically. In the case of suicide or any other problem, the more ways we can contextualize the matter, the greater our understanding of it and the more likely we are to solve it.

We are vitally concerned with teachers and students being able to produce knowledge. Indeed, one of the key differences between education in the old paradigm and in the new paradigm is that the old model emphasizes the *discovery* of knowledge while the new one emphasizes the *invention* of knowledge. Thus, teachers are scholars who both contextualize and produce knowledge, all the while sharing their abilities with students. Thus, the classroom takes on the appearance of a "think tank," an institution in which important knowledge is produced that has the value outside of the classroom. In modern positivism, teachers were instructed to say: "Give me the truth and I will pass it along to students in the most efficient manner possible." In the new paradigm, teachers are encouraged to support themselves, to assert their freedom from all-knowing experts, to operate in an unauthorized manner. Such teachers often say: "Please support me as my students and I explore the world of mathematic, sociology, or whatever." Teachers in the new paradigm refuse to accept without question the validity of the Western canon (the great books and ideas that have been taught in the traditional Western curriculum) as they seek knowledge from other cultures and traditions. Indeed, they are not content to operate within the framework that is taken for granted—they seek to recontextualize questions that have been traditionally asked about schooling and knowledge production in general. While they respect earlier insight and are reverential in respect to the genius of past eras, such educators display their veneration by continuing to question the work of their intellectual ancestors. Your own personal context and understanding may lead you to revise and to expand many of the ideas presented in this book.

Teachers in the new paradigm seek new ways of conceptualizing the world. Thus, in the spirit of Brazilian educator Paulo Freire, they problematize the information that confronts them. Freire and other educators (including Jo Anne Pagano, Deborah Britzman, Donaldo Macedo, Michael Apple, Philip Wexler, Joyce King, Gaile Canella, Ivor Goodson, Henry Giroux, Peter McLaren, William Pinar, and Tomas da Silva) have argued that any paradigm shift be viewed in a critical or socially transformative manner. Such a position maintains that knowledge always reflects larger power relationships in society. This means that those with social, economic, and political clout will have more say in what the schools consider official, validated knowledge than those without clout. Critical teachers understand this tendency and account for it in the way they work to problematize classroom information. Problematization in this critical new paradigm would, of course, involve asking questions such as where did the knowledge come from or who benefits as the result of the canonization of this knowledge. The ability to recognize these power-related dynamics lays the foundation for what Paulo Freire has called "critical consciousness." Such a way of seeing moves individuals to reconceptualize their world in a manner that leads to transformative action, to social change.

Teachers who embrace these critical goals help students develop an awareness of themselves as social agents. This goal requires that teachers and students contextualize what happens in the classroom in relation to power and social justice issues as well as in relation to real lived experience. Thus, when students read a section of a science textbook that touts the virtues of nuclear power without references to environmental questions or allusions to Three Mile Island or Chernobyl, critical teachers insist that power questions be asked. Who benefits if we buy into such a description of nuclear power or who loses? These are central questions in such a context. A key question of this book is: *How do we construct contexts for critical growth in our classrooms?* We will present activities and methodologies that teachers have used to encourage student reflection of the cultural values that shape personal views of the world and one's place in it. Understanding the ways our consciousness is constructed is a fascinating exploration that not only provides insight into who we are but also into how the world works. Critical teachers in the new paradigm are enthralled by such questions.

As Teachers, We Have a Responsibility to Become Scholars and Self-directed Agents

Teachers becoming excellent scholars will certainly not solve every problem in education, but we believe such a vision would constitute a damn good start in long-term educational reform. As we apologize for our glibness, we understand the structural problems that undermine education—not the least of which is an unequal distribution of wealth that robs the poor and marginalized of an equal opportunity to educational resources. Indeed our call for scholarly teachers in a more complex new paradigm is always accompanied by the belief that critical scholarly insight will render teachers better prepared to lead the struggle for political and economic democracy and social and educational justice. In the old paradigm elementary and secondary teachers were not even considered members of the traditional scholarly culture of higher education. Too many teachers have worked in the culture of the time clock, anti-intellectualism, ideological naivete, limited interpretive practice, and minimal analysis of the assumptions of the professional world. The logic of such working conditions emphasizes something quite unlike interpretive thinking. There is a tendency to surrender to the given, to view existing institutional arrangements, *authorized* arrangements, as objective realities. Without the catalyst of interpretation, and of an intellectually active analytical community, pronouncements tend to speak at a literal level—they speak "for themselves." Without an analytical view of the everyday and of institutional requirements and activities, thought is fragmented and conceptual synthesis is blocked. Indeed, our relationship to knowledge is severed. As a result, our role as participants in social and institutional life is unexamined and our power to anticipate the consequences of social actions is devoured (Zeuli and Bachmann 1986; Greene 1988; Britzman 1991).

The implicit message of older paradigmatic teacher education, the positivistic research that often grounds it, and the state and provincial reform movements that share the same epistemological assumptions is that teachers must do what they are told, what they are authorized to do, and that they must be careful about thinking for themselves. Such caution eventually turns into apathy as teachers lose interest in the creative aspects of pedagogy that originally attracted them to the profession. Teacher thinking is profoundly affected by the top-down flow, the teacher-proof curriculums that assume practitioner incompetence. As they are rewarded in teacher training for their passive acceptance of expert-generated knowledge, prospective teachers gain little experience in contextually grounded interpretive thinking about the purpose of teaching in a democratic society. Management science is geared to the control of human beings in line with visions of institutional efficiency and standardization. Teacher education often contributes to such management orientations by conveying the belief that the laws of social and educational life are well known and devoid of ambiguity (Glickman 1985; Baldwin 1987; Popkewitz 1981).

In this context consider Madeline Hunter's popular teaching/supervision model (an authorized model) used in thousands of teaching education programs and school districts. Hunter's model assumes a predetermined, prescribed version of teaching based on "seven essential steps." Teachers guided by Hunter follow these specific (and measurable) steps in every lesson regardless of the subject matter. Supervisor evaluation is simplified, standardized, and streamlined as administrators come to define good teaching as that which conforms to Hunter's model. Accountability is ensured, Hunter and the technicists argue, as teachers come to understand what is expected of them so they can perform appropriately.

The range of teaching behaviors that may be considered appropriate is narrowed under Hunter's model. Supervisors and teacher educators admit that innovative lessons that fail to follow the model must be evaluated as unsatisfactory. Thus, rewards for teaching are not based on reasoned notions of competence and creativity but on adherence to format, or, teacher compliance. Teacher education becomes a conformity mill, an adjustment procedure in which novices are fine-tuned to the Hunter channel. Like workers in Frederick W. Taylor's scientifically managed factories of efficiency, the technicist system a la Hunter strips teachers of their role in the conceptualization of the teaching act. Teachers become executors of managerial plans. The moral and ethical dimensions, not to mention the cognitive aspects of the teaching act, are submerged in a pool of standardization and conventionalism (Garman and Hazi 1988). Practitioners in this context are operating only with *authorized* teaching methods.

When teaching methods are taught in old paradigm professional teacher education, they are rarely conceived in the context of high-order scholarly demands on the teacher. Yet, we maintain that teachers must understand educational psychology and cognitive theory in paradigmatic context. Cognition studied in such a rigorous manner would provide educators with insights into the type of scholarly/cognitive abilities that are possible and how they can teach themselves and their students to operate at a higher cognitive level. In the old paradigm of teacher education, however, modernist cognitive theories are typically presented one after another without any attempt to critically assess or relate them to actual classroom practice. Such information is presented at a concrete cognitive level, as students commit to memory what B. F. Skinner, Kurt Lewin, S. Freud, or J. Piaget said. Because of a particular emotional attachment, particular students latch on to certain cognitive theories. Many theories are useless and have little to do with the everyday life of teachers. Consistent with the technicist assumptions about neutrality and objectivity, many education professors believe that students should learn a little about every major cognitive theory so they can make their own choices. Such an approach is in many ways an abrogation of pedagogical responsibility, as it ignores each theory's significance, its explanatory power, its epistemological dimensions, and its political implications. If teachers were empowered to understand the relationships between Piagetian constructivism and, say, Skinnerian behaviorism from pedagogical, epistemological, and political perspectives, they would not allow the simpleminded imposition of lesson plan *formats*, behavioral objective writing, or bulletin board making to dominate their pre-service and in-service teacher education (Kamii 1981).

Most teachers agree with the proposition that it is important to induce students to think critically but few are sure how such a goal should be achieved. It seems obvious—but it is commonly overlooked in the old paradigm—that teachers must learn to operate in a cognitively sophisticated scholarly way before they can teach students to do so. This simple observation forms the foundation for much of our work as educational scholars. We have attempted to develop a specific description of what such cognitively sophisticated scholarly activity entails. Labeling our description post-formal thinking (see Kincheloe and Steinberg 1993; Kincheloe 1995), we have delineated a cognitive mode that is post-Piagetian and post-Vygotskian. Drawing upon but moving beyond these important cognitive theorists, post-formalism engages a form of self-reflection and cognitive self-monitoring. It transcends Piagetian formalism (his highest level of human thought) via the questioning of his untroubled acceptance of Cartesian-Newtonian logic. It transcends Vygotskian socio-cognition by specifying the social theory that helps shape cognition—a specification Vygotsky never had time to articulate before his early death. Drawing upon the anti-positivist tradition of philosophy from Giambattista Vico in the early 1700s, to Soren Kierkegaard in the first half of the 1800s, to John Dewey in the early twentieth century, to more recent phenomenology, critical theory, feminist theory, and post-structuralism, post-formal thinking attempts to map new cognitive territories for both teachers and students.

The cognitive demands of teaching are unique. They differ from the technical, scientific ways of knowing traditionally associated with professional expertise. Post-formal teacher thinking draws upon Donald Schon's (1983) notion that professional expertise is an uncertain enterprise as it confronts constantly changing, unique, and unstable conditions. Teachers never see the same classroom twice, as teaching conditions change from day to day. The students who reacted positively to a set of pedagogical strategies yesterday, respond differently today (despite William Bennett's assurances of "what works"). Schon's practitioners relinquish the certainty that attends to professional expertise conceived as the repetitive administration of techniques to similar types of problems. In the post-formal reconceptualization of practitioner thinking, the ability to develop research strategies that explore the genesis and efficacy of comfortable assumptions and implicit objectives is extremely important. In education, post-formal teachers become teachers-as-researchers who question the nature of their own thinking as they attempt to teach higher order thinking to their students. What are the limits of human ways of knowing? Where do we begin conceptualizing post-formal modes of teacher thinking that lead to a metaperspective, to empowerment? Drawing intellectual sustenance from its familiarity with paradigmatic dynamics and social theoretical challenges to traditional psychological assumptions, post-formal teacher thinking reconceptualizes the highest cognitive expressions of Piaget, Vygotsky, William Perry, and other psychological theorists.

TRANSCENDING FRAGMENTATION

Post-formal thinking provides the concrete grounding necessary for teacher self-direction, teacher empowerment. If teachers are to employ unauthorized methods to create their own knowledge, they must be able to disengage themselves from the tyranny of unequal power relations and dominant discursive practices. It is by "getting smart" (thanks to Patti Lather) that teachers and students will exert more conscious control over their everyday lives. Hyperrational, positivist thinking emerging from modernism's one-truth epistemology produces not only a congregation of nervous right-answer givers and timid rule followers, but a rather mediocre level of education unrelated to any ethical effort to use constructively our ability to reason. The old paradigmatic efforts to cultivate higher order or critical thinking among teachers too often involved removing prospective practitioners from their lived worlds in order to control the variables of the situation. As a result, thinking was sequestered in artificial laboratory settings where passion and authentic feelings of love, hate, fear, and commitment were scientifically removed. Cartesian-Newtonian models of the rational process are always culturally neutral, always removed from the body and its passions. These modernist models assume that a practitioner can be removed from his or her embeddedness in a physical context without affecting cognition (Hultgren 1987; Bobbit 1987; Bowers and Flinders 1990).

But this separation of context from cognition is exactly what's wrong with teacher education. Whether we are teaching high school math, elementary language arts, or teacher education, the approach is the same: break down the information to be learned into discrete parts that can be easily memorized. Thus cognitive theories, grammatical rules, vocabulary, math computation skills, the "causes" of the Civil

11

War can all be "learned" in this way. As long as the curriculum is conceived in a technical way with prespecified facts to be learned, with improvement of standardized tests the goal of instruction, with little concern granted to connecting school and life, with no debate over the role of learning in a democratic society, then maybe science has proven that we know how to teach (Jones and Cooper 1987).

Take the way science has "authorized" us to teach reading. Mastery learning programs break reading skills into subskills such as beginning consonant sounds, vowel sounds, ending consonant sounds, consonant blends, and vowel diagrams. Teachers learn to teach these in a structured, sequenced manner until students pass the mastery test on each subskill. Again, the common sense, linear methodology seems to satisfy everyone's demands. Upon deeper examination, however, problems begin to materialize—even on the superficial level on which such programs are assessed. Researchers have found that in the first few years of the program, reading skill scores among early elementary students increased. But, by the time the children were in the sixth grade, reading levels decreased, and students were not reading. Although students were scoring high on achievement tests, the examinations only measured what early grade teachers had taught: the subskills. Reading or language arts classes had revolved mainly around worksheets or dittos on the subskills. Very little actual reading was taking place. Students had learned the fragmented curriculum well. They had indeed learned the isolated subskills and had reflected that knowledge on the standardized tests. Even so, they were not reading for knowledge, enjoyment, or meaning—they were not even reading. The reading program had committed a fatal modernist error: It had assumed that the parts add up to the whole. As with most human endeavors the whole was far greater than the parts (Fosnot 1988; Shannon 1989).

The above case exemplifies what happens when knowledge is fragmented, separated from its context—when teaching methods are isolated from subject matter. Getting beyond traditional, authorized forms of teacher education involves uniting pedagogical method with a detailed knowledge of subject matter. The way we approach a body of knowledge (especially knowledge we have created), determines what is important about it, decide how it relates to other subject matter, massage it for an engagement with a target group, and ascertain the ways it affects our lives and the lives of others are all part of what are called teaching methods. Thus, teaching methods in the new paradigm are never considered outside the context of an engagement with a body of knowledge. Teaching is more than the mere application of a set of prearranged activities to a set of generic, standardized students. Methods classes that attempt to provide teachers with a set of pre-arranged behaviors assume a positivistic universe where learning outcomes are measurable and predictable. Authentic, spontaneous interaction between students and teachers in this worldview is deemed uncomfortable and disconcerting in its improvisational uncertainty. From the post-formal, new paradigmatic perspective the well-prepared teacher is not one who enters the classroom with a fixed set of lesson plans but a scholar with a thorough knowledge of subject, an understanding of knowledge production, the ability to produce knowledge, an appreciation of social context, a cognizance of what is happening in the world, insight into the lives of her students, and a sophisticated appreciation of critical educational goals and purposes.

The paradigm shift is still in its early stages—as a society we are extremely confused about what it means. Arguing for a move to a new paradigm, we do not call for a complete break from that which has preceded us. Indeed, the new paradigm takes strength from a combination of ancient, new, and even modernist ideas. Ancient wisdom of indigenous people from around the world, the great contributions of modernist science in gaining new insights into the world, modernist political notions of justice, freedom, and liberty, and, of course, the new insights emerging from our understanding of the interconnectedness of all "living" and "non-living" things shape our eclectic view of the new paradigm. We are interested in synthesizing this diversity of ideas and insights in a way that helps students gain a multifaced view of the world and themselves. Reuniting context, content, and methods, we attempt to make school an integral part of life—not a superfluous hoop that holds little intrinsic meaning for students. Without this connection to the lived world of students and dedication to meaning making, schooling becomes what Paulo Freire so aptly described as a banking process, where data deposits are made into the inactive mental vaults of students' brains. When this occurs dispirited teachers face a corps of passive, uninterested students and the potential for a meaningful, exciting learning experience quickly fades away.

REINVENTING LESSON PLANS AND TEACHING METHODS FOR A NEW WORLD

In modernist positivism, teachers are often disempowered in their role as information deliverers, servants of knowledge and curricula produced elsewhere. In the new paradigm we advocate that classroom teachers take charge of developing courses of study emerging from their conceptions of both what is truly important and useful in the lives of the particular students they are teaching. We don't want system guidelines to cease to exist or for teachers to ignore subject delineations of governmental departments of education. We do want teachers to take more responsibility for interpreting how such guidelines fit into their classroom contexts. Such teacher interpretation may take shape around what a practitioner decides not to cover in his or her classroom. Maybe a detailed examination of the novels of James Joyce with analysis of his life, writing style, literary innovations, and literary criticism of his work might provide students more insight into the purpose and benefits of literary studies than a cursory, fragmented, fact-oriented survey of twentieth-century novelists. Higher orders of cognitive activity would replace modernist fact gathering, expanding, as we put it, the cognitive envelope. In no way are we making the argument that subject matter doesn't count. Content is extremely significant, so important that it demands to be studied in sufficient detail to allow us to make meaning around it. We need to understand the conditions of its production and validation, who benefits from it and who does not, and how it relates to knowledge and information. Such conceptual understanding cannot be learned in a superficial survey of a discipline's subject matter.

Empowered teachers work together to thwart supervisors' efforts to evaluate them on the basis of how much content they cover during the school year. Such expectations reflect modernist positivism's obsession with quantification and measurability, as supervisors speak of how the teacher covered only sixty percent of the required subject matter. Few questions are asked, of course, about how students made use of the data or even how long they remembered it. Advocates of less but deeper and more analytical coverage of content understand that force-feeding students massive amounts of data dulls their interest in a subject and their appreciation of the meaning of the material. Students' relationship to the survey curriculum that focuses on quantity of coverage is similar to contestant preparation for an appearance on *Jeopardy*. The breadth but no depth form of learning that pays dividends on *Jeopardy* can be put to use only in a few other life circumstances—maybe in a game of *Trivial Pursuit* or in an attempt to impress prospective in-laws. As we learn to make meaning, to search for connections between subject matter and student-produced knowledge, and to relate students' worlds to the lived reality of schools, our methods of teaching and curriculum making begin to change.

Such a change, as we argued previously, demands a reconceptualization of the modernist methods courses with their emphasis on providing teachers with methods of information delivery. Such an orientation renders teachers deskilled paraprofessionals who are the executors of some expert's lesson plans, not empowered conceptualizers of their own professional practices. In methods classes grounded on these assumptions teachers often come to internalize their reduced role. They begin to demand teacher education classes and crudely practical in-service programs. Such victimized teachers are uncomfortable with our vision of teachers as scholars, as they seek out teacher-proof materials that can be plugged into their classes on Monday morning. Tragically, these teachers adopt a deskilled ethic that glorifies paint-by-numbers education and denigrates and even ridicules those who seek to understand teaching methods in relation to the context of students' lives, the discourses of academic subjects, social/economic justice, and educational purpose. A few months after taking an education course with Joe Kincheloe that emphasized the limitations of modernist forms of teacher training with their inculcation of technical methods of skill delivery, a group of his education students ran into his office to describe a final exam given in a technical audio-visual education class. They were excited to describe the way the exam served as an example of (in their words) "the ultimate technocratic form of evaluation." Fragmenting all aspects of the teaching act, the test required students to list the five steps involved in making a bulletin board. All five had to be in correct order or they would all be marked incorrect. One of the students had missed all five steps because he forgot the first step: "Get an idea." The absurdity of the exam struck us all as very funny, reminding us of a George Carlin comedy sketch. We imagined a future teacher after making a bulletin board proclaiming in frustration: "Damn, I forgot to get an idea!"

Donaldo Macedo picks up on the pedagogical implications of this story, arguing that a critical pedagogy is always an anti-method pedagogy. It is anti-method in the sense that critical teacher education provides no specific road to the way a critical educator must teach or a student must learn—there are not five correct ways to construct a bulletin board. Drawing upon the poetry of Antonio Machado, Macedo understands that critical teachers will make their road as they walk (Macedo 1994). Macedo doesn't mean that we simply throw young teachers into classrooms with no experiences with teaching methods. His point here is that we don't present simplistic notions of the "correct way to teach." Prospective teachers need examples of teaching methods as we provide in this book—methods that are described in the context of all the dynamics that make the lessons valuable. And we invite our readers to change these ideas, take from them, and add to them—we hope the "methods" discussed in this book will be elastic and stretch and shrink to each person's needs and tastes. Indeed, in this context, we found the title of this book, *Unauthorized Methods*, creating a resource that provides examples of lessons for analysis, not recipes.

The methods courses we envision necessitate a reconceptualization of teacher knowledge, that is, what teachers need to know to perform their jobs successfully. Teachers develop what many have called "practitioner knowledge," in a variety of ways, including experience. This practitioner knowledge alerts teachers to the fact that the classroom is a complex and chaotic place with significant and peripheral variables. Such an understanding alerts teachers to the innate problems with modernist attempts to produce empirical generalizations about the best way to teach. Even though they intuitively understand the limitations of these empirical generalizations, teachers are unable to escape the shadow of their scientific power. In their seemingly perpetual vulnerability to the vicissitudes of public opinion, teachers are unable to prove their competence through their practitioner knowledge. Because it has not been scientifically validated, it holds no legitimacy in the court of public opinion. Thus, state and provincial legislatures demand scientific validation of teacher practice. As a result, teachers are forced to abandon practitioner knowledge in favor of practices the research base has scientifically endorsed—practices that may directly contradict subtle practitioner understandings (Alrichter and Posch 1989; Madaus 1985; Garrison 1988).

Knowledge about teaching produced by modernist science smashes the experience of teaching into discrete fragments that are one generation removed from the subtle interplay of forces that made experience what it was originally. As educational science issues its injunction to keep experience away from verified knowledge, a chasm develops between the official discourse and the one that teachers develop in action. Teachers come to be personally excluded from the process of producing knowledge about their profession. The concept of teachers as virtuosos who create brilliant pieces of pedagogical performance is alien to the modernist conception of educational knowledge. In a modernist context teachers are expected to follow imperatives that are scientifically derived, not to produce teaching masterpieces (Britzman 1991; Clark 1987).

The authorized methods course that emerges from this modernist dismissal of practitioner knowledge involves transmitting the forms of teacher behavior that researchers have connected to improved student standardized test performance to prospective teachers. Yet, these forms of teacher activity and cognitive schematas are not transportable from the teacher education classroom to the elementary or secondary classroom. A critical teacher education would attempt to expose the assumptions about the epistemology and the nature of modernist research that are buried in the officially approved teacher actions. As it deconstructed the teacher activities and cognitive schematas, a critical teacher education would reconceptualize the ways that practitioner knowledge is analyzed and shared with teacher education students. The attempt to extract generalized methods would be replaced by an analysis of the way practitioners think and operate in action (Lampert and Clark 1990; Haroutunian-Gordon 1988). Teachers in action acquire and employ knowledge in context, in interaction. With this in mind, critical methods courses engage novices in the analysis of the context in which teaching takes place.

Such a study opens new vistas for methods courses. Assuming that teachers' knowledge cannot be separated from the socio-educational and the classroom context in which it is generated, students analyze the process of teacher thinking. What conditions contributed to the cognitive processes employed? What subliminal signals did the teacher pick up and how did such codes and signs help shape the cognitive schemata adopted? What implicit social and cultural assumptions were at work and how did they affect the teacher's thoughts and actions? Thus, students of teaching begin to recognize that practitioner knowledge is elusive, so elusive in fact it cannot be transferred like the knowledge of multiplication tables or parts of speech. The contextual contingency, the uniqueness of particular teaching situations can no longer be ignored: The elusiveness, the uncertainty of the practitioner's cognition and knowledge must be addressed (Schon 1987; Lampert and Clark 1990).

In this context the concept of teachers as researchers becomes extremely important to the reconceptualization of the methods course. If teachers are to be empowered to move beyond the static modernist views of teacher cognition and practitioner knowledge, they must become researchers of educational contexts. As prospective teachers study the interaction between context and teacher cognition/behavior, they must employ the tools of qualitative research. Ethnography (the study of events as they evolve in natural settings) and semiotics (the study of the codes and signs that enable humans to derive meaning from their surroundings) become important subjects of study. Learning such research strategies in preservice education allows novices to become meta-analysts of teacher knowledge and thinking. This means that they are empowered to review the deep structures that determine the professional activities of teachers. In the process they develop a reflexive awareness that allows them to discern the ways the teacher perception is shaped by the socio-educational context with its accompanying linguistic codes, cultural signs, and tacit views of the world.

This reflexive awareness, this stepping back from the world as we are accustomed to seeing it, requires that the prospective teachers construct their perceptions of the world anew. This reconstruction of their perceptions is not conducted in a random way but in a manner that undermines the forms of teacher activity that appear natural, that opens to question expert knowledge that has been officially verified. Reflexively aware action researchers ask where their own cognitive forms come from, in the process clarifying their own educational goals as they reconstruct the role of teacher. The ultimate justification for such research activity is practitioner empowerment—an empowerment that provides teachers the skill to overcome the modernist tendency to discredit their integrity as capable, reflexively aware professionals (Slaughter 1989; Carr and Kemmis 1986).

TEACHER EMPOWERMENT VIA TEACHERS PRODUCING KNOWLEDGE

Thus, there is more to teaching than meets the traditional modernist paradigm's eye, more than is included in the traditional methods course. The purpose of the critically reconceptualized methods course is not to learn the right answers, the hand-me-down methods of the research experts; on the contrary, the critical methods course attempts to convey an understanding of the unanticipated complications of classrooms. Such an understanding forces methods instructors to avoid the provision of generic methods applicable to all students in all contexts. As an alternative new paradigmatic methods classes engage students in the production of their own knowledge. Teachers as researchers audaciously claim the right to participate in the production of knowledge, while at the same time retaining their humility concerning the tentative, provisional nature of the knowledge. The production of new knowledge gleaned from the lived world of the students and the members of the community surrounding the school is very much a part of a critical effort to reconstruct culture and to reconceive the role of education around a democratic system of meaning. As long as officially certified experts retain the power to determine what counts as knowledge, little reform is possible. If we hold the power to produce our own knowledge, then we are empowered to reconstruct our own consciousnesses. The tyranny of expert-produced interpretations of traditions can be subverted and our futures can be reinvented along the lines of a critical democratic vision.

Teacher knowledge is created when teachers and students confront a contradiction, when students encounter a dangerous memory, when teacher-presented information collides with student experience, or when student-presented information collides with teacher experience. When we speculate on the etymology and deployment of knowledge, new knowledge is created. Generally speaking, Western culture is unaware of the origins of knowledge and the social processes by which knowledge is legitimated. Without such understandings, teachers are unable to separate non-conventional thinking from expressions of intellectual deficiency, highly moral behaviors from deviant behaviors. Teacher education that is grounded on the attempt to produce knowledge must focus attention on linguistic analysis, the study of power and its relationship to the individual, and the examination of the rational process. Teaching in multicultural settings provides a situation where the creation of knowledge takes on an even more profound significance. When a critical teacher who doesn't share the culture, language, race, or socioeconomic backgrounds of students enters the classroom, he or she becomes not an information provider but an explorer who works with students to create mutually understood texts. Based on their explorations, teachers and students create new learning materials full of mutually generated meanings and shared interpretations. At a time when educational dilemmas resulting from the rapid increase of diverse students in schools portend the future of North American education, such a pedagogical perspective becomes extremely important. If educators are unable to meet the challenges issued by this expanding diversity, disastrous consequences will result.

Such explorations cannot take place until teachers begin to learn about the diverse lives of their students and the specifics of their thinking processes. Methods courses in new paradigm teacher education programs teach beginning teachers to overcome the paucity of dialogue in classrooms and the impersonal relationships such an absence produces. One of the first lessons such students learn is to surrender their position as an expert when they stand as a teacher in front of the class. When we are ready to admit to our role as imposter, that we are not omniscient providers of truth to our disciples, we begin to actually listen to our students. We become open to the stories of students, analyzing how the stories inform educational and social theory and how educational and social theory inform the stories. The cultivation of such abilities forms the core of the critical methods course curriculum. Prospective teachers learn to engage students in genealogical projects, autobiographical writings, journal keeping, and collaborative methods of assessing and interpreting these activities. Student lives become the primary sources for writing and reading exercises. In the process, teachers learn forms of linguistic analysis, which they use to engage students in meta-analytical examinations of their consciousness construction. Such examinations elicit the type of critical thinking that we have labeled *post-formalism* (Greene 1986, 1995; Maher and Rathbone 1986; Kincheloe and Steinberg 1993).

Paulo Freire facilitates our attempt to conceptualize a democratic form of teaching what we call "unauthorized methods." Our democratic post-formal teacher education prepares prospective practitioners to build curricula around the construction of knowledge using the themes and conditions of people's lives as primary building blocks. Prospective teachers learn to study their students' experiences in classrooms and in their communities in order to identify the words, conditions, concepts, and ways of seeing basic to their lived worlds. Freire has taught us that by using this information teachers identify "generative words and themes" that signify the most important subject matter for an emancipatory curriculum. Contrary to the belief of some critics of our critical pedagogical position, this subject matter is not simply passed uncritically along to students. The information is presented back to students for interrogation as part of a critical dialogue. As Freire puts it, the subject matter is "problem-posed," that is, students and teachers reflect on the lives they lead asking questions of meaning and value. From a post-formal perspective they come to think about their own thinking and about the political dimensions of their daily lives. Such reflection provides students and teachers with a cognitive distance that leads to transformative action (Freire 1989; Freire and Macedo 1987; Shor 1992).

An understanding of Freire is important to prospective teachers learning to create knowledge. Critical methods courses help students learn sophisticated research techniques and deploy them in inquiries about student experience; the ways dominant interests manifest themselves in schools, society, and individual lives; and the ways that individuals resist the domination of these interests. Knowledge is no longer made to appear as if it is immutable, a secret known only by the elect, the privileged. Umberto Eco writes in *The Name of the Rose* about the evils of immutable, secret knowledge that is viewed as an entity to be possessed rather than to be diffused among the people.

Speaking of Aristotle's work, the blind monk who guards the great books in the monastery argues that if he were to allow the books to become objects open to anyone's interpretation "we would have crossed the last boundary." The last boundary is democracy, the right of individuals to create their own knowledge rather than having to rely on the official interpretations of the experts. We have yet to cross that boundary; critical teacher education pushes us toward it (Ross and Hannay 1986; Greene 1986).

CONCLUSION

The lesson plans delineated in this book reach to the outer limits. They are dedicated to the principles of democracy, empowerment, research, and academic rigor that we have discussed in this chapter. In the short run these methods remain unauthorized, even dangerous in the minds of many—hopefully they will be less threatening as time passes. The following chapters attempt to make teaching sophisticated subject matter a teacher-friendly, not a teacher-proof exercise. We contend that it is important to include examples of critical teaching methods in a wide variety of disciplines so that teachers in one academic domain can see what it means to teach critically in another subject area. In this way curricular integration and interdisciplinary work can be encouraged so as to provide another means of preventing the modernist curricular fragmentation we have frequently referenced in this chapter. We understand that we are asking much of teacher educators, teachers, and students, inducing them to go beyond typical educational practice. We also understand that there are a multitude of forces that are working and will work to thwart such efforts. Nevertheless, our vision of critical pedagogical and political frontiers calls us to redefine human progress in new non-colonial, non-oppressive ways that celebrate democracy, social/economic justice, new levels of cognitive understanding, and innovative community building.

The next chapter is a classic essay by Ivor Goodson. His timeless observations on teaching remind us that in the last twenty years, we have still not created a student-centered pedagogy. Other chapters follow, written by teachers and students who have failed and succeeded with critical teaching strategies. Each piece celebrates these ups and downs in teaching and serve to exemplify what *can* be done in teaching—never what *should* be done.

REFERENCES

Altrichter, H., and P. Posh. "Does the 'Grounded Theory' Approach Offer a Guiding Paradigm for Teacher Research?" *Cambridge Journal of Education* 19 (1989): 21–31.

Baldwin, E. "Theory vs. Ideology in the Practice of Teacher Education." *Journal of Teacher Education* 38 (1987): 16–19.

Bobbitt, N. "Reflective Thinking: Meaning and Implications for Teaching." In *Higher-Order Thinking: Definition, Meaning and Instructional Approaches*. Ruth G. Thomas, Washington, DC: Home Economics Education Association, 1987.

Bowers, C., and D. Flinders. *Responsive Teaching: An Ecological Approach to Classroom Patterns of Language, Culture, and Thought*. New York: Teachers College Press, 1990.

Britzman, D. *Practice Makes Practice: A Critical Study of Learning to Teach*. Albany, NY: SUNY Press, 1991.

Carr, W., and S. Kemmis. *Becoming Critical*. Philadelphia: Falmer Press, 1986.

Clark, C. "Asking the Right Questions About Teacher Preparation: Contributions of Research on Teacher Thinking." Occasional Paper Number 110. East Lansing: Michigan State University, Institute for Research on Teaching, 1987.

Fosnot, C. "The Dance of Education." Paper presented to the Annual Conference of the Association for Educational Communication and Technology, New Orleans, 1988.

Freire, P. *The Politics of Education: Culture, Power, and Liberation*. South Hadley, MA: Bergin & Garvey, 1985.

———, and D. Macedo. *Literacy: Reading the Word and the World*. South Hadley, MA: Bergin & Garvey, 1985.

Garman, H., and H. Hazi. 1988. "Teachers Ask: Is There Life After Madeline Hunter?" *Phi Delta Kappan*, 69 (1988): 670–72.

Garrison, J. "Democracy, Scientific Knowledge, and Teacher Empowerment." *Teachers College Record*, 89, 4 (1988): 487–504.

Glickman, C. "Development as the Aim of Instructional Supervision." Paper presented at the Association for Supervision and Curriculum Development, Chicago, IL, 1985.

Greene, M. *The Dialectic of Freedom*. New York: Teachers College Press, 1988.

———. *Releasing the Imagination: Essays on Education, the Arts, and Social Change*. San Francisco: Jossey-Bass, 1995.

Haroutunian-Gordon, S. "Teaching in an 'Ill-Structured' Situation: The Case of Socrates." *Educational Theory*, 38, 2, (1988): 225–37.

Hultgren, F. "Critical Thinking: Phenomenological and Critical Foundations." In *Higher-Order Thinking: Definition, Meaning and Instructional Approaches*. Ruth G. Thomas. Washington, DC: Home Economics Education Association, 1987.

Jones, N., and M. Cooper. "Teacher Effectiveness and Education: A Case of Incompatibility." Paper presented to the American Educational Research

Association, Washington, DC, 1987.

Kamii, C. "Teacher's Autonomy and Scientific Training." *Young Children*, 31 (1981): 5–14.

Kincheloe, J. *Teachers as Researchers: Qualitative Paths to Empowerment*. New York: Falmer Press, 1991.

———. *Toward a Critical Politics of Teacher Thinking: Mapping the Postmodern*. Westport, CT: Bergin & Garvey, 1993.

———. *Toil and Trouble: Good Work, Smart Workers, and the Integration of Academic and Vocational Education*. New York: Peter Lang, 1995.

———, and S. Steinberg. "A Tentative Description of Post-Formal Thinking: The Critical Confrontation with Cognitive Theory." *Harvard Educational Review*, 63, 3 (1993): 296–320.

Lampert, M., and C. Clark. "Expert Knowledge and Expert Thinking in Teaching: a Response to Floden and Klinzing." *Educational Researcher*, 19, 5 (1990): 21–42.

Lather, P. *Getting Smart: Feminist Research and Pedagogy within the Postmodern*. New York: Routledge, 1991.

Macedo, D. *Literacies of Power: What Americans Are Not Allowed to Know*. Boulder, CO: Westview Press, 1990.

Madaus, G. "Test Scores as Administrative Mechanisms in Educational Policy." *Phi Delta Kappan*, 66 (1985): 611–17.

Maher, F., and C. Rathbone. "Teacher Education and Feminist Theory: Some Implications for Practice." *American Journal of Education*, 94, 2 (1986): 214–35.

Popkewitz, T. "The Study of Schooling: Paradigms and Field-Based Methodologies in Education Research and Evaluation." In *The Study of Schooling*, T. Popkewitz and B. Tabachnik, eds. New York: Praeger Publishers, 1981.

Ross, E., and L. Hannay. "Toward a Critical Theory of Reflective Inquiry." *Journal of Teacher Education* (1986): 9–15.

Schon, D. *The Reflective Practitioner: How Professionals Think in Action*. New York: Basic Books, 1983.

Schon, D. *Educating the Reflective Practitioner*. San Francisco: Jossey-Bass Publishers, 1987.

Shannon, P. *Broken Promises: Reading Instruction in Twentieth-Century America*. Granby, MA: Bergin & Garvey, 1989.

Shor, I. *Empowering Education: Critical Teaching for Social Change*. Chicago: University of Chicago Press, 1992.

Slaughter, R. "Cultural Reconstruction in the Post-Modern World." *Journal of Curriculum Studies*, 3 (1989): 255–70.

Steinberg, S., and J. Kincheloe. *Kinderculture: Corporate Constructions of Childhood*. Boulder, CO: Westview Press, 1997.

Zeuli, J., and M. Bachmann. "Implementation of Teacher Thinking Research as Curriculum Deliberation." Occasional Paper Number 107. East Lansing, Michigan State University, Institute for Research on Teaching, 1986.

PART ONE

FROM THEORY...

II

TOWARDS AN ALTERNATIVE PEDAGOGY

Ivor F. Goodson

Current classroom practice is largely derived from the belief that the teacher's basic task is the "transmission of knowledge." At one level this statement is obviously true—any pedagogy is concerned with the transmission of values and ways of knowing—but at the level of rhetoric "transmission" has come to characterize a particular view of practice and an associated view of knowledge as a commodity. The distinction between transmission as an aspect of pedagogy and transmission *as* pedagogy is in this sense crucial. What may seem a superficial confusion in educationists' language might mark a deeper confusion of considerable importance. Implicit in the notion of transmission is a one-way communication; it is to "pass on, hand on"[1] knowledge *from* the teacher *to* the pupil. In this chapter I take "transmission" as characterizing any educational incident that sets the learning of knowledge *previously* planned or defined by the teacher as the basic objective. In thus characterizing transmission I am echoing practice derived from this model in that curricula and lessons center on the prior definition of knowledge *for* transmission. The transmission pedagogue works to defend this prior definition against interactive redefinition.

By this definition a broad spectrum of teaching styles—"chalk and talk," "question and answer," "discovery projects," "discussion," "individualized worksheets"—might be seen as following the transmission model. Hence in "chalk and talk" the teacher will have decided beforehand what content, concepts, or skills he or she wants to get across. In the "question and answer" he will have decided what answers are the right ones. In "discovery" he or she will know what he is aiming to help the child discover. In all cases the style of the encounter and the outcome are previously prescribed.

This chapter will argue that if the intention of teaching is to involve *all* pupils in learning, then transmission, with its dependence on the viability of preplanned educational incidents and outcomes, is particularly ill suited. In arguing this way I do not wish to imply that pupil-teacher interaction should go on without using previously defined ideas, material, and conceptual structures, or that at no stage should ideas and content be transmitted from teacher to pupil. I am, however, arguing that it is misguided to set transmission as the basic role of the classroom teacher.

The substantial forces maintaining transmission as the dominant pedagogy only partly explain why the development of radical alternatives has largely disappeared. In spite of the enormous validity of its critique of transmission teaching, child-centered progressivism remains for most a negative creed: sure that to transmit to an unwilling child is pointless, but unsure what to do instead. As a result, the "failure" of the transmission classroom often becomes the "problem" of the progressive teacher. By only reacting negatively to transmission pedagogy, progressivism is in danger of becoming an extension of it.

It is time to move on from the negativity of progressivism to the definition of a positive alternative pedagogy. To do so might transform educational debate from the present "no contest" between ideologies that both faithfully reproduce the social system into a dialectic concerned with educational priorities. Much is to be gained by teachers exploring the possibilities of changing their classroom practice, but to do so they need to move beyond the potent but frustrated plea: "OK, but what's the alternative?" In this chapter I pursue a tentative search for an answer.

CLASSROOM LEARNING

The assumption underpinning transmission pedagogy is that what is decided in the preactive context can be made to work in the interactive context.[2] I want to question this assumption and argue that what is decided at the preactive stage of curriculum planning is commonly contradicted and subverted at the interactive stage.

The assumption that preactive decisions can and should be made to work in the interactive context is inevitably allied to the belief that learning consists of the child coming to understand and accept the teacher's expositions and definitions. In arguing that preactive decisions seldom stand up in the interactive context I am, by implication, arguing for a new model of classroom learning. Modern studies of learning show how information is idiosyncratically processed by each learner. Recognition of the uniqueness of individual processing and of the variability of interests is the prerequisite of any understanding of classroom life and of any move to describe a new pedagogy. The new pedagogy would seek to define a strategy that sensitized the teacher to individual processes and interests and positioned his response to these at the center of his teaching: broad collective plans and decisions would be ancillary to this central response.

In many ways the new pedagogy would be seeking to formalize at the theoretical (preactive) level what already sometimes goes on at classroom (interactive) level: As we have argued, transmission is commonly subverted in the classroom. Studies of classroom interaction offer boundless evidence of such recurrent subversion. Philip Jackson's studies of "Life in Classrooms" are widely regarded for their authentic flavor:

> As typically conducted, teaching is an opportunistic process. That is to say, neither the teacher nor his students can predict with any certainty exactly what will happen next. Plans are forever going awry and unexpected opportunities for the attainment of educational goals are constantly emerging. The seasoned teacher seizes upon these opportunities and uses them to his and his students' advantage . . . in the classroom as elsewhere, the best laid schemes suffer their usual fate.[3]

The unpredictability of classroom life described by Jackson explains the most common classroom phenomena: one group of children working along the lines the teacher has laid down (e.g., listening, answering, or filling in the worksheet); some just going through the motions by copying out bits or doodling, and another group thoroughly alienated, talking among themselves, staring out of the window, thinking of last night at the disco.

This range of responses is what most teachers will readily recognize as the "reality" of their classrooms. The myth of transmission claims that it is only the teacher's inadequacy that explains why more children are not working along pre-determined lines. I am arguing that the recurrent failure to involve so many children in classroom learning is most convincingly explained by fundamental flaws in the transmission model. A pedagogy so firmly situated in the preactive vacuum can only expect partial success, given the variabilities of interactive reality; no pedagogy so all-dependent on prediction could hope to encompass the diversity of the classroom.

Even more disturbing, the fatal flaws of transmission pedagogy mean that teachers' expectations inevitably come to fit the partial successes that are transmission's inevitable achievement:

> The most wasteful and destructive aspect of our present educational system is the set of expectations about student learning each teacher brings to the beginning of a new course or term. The instructor expects a third of his pupils to learn what is taught, a third to learn less well, and a third to fail or just 'get by.' These expectations are transmitted to the pupils through school grading policies and practices and through the methods and materials of instruction. Students quickly learn to act in accordance with them, and the final sorting through the grading process approximates the teacher's original expectations. A pernicious self-fulfilling prophecy has been created.[4]

If the involvement of all students is to be our aim, and this article takes that view, then a pedagogy firmly situated in the interactive reality of the classroom is required: a pedagogy that accepts and works with the individual interests and processes that are at the center of classroom learning.

ALTERNATIVE THEORIES AND PRACTICE

In discussing an alternative pedagogy I am conscious that I am merely presenting a pedagogy in embryo, yet it is an embryo with a long history. Central to an alternative theory is the focus of investigation upon the *individual* process of learning. Each individual pupil exhibits the most positive response in the learning process when the information to be learned somehow "meshes" with his interests. As P. S. Wilson notes, "A child's education (as opposed to schooling) can only proceed through the pursuit of his interests since it is only these which are of intrinsic value," and further, "whatever enables him to appreciate and understand his interest more fully and to pursue it more actively and effectively is education."[5] Over half a century ago Dewey was similarly disposed to focus on the individual experiences of the pupil. He saw the need of reinstating into experience the subject matter of the studies, or branches of learning. It must be restored to the experience from which it has been abstracted. It needs to be psychologized, turned over, translated into the immediate and individual experiencing within which it has its origin and significance...[6] If the subject matter of the lessons be such as to have an appropriate place within the expanding consciousness of the child, if it grows out of his own past doing, thinking, and suffering, and grows into application in further achievements and receptivities, then no device or trick or method has to be restored in order to enlist 'interest.' The psychologized is of interest—that is, it is placed in the whole of conscious life so that it shares the work of that life. But the externally presented material, conceived and generated in standpoints and attitudes remote from the child, and developed in motives alien to him, has no such place of its own. Hence the recourse to adventitious leverage to push it in, to factitious drill to drive it in, to artificial bribe to lure it in.[7]

Acknowledgment of the crucial role of each individual pupil's interests and experience in the learning process is only a starting point for exploring a new pedagogy. Certainly such acknowledgment could be, and often is, used in amplifying transmission method pedagogies. But, "this regard for children's interests in teaching has more relevance to the method of teaching than to its content. . . . Children's existing interests can be used as a starting point from which they can be led on to take an interest in realms of whose existence they never dreamt."[8] By this argument the child's interest can be used as a method yet has little relevance to content: The teacher defines the content and uses the child's interest to transmit it to him or her. Acknowledgment of the importance of the child's experience and interests *and* acceptance of these as valid knowledge content in class-room learning can lead to two distinctive alternative pedagogies. The first pedagogy, child-centered progressivism, would focus on the child's interest, *and* in so doing conclude that the pedagogy should aim to allow him or her to personally direct his or her own learning. W. H. Kilpatrick's views are closest to advocating this pedagogy; education starts where the child is so as to capitalize on the child's personally directed activity springing from his or her real interest:

> It is what pupils do of themselves that brings the best learning results, both in direct learning and in concomitant learnings. We can thus say, paradoxically, that the teacher's aim is to give as little help as possible, that is, to give the least degree of direct help consistent with the best personal work on the part of the pupils.[9]

Charity James describes a similar style of pedagogy:

> At its most elementary, if a group of students is engaged on Interdisciplinary Enquiry, within the area of investigation (say, some aspect of life in a technological society, or of human growth and development in childhood and adolescence) students formulate the questions they want to answer,

identify the problems which they want to solve, create hypotheses for their solutions, test them and revise the hypotheses.[10]

For James, as for Kilpatrick, the teacher is seen "as a consultant to students in their self-directed enterprise."[11]

While sympathetic to the emphasis of Kilpatrick and James, I think the pedagogy they recommend is over-dependent (one might say solely dependent) on "what pupils do themselves."[12] Such an emphasis seems to be ill suited to the interactive character of classroom learning in two ways:

(a) A major part of the rationale for classroom learning must surely turn on those aspects the pupil learns in interaction with his peers and his teacher. This interactive dimension in learning can aid the development of the pupil's interests and ideas into other areas from those he might independently explore. Learning associated with the kind of pedagogy Kilpatrick and James advocate seems to miss most of the potential present in classroom interaction.

(b) A further aspect of classroom interaction is that the pupil's independent studies may well be subject to a good deal of interruption. The Kilpatrick model never seems to come to grips with the question of "control" within the classroom. Any pedagogy that fails to address this question is surely doomed. This is not because the classroom teacher is an irremediable authoritarian by nature but because part of his/her job must be to ensure that pupil's work can go on uninterrupted. This means that he must be more than a consultant in his classroom. A viable pedagogy must acknowledge that in the classroom "the crowds remain" to pull at the student's attention and divert the teacher's energy.[13]

A second pedagogy based on the child's individual interests and experiences addresses the interactive potential and reality of the classroom. Acknowledgment of the paramount role of individual process is self-sufficient. The paramountcy of individual process in learning does not preclude the role of external challenge and collaboration in that process; rather, it argues for such a role to be at the center of the teacher's actions.

Towards an Alternative Pedagogy

A number of accounts of the introduction of innovation teaching courses, besides underlining the pervasive flaws of transmission, also indicate how an alternative pedagogy could remedy such flaws. The following quotation by M. Armstrong refers to a fourth year humanities course in a comprehensive school:

> A theme is chosen, strategies worked out to relate it to the pupil's experience and interest, materials prepared, resources mobilized. The process is intensely exciting, above all, I think because it incites us to pursue ourselves to the course of study we are preparing to advocate to our pupils. Ironically, by the time the programme is ready to be presented to the pupils for whom it is intended, our own enthusiasm as teachers if often half-spent, or else has become so self-absorbing that we cannot appreciate that it will not be shared by everyone else. We have become our own curriculum's ideal pupils; our resources are beautifully designed to satisfy not our pupils' intellectual demands, but our own![14]

An account of a first year undergraduate course in economics makes similar points:

> One puzzling factor in the situation was that, whilst students appeared to get very little out of the Demand Theory Package, the members of faculty who prepared it felt that they had learnt a lot. In preparing the Factor Pricing package, therefore, our attention began to shift towards the problem of getting the students to share the experience which the faculty had had. It became clear that it was the process of "sorting it all out," so important and necessary in developing self-instructional materials, which was the key to this problem. In presenting the students with a completed analysis we were concentrating their attention on predetermined solutions at the expense of focusing it on either the nature of the problem or the analytic process itself. [15]

These two accounts indicate what is needed is to involve the student in the process of "sorting it all out," what Dewey called "the need of reinstating into experience the subject matter." We must move the pedagogic focus from the preactive situation where it is divorced from the pupils to the interactive situation where the pupils are involved. By so changing the focus, learning becomes less a matter of mastering externally presented material and more a case of actively reconstructing knowledge.

We have stated before that moving the pedagogic focus from implementing the preactive to interpreting the interactive does not imply an absence of planning (or for that matter, of evaluation). As before, the teacher will be concerned to plan for his lessons but in the new situation will seek to ensure that the predictive does not become the prescriptive. E. W. Eisner comes near to the spirit of such a plan in describing expressive objectives: "An expressive objective describes an educational encounter: It identifies a situation in which children are to work, a problem with which they are to cope, a task in which they are to engage; but it does not specify what from that encounter situation, problem or task they are to learn."[16] In short, planning is concerned with the process of learning and does not prescribe what is going to be produced.

A number of examples of work based on this kind of pedagogic ideal are already in operation. An important minority of "progressive" teachers in British primary schools and a growing body in middle schools already employ an alternative pedagogy:

> At her best the primary school teacher working in a more or less progressive English primary school is perhaps the only contemporary polymath, even if to herself she seems more like a jack of all trades. She is something of an expert in the psychology of learning and the nature of childhood, passionately committed to intellectual exploration within the most widely ranging areas of experience, rarely afraid to tackle, at the invitation of her pupils, new disciplines, and often the master of some particular part of experience which she teaches—art or nature or language. Doubtless to put it so badly is to idealize, but it is an idealization drawn from life.[17]

The guiding principle of this primary school tradition is "intellectual exploration." Such exploration demands a working plan of principles of procedure as well as predictions of worthwhile activities and useful resources. The controversial American Social Science Curriculum, *Man: A Course of Study* of the 1970s, goes some way towards defining principles of procedure for an alternative pedagogy:

(1) To initiate and develop in youngsters a process of question-posing (the inquiry method).

(2) To teach a research methodology where children can look for information to answer questions they have raised and use the framework developed in the course (e.g., the concept of the life cycle) and apply it to new areas.

(3) To help youngsters develop the ability to use a variety of firsthand sources as evidence from which to develop hypotheses and draw conclusions.

(4) To conduct classroom discussions in which youngsters learn to listen to others as well as express their own view.

(5) To legitimate the search: that is, to give sanction and support to open-ended discussions where definitive answers to many questions are not found.

(6) To encourage children to reflect on their own experiences.[18]

While not recommending the whole curriculum as exemplifying an alternative pedagogy, I believe this definition of principle offered useful guidelines of a broad plan of interaction.

As well as having broad principles of procedure it is also useful for teachers to have a working list of likely criteria to judge classroom activities. Raths recently attempted to produce such a list that suggested "All other things being equal, one activity is more worthwhile than another if it permits children to make informed choices in carrying out the activity and to reflect on the consequences of their choices."[19] But clearly lists of procedural principles and worthwhile activities might fall into the trap whereby preactive definition prescribes interactive interpretation. To avoid this it is important to try to "catch the spirit" in which such lists should be used. "The problem is to produce a specification to which teachers can work in the classroom, and thus to provide the basis for a new tradition. That specification needs to catch the implication of ideas for practice."[20]

What might fulfill this need is a description of the kind of encounter that best characterizes the new tradition: an exemplar of the pedagogy in interaction. Peter Medway and I attempt to define an exemplar of what, for want of a better phrase, we called cooperative learning.

Imagine this situation in a secondary school. A male teacher with a group in his classroom. He spends two mornings and two afternoons with them each week. He has set up a room that reflects many of his own interests and his predictions of what might grab his kids. There are charts and paintings on the wall, a trolley of assorted materials in the corner, some records, filmstrips, paint and brushes, and so on. It's an environment deliberately set up for learning.

It's noticeable that the teacher is relating very differently to different groups and individuals. Some he leaves alone; with others he sits down and looks at what they've done and make vague situation-maintaining remarks, "Yes, that's good, go on"; with others he's engaged in specific and animated point-by-point argument, explanation, planning, disagreement.

This situation exemplifies cooperative learning—cooperative, that is, between teacher and student. There may well also be cooperation between students, but we want to single out for attention here the type of relationship between the teacher and either individual students or small groups of friends. It's cooperative in that teacher and student look together at a topic, each presenting to the other his own perception of it, both feeling their way through dialogue towards a common perception. Cooperation is not a euphemism, a gentler way of doing the same old thing by persuasion rather than imposition. We take the implied equality seriously, and the learning relationship, starting on the teacher's side with a commitment to the principle of reciprocity, progresses to the point where reciprocity is experienced as a reality.

A cooperative learning enterprise that reaches the crucial learning threshold might pass through three stages:

First stage:

The student says "I want to do something on the second world war" and gets the reply, "OK, get started. Here's some books and magazines, there's a filmstrip you can look at." During the following period the teacher may feel quite anxious about what's going on: There may be a lot of copying out of books, drawing of pictures, collecting of unrelated bits and pieces of knowledge—useless knowledge it may seem, and so indeed it may sometimes turn out to be. But what *may* be going on is a process of exploration in which the student, often unconsciously, feels around the topic to locate the real source of its attraction for him—some problem or worry or preoccupation or powerful feeling related to it.

Second stage:

The teacher, after watching all this and trying to detect underlying themes and concerns in the student's busy activity, while very gently maintaining it and restraining himself from criticism, and the student, who is beginning to understand why the topic holds his interest, get together to bring it into focus. "So what you're really on about is the casual, pointless way people could get killed, in ways that couldn't make any sense to them—you live your whole life, have an education, a family, fillings in your teeth, and end up in a ditch after some minor skirmish with an unimportant enemy outpost that was going to withdraw one minute later anyway." The teacher goes on to suggest further ways of exploring the central interest.

Third stage:

The student is now experiencing the satisfaction of successfully investigating a topic alone and bringing it under control. The student has developed tenacity and perseverance, is making statements he can back up, is hypothesizing with confidence, and can improvise from knowledge. The project is out of the intensive care unit and the teacher can speak his mind about it without fear of killing it stone dead or putting the student down. The relationship has become robust and stimulating to both sides. The student enjoys the teacher's company and finds it challenging. The teacher has gotten interested in the student *and* in the topic—about which he or she now knows a lot more. The teacher takes the student's challenges and suggestions seriously, and now experiences the cooperation which started off as abstract ideal.

This is the stage of synthesis. The student has a perspective on the whole topic that may be expressed in a piece of writing that integrates generalizations, facts, attitudes, and the students' whole view of the world. The final writing or presentation will express the dynamic vigour of the reconstruction of knowledge that has gone on.[21]

If, as I intend, this description is taken as characterizing a new pedagogy at work, a number of important implications must be clearly enunciated. First, learning will often involve *individual* negotiation between pupil and teacher: The teacher learns alongside the pupils, an adult learner among young learners, though with additional responsibilities to those of his charges. The teacher helps the child isolate a problem that is puzzling him (the example given related to the second world war), together they devise a plan for investigating the problems, the investigation promotes a number of hypotheses, these are worked through and reformulated, and together the teacher and child discuss and define a mutually acceptable solution. In this case the teacher's energy, resource preparation, and stock of common sense and specialist knowledge is used in facilitating the child's inquiry into something he or she has become interested in. (In transmission the teacher puts much energy and resources into preparation *before* confronting the variety of children's interests—a fatiguing gamble that too seldom pays off.)

Second, the pedagogy implies a radical re-ordering of the way in which knowledge is defined. The rhetoric of transmission maintains that the child gets a balanced "diet" of "subjects" that cover the main disciplines of knowledge. But this must be recognized as rhetoric: The knowledge that teachers transmit has *never* been "received" by most children. That is why there are millions of acknowledged adult illiterates, why I cannot use mathematics and speak no foreign languages (not even Latin), why in many schools only the minority are even *offered* subject transmission while the rest do "Parentcraft," "Personal Development," and "Motor Cycle Maintenance." Barnes has described knowledge as transmitted in schools as: "Knowledge which someone else presents to us. We partly grasp it, enough to answer examination questions, but it remains someone else's knowledge, not ours. If we never use this knowledge we probably forget it."[22]

Although optimistic, this description catches the essence of school knowledge and Barnes goes on to argue for a new view of knowledge known as "action knowledge":

> In so far as we use knowledge for our own purposes ...we begin to incorporate it into our view of the world, and to use parts of it to cope with the exigencies of living. Once the knowledge becomes incorporated into our view of the world on which our actions are based, I would say it has become "action knowledge."[23]

Only if the teacher gives the child access to "action knowledge" can learning take place. An alternative pedagogy would seek to offer the child such an opportunity whilst transmission pedagogy pre-empts it. In placing the individual pupil in such a central position in defining the approach to knowledge there is not only a psychological rationale (which some traditionalists concede) but a logical rationale too. All subject matter begins with an original attempt to solve problems and it is this unitary process of knowledge creation that should be the focus of pedagogy, not the transmission of its differentiated products. Only by involvement in this process can the pupil begin exploration of the wider fields and forms of knowledge: that successive broadening and deepening of knowledge which is the only route to a "balanced curriculum" for each child.

SOME CONSTRAINTS AND PROBLEMS

The most obvious constraint to centering a pedagogy around the pupil's inquiry in cooperation with the teacher is that pupils have to attend school and the teacher is responsible for such attendance. Yet this is the constraint within which any style of classroom learning has to operate; it is not a constraint that demands a transmission model, rather an alternative pedagogy would better accommodate this fact of classroom life.

A more specific problem relates to the nature of classroom life, for *the crowds remain to pull at the student's attention and to divert the teacher's energy*. There are two problems associated with an alternative pedagogy. (a) Is "individual negotiation" possible in the hurly-burly of the classroom? (b) Does a role as an equal learner interfere with the teacher's control capacity? Undoubtedly most people would answer "yes" and conclude that only transmission can cope with classroom realities. A number of facts indicate that this perception is outdated. In a number of primary school classrooms with forty or forty-five pupils, of often noisy and mobile inclination, an alternative pedagogy has been made to work quite successfully. Exceptional teachers, perhaps, but what of the average teacher? In the upper secondary school the average teacher works in an organization that maximizes his opportunity for short, specialized sessions of transmission. As widely reported, it is at this level that "control" is most difficult: where transmission is maximized "control" problems are greatest. Even as "survival technique" it would appear that transmission is outmoded: The pedagogy and associated organizational structure work against the establishment of those individual and personal relationships, which as well as alleviating "control" problems might serve to increase the educative potential of the teacher.

The contradictions in transmission pedagogy have already encouraged new developments in our classrooms. Clearly the development of an alternative pedagogy can only be part of a much larger scheme of transformation, but acknowledgment of the enormity of the task should not inhibit developments; indeed exploration of alternative pedagogies would seem one important place to begin. By exploring an alternative pedagogy in their classrooms, teachers can clarify what is possible in schools, what purposes schools serve in our society, and perhaps bring new understandings of the rhetoric of transmission. That is a long way from accepting that transmission *is* teaching.

For "progressive" models of education the development of an alternative pedagogy would provide that coherent and positive view of the teacher's involvement that has so far seemed lacking. An outmoded pattern of teacher domination would give way to a new active collaboration with the child. Finally, an alternative pedagogy should move beyond the individual negotiations that this paper has concentrated on; collective and group aspects need to be developed. But, only from an individual knowledge of and relationship with each student can the teacher broaden his curriculum and group involvement. And from a clear definition of pedagogy new definitions of school and classroom might begin.

NOTES

1. *Concise Oxford Dictionary.*
2. P. W. Jackson, *Life In Classrooms*, (New York: Holt, Rinehart & Winston, 1968), 152. Using Jackson's distinction, what the teacher does before the lesson in the empty classroom is preactive; when the children enter the classroom it is interactive. Nell Keddie has drawn attention to a similar dichotomy between the "educationist context" and the "teacher context" N. Keddie, "Classroom Knowledge" in M. F. D. Young, ed., *Knowledge and Control*, (London: Collier-MacMillan, 1971).
3. op. cit. Jackson, 166.
4. B. S. Bloom, "Mastery Learning" in J. H. Block, ed., *Mastering Learning: Theory and Practice*, (New York: Holt, Rinehart & Winston, 1971), 47.
5. P. S. Wilson, *Interest and Discipline in Education*, (London: Routledge and Kegan Paul, 1971), 67.
6. J. Dewey, *The Child and the Curriculum*, (Chicago: University of Chicago Press, 1902, reprinted 1971), 22. I share the severe reservations about Dewey expressed most recently in the work of Clarence Karier.
7. Ibid., 27.
8. R. Peters and P. Hirst, *The Logic of Education*, (London: Routledge and Kegan Paul, 1970), 37–38.
9. W. H. Kilpatrick, *Philosophy of Education*, (New York: MacMillan, 1951), 307.
10. C. James, *Young Lives at Stake*, (London: Collins, 1968), 65–66.
11. Ibid., 65.
12. op. cit. Kilpatrick, 307.
13. op. cit. Jackson, 111.
14. M. Armstrong, "The Role of the Teacher," in P. Buckman, ed., *Education Without Schools*, (London: Souvenir Press, 1974), 51.
15. M. Eraut, N. MacKenzie, and I. Papps, "The Mythology of Educational Development," *British Journal of Educational Technology*, Vol. 6, No. 3, (October 1975).
16. W. J. Popham, E. W. Eisner, H. J. Sullivan, and L. L. Tyler, *Instructional Objectives*, (Chicago: Rand McNally, 1969), 15-16.
17. op. cit. Armstrong, 56.
18. J. P. Hanley, D. K. Whitla, E. W. Moo, and A. S. Walter, *Curiosity, Competence and Community. Man: A Course of Study*, (Cambridge, MA.: Education Development Center, 1970), 5.
19. J. D. Raths, "Teaching Without Specific Objectives," *Educational*

Leadership, (April 1971), 714–20.

20. L. Stenhouse, "Defining the Curriculum Problem," *Cambridge Journal of Education*, Vol. 5, No. 2, (Easter 1975).

21. I. Goodson and P. Medway, "The Feeling Is Mutual," *Times Educational Supplement*, (20 June 1975), 17.

22. D. Barnes, *From Communication to Curriculum*, (Harmondsworth: Penguin, 1976), 81.

23. Ibid.

III

NURTURING THE IMAGINATION OF RESISTANCE
YOUNG ADULTS AS CREATORS OF KNOWLEDGE
Kathleen S. Berry

Young adult learners are in a state of negotiating between their play world and the expectations of becoming adults. School appears to be the last place that encourages self-expression and cultural/critical imaginations. The state of limbo between the two eras of student life is the very place in which cultural/critical literacy should find a place. Younger students (e.g., elementary school level) and their teachers are consumed by a multitude of cultural worlds while at the same time consuming the knowledge, values, beliefs, histories, structures, and representations of culturally constructed worlds based on gender, race, class, age, sexuality, and so forth. Most likely, young adult students are at a point where they have consumed most of the knowledge and beliefs about their world that will carry them into and through their adult life. Therefore, school, as an educational site, confirms the statement that knowledge is to be consumed by young adults as areas of specialization or disciplined knowledge, e.g., science, math, arts, and humanities. This places young adult students in a position where they are mainly, if not consistently, consumers of knowledge instead of creators of knowledge.

One of the first assumptions of cultural/critical literacy is that knowledge is a cultural artifact constructed in large part by dominant groups socialized and positioned by history, institutional structures, gender, race, and so forth. This point of view supports the architecture of curriculum in which the student is shaped by, but has no role in the creation of knowledge, beliefs, values, histories, and so forth. Therefore, students are immersed in an epistemological world not of their making. In fact, their worlds are created, produced, circulated, and maintained by the authority, especially of epistemological disciplines, known as bodies of knowledge in a special field, and organized accordingly. The task for young adults becomes one of learning the content and structure (logocentrism) of subject disciplines, ranging from literature to the sciences, and to do so without challenging the inconsistencies among various experiences, backgrounds, and truths of the logocentric knowledge.

A second factor of cultural/critical literacy and consistent with epistemological objectivity is that knowledge is separate from the learner, in this case, the imagination of the young adult. This condition positions the learner as a passive recipient of knowledge that makes claims of truth, legitimacy, and universality distinct from the cultural/critical imagination of the young adult learner. In modern curricula, especially in the disciplines of sciences and technology, knowledge and the knower live in a world of dualisms. The student as knower has no responsibility and is not in a privileged position as a constructor of knowledge. These dualisms can be found in many forms: learning the facts, filling in the blanks, computer tests, standardized testing, memorizing information for exams, writing formatted essays, and a plethora of other means. These "objective" methods of teaching, learning, measuring, and evaluating the knower eliminate any responsibility on the part of the student to construct knowledge or to challenge mainstream thinking.

A third issue for cultural/critical literacy is that culturally constructed knowledge shapes the young adults' consciousnesses in ways not inclusive of their knowledge and experience. Or in other ways, it misrepresents or distorts their world, unless they are the children of the status quo, which in North American usually means beholden to Euro/American–centric truths. From a feminist point of view, we claim knowledge is gendered by males. Non-whites also argue that knowledge is racist when it is constructed by whites. Similarly, knowledge constructed by people of different physical and mental abilities, sexualities, histories, institutional policies, nationalities, religious and ethnic experiences that are different from the mainstream bodies of knowledge are also excluded.

For our purposes here, the dominant knowledge (which includes more than just facts and logic, but also values, attitudes, institutional structures, history, etc.) of the modern era is assumed to be structured and validated by Western, European, white, middle-class males. Excluding all other knowledge, Euro/American–centrism has permeated every aspect of late, modern consciousness including those nations in varying states of modernization, such as some Asian populations. Another major constructor of knowledge in late modernity has been the influence of media and computer technologies. Whatever the influence, students, specially those not privileged by the status quo, are eventually robbed of their participatory consciousness—in other words, limited to nil nurturing as creators or as oppositional readers of knowledge.

I would like to argue that cultural/critical literacy would not only reestablish the young adult as a learner but more importantly, as a creator of knowledge. A fundamental principle of cultural/critical literacy encourages challenge or opposition to the dominant knowledge established and legitimized by Euro/American-centric culture. For examples of this dominance look to textbooks (traditionally authored by males) that privilege European white male history and ignore the accomplishments of women, African-heritage, and the physically different. Whose knowledge do we learn in school? The dynamics of opposition to established knowledge, truths, beliefs, structures, and so forth, become a constant element in every aspect of curriculum including teaching, learning, and materials. Responsibility is shifted from teachers and students as consumers of knowledge to creators of knowledge. In turn, education becomes a political site where dominant knowledge is deconstructed and new knowledge is constructed.

QUESTIONS AS SITES OF KNOWLEDGE CREATION

Because students are inserted into a world of knowledge and representations through predetermined curriculum content and structure, there is no opportunity for them to create knowledge since it is determined beforehand what knowledge is to be acquired and the order in which it is to be learned. Such an approach denies the students the priority to ask questions. To ask questions is to cocreate knowledge. A return of authentic questioning to students is a reclaiming of unknown territory, of knowledge. Children at a very early age begin asking questions about their world—authentic questions in that there is no predetermined knowledge or answer to their questions. Adults are quite frequently astonished at the level of questioning that young children can produce and are even more surprised by the authenticity with which they create the answers. "Out of the mouths of babes" comes knowledge that sounds as if never thought about or said before. The creation of knowledge through the question is an intrinsic part of being a learner.

The questions that young children ask are extremely high level, deep, scientific, philosophical, and engaged in a search for knowledge, truth, and justice. Questions such as "Why is the sky blue?"; "Is it true that God lives up in heaven?"; or "Why does he get more than

I do, I don't think it's fair" are only a few that young children voice. They create knowledge through their adventurous and serendipitous attempts at answering questions, sometimes in negotiation with adults and frequently in their own world (think of teenagers constantly engaged in conversation with their peers.).

In school however, students' questions are inauthentic and merely asked as procedural, conformist, or intellectual capital. Procedural because routine is important to the schooling process and conformist because the teacher already knows the answer and the student is expected to guess what the correct answer is. Questions are merely a way of testing, controlling, and determining students' acquisition of predetermined, preconstructed knowledge. The students' role in this type of classroom questioning is to compete against one another in a manner similar to the game of *Trivial Pursuit*, in which knowledge is categorized under science, literature, sports, history, geography, and entertainment. Like the game, knowledge in classrooms becomes a pursuit of trivia and a competition against the "authorities of knowledge."

In the classrooms in which students create their own knowledge from preexisting knowledge they learn to create and to value their own questions. From their questions, they attempt to create knowledge by challenging and opposing the status quo or mainstream thinking of the authoritative texts before them, whether visual, computered, media-ed, printed, or otherwise. In this way students claim the knowledge as their own simply because they have produced the questions.

SO WHAT QUESTIONS CREATE KNOWLEDGE?

In a reductionist notion of questioning, knowledge is something to be acquired, developed, and tested instead of questions that permit students to create their own knowledge. Because of the important nature of questions, it is crucial for students to receive and to learn a repertoire that creates and shapes knowledge instead of a technique that simply conforms to, develops, and furthers dominant and authorial knowledge. In the traditional questioning format of schooling, students answer questions that require correct answers to preferred or mainstream knowledge. The nature of such questions is to circulate and maintain the status quo.

Traditional questioning of texts, for example, range from factual to analytical questions, from synthesis to evaluation, and at all times are to be answered in order to maintain the authority of the text and the concurrent subjection of the student. The knowledge contained within these texts is not to be challenged or to be seen as inconsistent or contradictory to the knowledge or questions of the students. The ultimate point here is that the text is the authority and is legitimized throughout the educational system by people and policies. In other words, the text contains the universal, absolute, fixed knowledge, truths, values, and so forth. Traditional questions find answers within the text, accept its knowledge and authority.

Questions, even of the reader/personal response kind to a text, embrace a mode of questioning that refuses the creation of student knowledge. In this format, negotiated responses to the knowledge in the text are asked instead of authentic student questions. The format tends to take the shape of "What do you think? How do you feel? What is your opinion?" and so forth, and thus, only negotiate the representations of the text with those of the reader.

To truly return to the creation of knowledge, young adult students must oppose or resist the knowledge contained in whatever symbolic texts they are exploring. Authentic questioning means that the prepackaged knowledge that is in a text needs to be actively deconstructed by the students before they can recreate and reconstruct the knowledge to be consistent with their questions. This is not to say that students naturally have access to questions that produce a state of creativity. The type of questions that students ask, whether traditional, negotiated, or oppositional, are modelled by the adults in their world—parents, relatives, teachers, television and newspaper reporters, and the many educational creators of knowledge that appear in their life. However, these "authorities" should be seen as sources for student resistance and oppositions to established knowledge. This is not a claim for rudeness or offensiveness on the part of students or for defensive and controlling actions on the part of authorities, but a call for authentic questioning that returns the responsibility for the creation of knowledge to the questioners in this case, students.

Consider the types of questions that were asked in traditional, basal reading programs designed by publishing companies in a format that was fairly well teacher-proof and controlling of student knowledge. Typical questions are: "Who is the main character?"; "Where does the story take place?"; "What happened when Fred's father left home?"; "What is the main problem in the story?"; "How was it solved?"; "How is the setting related to the mood of the story?"; "What is the atmosphere of the story?"; "What happened to the main characters?"; "What kinds of food did Grandma have in her cupboard?"; "What kind of animal is Oliver?"; "Why did the pirates kidnap Grandma?"[1] In almost every case, these types of questions required a preferred reading of the text, and students were required to regurgitate the knowledge of the text.

A whole language or negotiated reading of text requires that the students answer questions but not that they create their own knowledge of or from the text. Questions in this category are framed as follows: "What do you think the story is about?"; "Have you ever felt like Leora?"; "What kind of a person do you think the archduke is?"; "What do you think will happen to princess Leora when her father leaves?"; "What do you think will happen after the story?"; "When you were reading the story, what events are similar to those that have happened to you?"; "What do you think Princess Leora's father was thinking when he had to leave his daughter with the archduke?"[2] In each example, the questions ask for a negotiated reading of the text; in other words, the text has particular representations and meanings and the reader has a particular response to the text. The questions generate a negotiation between those of the text, and those of the reader. Framing the question with what do "YOU" think/feel/know is still a control of student knowledge in which the text holds a large part of the authority/authorship of the knowledge.

What changes when the students resist, oppose, or challenge the authority/knowledge of a text? How are the questions framed or produced that move the student into a position of power? Compare the nature of the following questions to those asked previously in the traditional, basal, or whole language approach to literacy: In what ways are the characters in power or oppressed by a dominant gender, race, class, age, and so forth? What racial knowledge is present in this text? In what ways? How has the author constructed men/women in this text that is consistent with or contradictory to mainstream knowledge of men and women? In what ways has the author constructed power/knowledge/relationships/representations/values based on gender, race, class, and so forth? In what ways would you challenge the exclusions of certain cultures (race, sexuality, etc.) in this text? Who do you think created the representations and knowledge in this text? And what do you oppose or resist about the representations/relationships based on age, class, history, dominance, privilege, marginalization, and so forth, in this text? In what ways has the author used mainstream knowledge to create a state of consent in the reader?

The answers or discussions that follow from this type of questioning nuture a cultural/critical imagination. They are not oriented at answers or personal/reader responses to the text that extract preferred or negotiated readings. Instead, each of the questions require students to reformulate the knowledge and, in turn, return the responsibility to the students for creating the knowledge, not as mere restructuring, but as knowledge that is inclusive of new truths, values, relationships, and representations.

Additional responsibility lies with the teacher/adult not only to model the questions, but to make this type of questioning an expectation of all students. To avoid or to resist a reductionist approach to questioning is the political burden of teachers. No longer can they avoid the dangerous, volatile, sensitive types of questions that are asked by cultural critics and those engaged in cultural/critical literacy. In addition, teachers shift their questioning from preferred and negotiated frameworks to politically active questioning by students. Politically active in that the teachers are shifting the production, circulation, maintenance, and control of knowledge from themselves and textbooks back to the students. Thus, students become political agents in the creation of knowledge. They create, produce, and shape knowledge and regain control of their initial entrance into the world of learning mainly through questions that challenge, resist, or oppose the dominant, exclusive, privileged, and legitimized status of established knowledge. When students consent to established knowledge (e.g. truths, relationships, and histories about gender, race, class, and so forth), they are gradually pressed into hegemonic practices. Cultural/critical literacy demands counter-hegemonic questioning and a differently nurtured imagination.

DISMANTLING THE CANONS OF KNOWLEDGE

A major source of knowledge in schools is the textbook. In it is found prepackaged, preordered, legitimized, objective knowledge. We find such knowledge in the texts of the sciences, arts, humanities, and the growing number of "how to" books, including the technologies of media, computers, and teaching. Knowledge in these textbooks is selected, ordered, and produced by authorities in the disciplines, to be consumed by the reader. Even at university, thoughts and knowledge are controlled by the authority of textbooks.

It seems that the first location for students to create their own knowledge would be at university. Yet, the textbook has become the dominant source of knowledge for students and in no way are they given the opportunity, encouraged to, or evaluated on their abilities to challenge, resist, or oppose that authority. Instead, they are evaluated and judged on their ability to consume, without negotiation or resistance, the prepackaged knowledge. Often, students relate how professors simply read from the textbook or have the students recall verbatim information from the textbook ("Great, we don't have to go to classes!"). Such comments recall the original nature of university when knowledge was created by professors mainly through their lectures to students. Alternatively, students were to create the knowledge through writing in collaboration with the professor's lectures.

A return to initial structures of higher learning is one important use of history that could be relevant to the creation of knowledge by students through their resistance and opposition to the established and dominant knowledge of mainstream thought. In middle school/junior high and secondary/senior high school curriculum policies could be developed and implemented that require students not to consume knowledge, but to create it. Again, this is not a cry for relevancy in education, but for a return to the fundamental purpose of educational institutions in which, teachers, administrators, parents, and students, through a process of collaboration, are opposed to prepackaged knowledge such as found in textbooks. Granted, this is a violent political statement that would require changes in attitudes, practices, and structures that are entrenched within educational settings. For example, in dismantling curriculum, the removal of dualisms in education such as: teacher/student, objectivity/subjectivity, knower/known, teaching/learning, testing/creating knowledge, authority produced/student produced textbooks are only a few of the implications for institutional structure. Such changes demand that students can and should be creators of knowledge.

MULTIPLE READINGS OF FIXED KNOWLEDGE

In the traditional approach to student learning, knowledge is held as power by authoritative teachers and textbooks. Such knowledge is perceived as absolute, total, and fixed with very clear boundaries between the disciplines. Even within the fields, there are clear boundaries; for example, within science: chemistry, biology, and physics; and within the humanities: literature, history, sociology, and psychology. At the end of the modern era, these boundaries between different knowledges are fixed so firmly that students cannot or must not cross them or challenge the knowledge within disciplinary borders. Even within a negotiated reader-response or relevancy approach to literacy (any symbolic representation of knowledge, whether print, oral, visual, media, etc.) in which students supposedly are given some responsibility for production, there is a limited opportunity to resist or to oppose the status quo knowledge base.

But a cultural/critical literacy, gives students no other option but to deconstruct and thus, to create new knowledge that is inclusive and decentered from the mainstream, legitimized knowledge (teachers, professors, textbooks, disciplines, and so forth). Students must create knowledge by challenging the canons or sacred texts (whether oral, printed, visual, or otherwise). In addition, once challenged and dismantled, canons of knowledge (i.e., texts that are produced, circulated, maintained, and legitimized by the dominant culture) can no longer stay at the center. Students create multiple readings and writings of cultural constructions with no need or expectation of absolutes, fixed truths, meanings, and knowledge. The implications of multiple readings and interpretations of knowledge have great impact on all aspects of education since all institutional policies, documents, and structures are dependent upon knowledge created by authorities other than students.

RE-SITUATED KNOWLEDGE

Claims to student-created knowledge re-situate both the known and the knower. Classrooms in which I work with teachers and students tend to position me uncomfortably if I am trying to introduce cultural/ critical literacy in the classroom. Teachers express discomfort with the types of discussions that follow from my visits. Whereas I am free, as a university professor, from certain political backlash from parents and administrators in the schools, the teachers do not feel the urgency or responsibility to "rock the boat." When I point out to them that cultural/critical literacy is now a stated fact in curriculum guidelines and documents, they hesitantly address the implications for a shift and decentering from mainstream knowledge, to the plurality of voices and reworkings of knowledge that the inclusion of differences generates.

Political support and theoretical discourse is needed for teachers and administrators before proceeding to implement cultural/critical literacy. Certain discourse has to enter educational documents and policies in order to provide an articulation and legitimization of the field. Professionals at school and district levels must unite to provide a political force that will influence the policy and decision makers.

Thus, there are parallel worlds in action: the world of theoretical awareness, political shifting, and the inclusion of cultural/critical literacy in policy and practice. Without these actions, there is limited support for teachers to institute cultural/critical literacy in their classrooms. Thus, knowledge remains as status quo; and textbooks, teachers, and other designated authorities remain as the producers of knowledge while students remain as the consumers of knowledge.

WHAT DOES A CULTURAL/CRITICALLY LITERATE CLASSROOM SOUND LIKE?

As mentioned before, the sound of students' questions being answered by students as they challenge, resist, and oppose the prepackaged knowledge, representations, information, values, history, and so forth, is a key element in a culturally literate classroom. And culture here does not mean merely ethnic or national cultures, but a whole host of symbolic representations (e.g., visual, oral, print, multimedia) that carry meanings situated in a social, cultural, and historical context. So students challenge the authority of any representational text that purports to contain knowledge of subject matter, with questions of race, class, relationships to that knowledge, contradictions to the mainstream, and so forth.

In their book, *Women's Ways of Knowing*, Belenky, Clinchy, Goldberger, and Tarule (1986) request that women (girls) create new knowledge and thus, in return, reclaim their selves, voices, and minds. Arguing that women have been silenced by the dominant structures and constitutions of knowledge, especially by white, middle-class, male knowledge, the authors discuss ways of knowing compatible with notions and practices of cultural/critical literacy. Since knowledge is gendered by the dominant status of males who have constructed a Euro/American–centric and logo-centric world based on their positioning, all others who do not fit into these categories are excluded.

This perspective was confirmed for me when I observed a student teacher in a high school class talk about Greek history, specifically the Peloponnesian Wars. While the students asked no questions of the text, the teacher bombarded the students with questions aimed at extracting information about men, battles, geographical locations, successes, and failures of the Greeks and of their enemies. At no time was there any mention of women nor any construction of the knowledge by the students. A few students were able to control the discussion based on the teacher's questions. The women in the class obviously did not have the resources or the awareness needed to challenge the knowledge that was being offered. Many of the male students were excited by the descriptions of bloody battles and the naming of several male heroes. When I asked the student teacher where were the women during this period, he shrugged his shoulders. The next day he attempted at least to incorporate some information on women who lived at this time. Nevertheless, he failed to provide any questions that would challenge or dismantle the text based on gender constructed knowledge. The same could be said for the Euro/

American–centric celebration in which the knowledge was embedded. In spite of the fact that the class contained multiple races, including Aboriginal, Arabic, Asian, and Eastern European peoples, there were no attempts to challenge the knowledge from the position of different races. The comment from the classroom teacher was that "You can't rewrite history." In other words, students cannot generate or create knowledge out of opposition to the fixed truths and absolute authority of the textbooks and of history.

STUDENTS WRITING KNOWLEDGE

When Toni Morrison recurrently and thematically askes "Why am I, an Afro-American, absent from [American literature]," she is in fact asking a question that students should be asking of their own learning. Why are they, with their plurality of differences, and thus, multiple knowledges, excluded from the knowledge-based curricula of educational institutions? Once having read against the grain of status quo knowledge, students are faced with the task of writing knowledge into the center instead of being left at the margins or invisible in texts. Not only are students required to create knowledge through challenge and opposition to the texts, they are to write themselves back into the cultures of knowledge. Their authorship would be the penultimate state of creating new knowledge.

Writing against the grain allows the students not only to create new knowledge but to produce it for others and for themselves to challenge and to oppose. In a continuous process of reading against the grain and writing knowledge out of its original social, cultural, and historical context, students engage in multiple readings, multiple writings, and the politics of plurality. Teachers must prepare for the onslaught of endless rereadings and rewritings of knowledge that is challenged by the students. Just as a body of knowledge is created and accumulated by the students, they must challenge their own creations—the art of revisiting and revising knowledge.

Classroom timetables, interactions, practices, materials, evaluation, and testing disappear into a realm in which students are intellectuals who are responsible and expected, in theory and practice, to challenge, and to resist knowledge as given. Timetables change to become schedules of seminars and laboratories of imagination in which students are presented with established, legitimized, dominant knowledge, and then given the task/expectation to deconstruct that knowledge as invalid, inconsistent, and contradictory. For example, in the natural sciences, a challenge to the objective, positivistic approach to the study of natural phenomenon could easily come from cultures that do not separate the natural world from the human world. Authors like Lyall Watson, Loren Eiseley, Lewis Thomas, and Aldo Leopold challenge the status quo knowledge base of most scientific disciplines such as biology and botany. In physical education, the dominance of sports knowledge would be challenged by alternative body awareness practices such as yoga and tai chi. In literature, bodies of knowledge established by the traditional canons such as Shakespeare, Frost, Steinbeck, Faulkner, and the ensuing literary critics would be dismantled by literature of other cultures based on differences of gender, race, class, sexuality, history, age, politics, nationality, ethnicity, religion, and a host of other cultural constructions.

IMPLICATIONS

Students creating knowledge has several implications, which, in many ways, will see the end of modern education as we know it. There have been very few major revolutions in modern Euro/American education, at least according to most educational philosophy. Rousseau, Piaget, and Dewey, to name a few of the boys, seem to be most commonly included as having the greatest impact on modern Western education. Although we have moved from a teacher-centered to a student-centered curriculum (mostly in theory), educational sites, especially schools, are still major arenas in which students acquire established knowledge.

If postmodern education moves students into a position as creators of knowledge, curriculum and notions of literacy also shift emphases and structures. Unlike paradigms in which knowledge is still regarded as fixed, absolute, and ordered, knowledge is neither dominant, shifted, or ordered. In fact, in postmodernism, challenge and chaos are the agencies out of which knowledge is created. And only if students challenge the logocentric does chaos emerge. That is the one consistent fact; that new knowledge emerges when that which is dominant and established no longer is ordered, legitimized, or inclusive. For example, in the sciences, arts, humanities, technologies, and professions, chaos is the emergent philosophy of knowledge in the disciplines. Furthermore, the distinction between the disciplines is no longer contained within borders of defined, ordered knowledge but within the process of seeking order out of chaos. In other words, students within the modern constructions of knowledge known as "disciplines," are engaged in a continuous process of questioning, challenging, resisting, and dismantling established knowledge especially that which is centered in traditional disciplines and institutions (family, school, church, business, popular culture and so forth).

Students use this chaos to create knowledge. More importantly, educational, pedagogical, and epistemological philosophy emerges as supportive of students as creators of knowledge. In order to do so, changes are required that dismantle and reposition the multiple dimensions of educational sites. Teachers, materials, structures, content, logic, methodologies, educational discourse, mainstreaming, administration, policies, classroom management and planning are only a few of the sites that would be accused of hegemonic practices that function to block students' creation of knowledge. Maybe governments and businesses will hire postmodern babies if they become experts in creating knowledge not consuming it?

NOTES

1. Thanks to Nora McLean and Sheri Smith-Ellis of Bathurst.
2. Thanks again to Nora and Sheri.

PART TWO

...TO PRACTICE

IV

GORILLAS...OOPS: GUERRILLAS IN OUR MIDST—
(RE)DUX: KITCHEN KNOWLEDGE

Karen Anijar, Joshua Anijar, Ron Gonzales, and Lana Krievis

INTRODUCTION

The announcement for the conference read: *Join us as we are Coming to a Place of Strength and are Developing Strategies for Action in Politically Conservative Cultures.* Ron, Lana and I (Karen) engineered our appearance with tremendous tactical élan, even though we were all exhibiting signs of battle fatigue.

As we returned from the conference to the "greater" Los Angeles area, many conversations ensued in our "guerrilla garrison." We present this chapter as an unauthorized form of pedagogy . . . an improvisational conversation with public school students. In between the dialogue, we insert original "pieces" from the paper we presented as we "came to a place of strength" and attempted to "develop strategies for action."

The setting: the familiarity of home where the warmth of the kitchen immediately lends itself to relaxed and spontaneous conversation. All the narrators know each other very well. The candor in our discussions may directly result from the informal ambiance, that comes from intimacy and acceptance. We have decided to label our methodology *Coffee Talk Research* in honor of a *Saturday Night Live* skit. With the exception of Lana, Ron, Joshua, and Karen all the other names in the chapter are pseudonyms. We are pleased that we have had the opportunity to place adolescent curriculum theorists in the body of this work. After all it is they who are profoundly affected by the frenetic backlash of retro-reforms.

Ron: Sometimes I feel like I am fighting a war of futility in a jungle of class!

Karen: I know exactly how you feel, Ron. Sometimes, I look around and think this

K. Anijar, J. Anijar, R. Gonzales, and L. Krievis

isn't real, this is a movie, and, somehow without preparation I was placed into the center of the action. I really want to find the exit door. Yet, the more I look the more it all becomes obscured. I feel as if I am wandering in a thick pea soup sort of fog. As if I was wandering in the midst.

At the conference, we were somewhat unwittingly conscripted. We attended a session on teaching *gifted* children. Suffice to say we were a captive audience.

Ron: Yeah, prisoners of war!

The speaker began her presentation with a cartoon. The presentation on strategies for the anointed few plunged downward into an hour long liturgy. The canon (or cannon) of institutional racism masked as technological efficiency under a rubric of care (for certain students) made the cute cartoon at the beginning of her presentation even more insidious. Each word, each stereotype, each expression in educationese shot through us like a bullet, a scud missile pointed directly at the children this young woman professed to serve. We dug our trenches deeper and buried our hands in our faces trying to protect ourselves from the onslaught.

Education in the 1990s bears a striking resemblance to the Gulf War. The Gulf War was fought much like a Nintendo game. The effects do not/did not seem real for the bombs do not/did not see people, or at least—people like US.

Language is transpositioned when we speak of saving lives with our missiles (or of acceptable losses). As J. Broughton exclaimed: "What a P.R. coup: doctoring the media to portray the bomb as Mother Teresa" (1996: 141). What a P.R. coup to do away with affirmative action to defend equality! What a P.R. coup to victimize the children at the altar of economic change and transformation!

Joshua: It was cool during the Gulf War. I was in Israel, and they gave out gas masks. The old lady next door barfed, I mean really hurled, in her gas mask. When I got back to North Carolina and we got to watch the war on TV it was weird because I mean there was this map of this place I had been. And, then the missiles hit my abuellos' town. But by then it was just like a point on the map. It got pretty dull watching CNN so I put my SEGA on instead.

Nobody saw the casualties. The war, much like the interplay between CNN and SEGA, presented technology apart from human beings. Technology remains merely human artifice. We create it, we shape it, we guide it. While we were digging trenches we began to let technology lead people, rather, than letting people control technology. Leo Marx today might have created a different metaphor than the oft-cited garden in the machine, or machine in the garden. The metaphor may well entail a holographic garden.

While we were watching, the New Right emerged and took most of the Left with them. With technological efficiency, and laser-like smart missile targeting, the resurgent Right shifted the discursive grounds of the political, "making conservative politics look mainstream when compared with overt bigotry, and numbing the public to racism and injustice in mainstream politics" (Quigley and Berlett 1995:20) and mainstream schooling.

"If I Had a Mouth, I Would Scream," was the title of a short story by Harlan Ellison. Cartoon characters do not necessarily have mouths. Deaf children have no language, bilingual children run on deficits, poor children, poor families, people of color, and immigrants are deficits. Essentially, essentialized as caricatures, as categories—but not as subjective entities living their own lives. Technically essentialized, dots on a map, quantified, and enumerated, but never the subjects of their own existence. Holograms that resemble humans, but, alas can never be human. If you pull the switch, a hologram having no control over "its" existence disappears into the darkness. In a virtual world you can be anything you want to be, in a virtual terrain you can (re)package reality for all to consume. This is not a gargantuan carnivalistic consumeristic frenzy without a bottom line. The bottom line is a befitting descriptor. Whoever pulls the switch has the right to cut you off, cut you out, and turn you off.

ANOTHER LOUSY DAY IN PARADISE

In the post–Gulf War world the triumphant Right portrays morality in ahistorical terms. Students seem to understand (with extraordinary clarity) issues contextualized in the binaries, black/white and absolute good/evil surrounding *certain* groups of people. One of our projects as guerrillas must be to recapture and to historicize morality, ethics, scruples, care, from the right.

Tony: The speaker calls herself a Christian. I wonder if a Latino ever made an A in that woman's class? She is a total hypocrite. And, it really made me mad last year at graduation, when that girl mentioned her as a role model. I saw her, sitting there on her ass: just smiling. Her smile was really bad, it could give you nightmares it was so fake. But, it was like she really believes she does good things.

61

Joshua: She would start screaming for no reason!

Jacob: After graduation, remember when we saw her in the supermarket. I wasn't going to say "Hi!" I mean it wasn't as if nothing ever happened. So, I avoided her. She saw me. And then she said to her friend that was standing there—"Well, he is so rude, you know some people don't know how to raise their kids . . . and then I am expected to teach them something".

Xavier: She once called my mom up on the phone and screamed: I said "Mom, mom why are you taking this shit from her? Do something." And my mom said, "Well, God has a plan!" And I said, "Sure, and it isn't for me to flunk English!"

Mark: She will sit there and smile ... and then you just want to hurl all over her, and say: "Liar!"

Joshua: My mom once called the school when she went ballistic on the phone and the principal said—"She never acts like that."   But, she did.

Tony: But the parents and the principal think she is a good teacher, but   they never see what she does in class.

TECHNO-RACES

Youth is simultaneously "transgressive and revered" (Ackland 1995:19), but it is always a threat. Young people are perceived as a disease, a pathologized condition that can be cured by reaching adulthood (which, unfortunately many young African-American men never get to reach). If schools would do their jobs, if mothers would stay at home, if there was not a breakdown in the family, the disease would not have spread with such impunity. Nevertheless, some young people are more threatening than others (some young people are more infected than others). Some people are perceived as more predatory, even by cohorts their own age.

"Skaters," Joshua exclaims "are a real problem in my school!"

A collage of consumptive images (re)creates our progeny as essentially deviant (Lewis 1992:54). Young people are not a homogenous aggregate waiting to descend on the good citizens of the heartland and to commit unspeakable acts of violence.

Young people, constitute an amalgamation of alternative collective subjectives shaped by aspects of their social identities (race, religion, region, social class, and age) that also provide them with rich alternative cultural identifiers.

Tony: The dress codes tell us we can't wear red or blue, we can't sag cause we will look like gang members. I don't think we can wear black or white, so what is left to wear? I don't want to look like a nerd!

In the post-Fordist world it is never merely style that makes the wo(man), rather, s/he emerges from the story that makes, creates, shapes, and sustains her. And the story is derived from the image. What is needed to transform the self? Enough capital to purchase the correct image.

"You know who the gang kids are by the way they dress," said Mark.

The schools buy into all of this as well. It seems pretty ludicrous that the students in suburbia are on color restriction because of gang violence. The dress code conceals the racial dimensions of the discussion. What appears to be a postmodern form of slippery selfhood (what you wear is who you are) is actually the dialectical doublespeak of the resurgent racist right.

"After all," Jacob remarks, "who wears the Lakers jackets and who sags?"

Dress codes (like the little Dutch boy, who put his finger in the dike) occur in the name of law and order. You can dress it up in plaids all you want, but the underlying problems of economic shifts are not addressed. The ruling class, the white ruling class can use law and order as a means of masking the realities of problems in schools. What do people of color have to "defend themselves against aggression . . . especially when aggression is done in the name of law and order" (Ross 1995:174)? Violence in schools is not a fashion statement. Poverty in schools is not a fashion statement. Who the clothing signifies is where the ideology reveals itself. The fashion statements erase economic inequities and injustices. You can't cure poverty by a new outfit.

Karen: The point is do the kids in your school get the same things as the kids in Ron's school, or Lana's school? You have got computers everywhere. Do you guys know who has access to all of this technology right now?

Joshua: I just read people with access to the internet have 92%   more something or other, I forgot, it was something academic.

Tony: We all have computers. What's the big deal?

Joshua: Not everyone has a computer.

Tony: I know not everyone but all our friends do. So we are 92% better . . .

He who has the most toys when he dies wins. The technological masks the economic base. If we are entering a world where technology reigns supreme, where technological literacy is the new literacy, then he who has access to technology is he who rules. Yet, you need a significant amount of capital to gain access to and to keep current with a rapidly changing technological world. The ruling class gets on the information highway a heck of a lot faster than those who do not have the capital to pay the toll. When children of the credit card classes enter the information highway with their Pentiums™, they do so with greater speed and power than those taking a broken-down 286, or an old style Mac. Some students don't even have computers. Perhaps the information highway in Hegelian language is a "highway of despair of modern consciousness" (Dallmeyer 1993:31) for the mode of production is obscured in the machine of 92% better.

We can call this a form of cyber-capitalism, which can be theorized as a virtual manifest destiny expressed unambiguously in the phrase *the rhetoric of the technologic sublime* (Leo Marx 1964). The technologic sublime constitutes an obscured version of hidden curriculum. The divisions are no longer buried, they are placed into the holographic, into the Star Wars, into the machine where war is peace, and defense is offense, and the fractions are always inverted in doublespeak and double entendres.

In retrospect, reflecting on the conference once again, we realize the young woman that presented her paper and offended us with her hyperbolized hypocritical categories, <u>did not see people</u>. She saw holographic caricatures of human beings. She saw objective characteristics: skaters, gangbangers, good gifted students, disabled students, losers, disruptive students, niggers, spics, wops, kikes, beaners, fags, and dykes. She saw collocations of paradigmatic easily packaged features. You know who the enemy is by how they dress. There is a hierarchy of signifiers of completely unequal value.

THINKING OF GUERRILLAS OR GORILLAS

Ron: We see ourselves as terrorists. Do other people see us as terrorists?

Joshua: Take a look at yourselves . . . Guerrillas don't get room service! Terrorists don't have down comforters . . . Look at Lana, for example. She looks like the perfect teacher . . . She certainly doesn't look like a guerrilla.

Karen: What does a terrorist look like? Whose face is the face of the terrorist? Is this all a part of the ideological aesthetic? And, is a terrorist the same thing as a guerrilla fighter?

I may need you to complete me (to paraphrase Bakhtin). But, I do not need you to define me. Who creates the definitions? How do the definitions become set in stone? Why do we constantly posit the categorical and why are we unwilling to see the dynamic and rich flux involved?

> On Sunday, August 4, 1996, Harry Thomas was winding down from a long hot weekend. He was half asleep watching the eleven o'clock news, when a story came on about the death of General Mohammed Farah Aidid, the self-proclaimed President of Somalia, who had humiliated U.N. and U.S. troops in a series of military skirmishes in 1993. When the newscast flashed a picture of the man who had taken Aidid's place, Thomas laughed and called out to his wife: hey, they have gotten the wrong guy! They are showing a picture of Hussein!
> Thomas was referring to Hussien Mohammed Farah, the soft spoken and impeccably polite part-time clerk who'd worked for him in West Covina's engineering department. . . (Goodman 1996:73)

The story in The *Los Angeles Times Magazine* continues. The adjectives that describe Hussien continually speak of soft-spokenness, and politeness: as if to be a warlord one can not be soft-spoken or polite. Who could have known Mohammed was a terrorist?

New right revisionist claims (re)capture the macho, the Rambo, the hard-bodied American male. To paint a terrorist or a guerrilla as soft weakens him/her as a formidable or even viable force.

> Asked if he was troubled by the fact he had been a Marine in Somalia, he replied "I always wanted to be a Marine." He explained, "I'm proud of my background and military discipline." With a soft smile, he added "Once a Marine always a Marine." (Goodman 1996:77)
> Terrorism has nothing to do with creating a just world, an equitable world or a peaceful world. "The intent is to create military and police forces upon which the social order can be based. Further, it is to create patterns of self-consciousness which amount to self-policing. . . ." It ensures a constitutional consent for the war against self-determination, for the perpetuation of a postmodern capital of rampant consumerism

for the sake of consumerism. "American citizens must adapt the policing model to their own lives. To do this they must feel the terror themselves . . . in a personal way so that people will beg the government to act decisively and do something." (Jones 1993:41)

To see one as a terrorist is a powerful and forceful (re)articulation. But, who is the terrorist here? Much like our justice system, terrorist (re)names the person in opposition to you as transgressive. It renames the person as criminal. Complexities and contingencies in a war of position and perspective (re)name and (re)articulate and (re)form for a different version of the same old same old. European nationalism paved the road for the tank of white supremacy in the guise of American Nationalism to roll through the highways and by-ways of the land.

Tony: Josh and I have a favorite sign: "International Borderzone State Park." Underneath is a smaller sign: "wildlife viewing permitted." I bet you know who the wildlife really is.

Joshua: Sometimes at night there are floodlights and they aren't for a used car sale. Why do you think that all the cars are supposedly inspected on the border of San Diego and Orange county?

In order to combat the measures that have been imposed we need to have a public pedagogy breaking the cycle and spiral of racism and hatred ensconced under the rubric of morality and technology.

We need to recognize that the political pedagogy practiced in the public schools is a direct result of the proto–facism that has emerged in the United States. In a post–Proposition 209 world (the removal of affirmative action) we must stop gingerly skirting the issues. We must continuously confront fascism in all of its forms ranging from the ridiculous: "The United States is a Christian nation, the United States is a White nation," to the sublime: "colonization of peace corps neo-liberals who cannibalize and exoticize our children" (for their own oftentimes voyeuristic, feel good, consumption). We are not being alarmist, but we are moved to action by a passion that comes from a historicized morality. We collectively define fascism in terms of the right that celebrates the nation or the race

> as an organic community transcending all other loyalties. It emphasizes a myth of national rebirth after a period of decline or destruction. To this end fascism calls for a spiritual revolution against signs of moral decay . . . and seeks to purge alien

forces and groups that threaten organic community . . . (Lyons 1995: 244)

We need to combat fascism in the schools in every hallway, in every room, in each concombinant (re)form—ranging from the nostalgic: "the resurgence of phonics, back to basics, and English only," to the overt: segregated school districting (which does exist in Southern California [San Diego for example has 43 separate school districts, we have also seen school districts with just one school]) or the incident in Bell Gardens where "a teacher asked students for their immigration papers" (Brugge 1995:204). "How many times have you heard white men are being discriminated against?" We must respond, no matter what the cost.

Ron: Never ever give power over to those who seek your acquiescence.

> Together we must hold, not only individuals, but governments accountable. The silence of the government equals permission to hate. Local governments must be responsible for the abuse of basic human rights of its citizens. State governments must stand up against intolerance. And the federal government must be the guiding force behind protection of human rights and human dignity in this country in which we claim all are created equal. Local, state, and federal legislation must be enacted and enforced to protect individuals and groups from racial, homophobic, and xenophobic intolerance. (Ross 1995:180)

But, instead of activism we have atrophy and silence. All is Quiet on the Western Front.

Who has the authority to name your conditions? Who defines the guerrilla as a terrorist? Why is Hussein a terrorist, and why is Pete Wilson governor? The positions, perspectives, paradigmatics, and prescriptions emerge at a dazzling rate of speed. We are peddling as hard as we can just to keep in place. What is needed here, what is necessary to survive is a bit of *pessimism of the intellect and optimism of the will.*

BACK TO THE LAND OR LIVING ROOM

Lana: You know the whole time I was in my teacher education program I made A's. Frankly, some of it wasn't for the work done. On occasion I didn't even hand in assignments . . . But, it is easier to give out an A than to have trouble or create trouble.
Mark: I wish it would happen to me.

Jacob: Yeah, but you know last week this kid, this skinhead threw a piece of metal at my sister and said 'ching chang gook' and what was I supposed to do sit there and do nothing?

Mark: The teacher would have seen it if it was a white kid.

Xavier: Everyone says Asians are model minorities . . .

Joshua: I won a biology award last year, everyone was happy I won. But, what was really funny is that there were comments made about how especially good it was cause I'm not Asian.

The shift in political orientation includes traditional liberals and conservatives as well. In a type of *Twister* both sides of the nonexistent political spectrum have been swept up into the rightist Hegelian vacuum. Students' comments disclose how pervasive this repackaged form of fascism is ("Democrats are Liberals and Republicans are Conservatives").

Signifiers do change, but the threat remains. The United States' economy is no longer hostage to Japan.

> There has been a recent shift from Japan bashing and Buy American to blaming immigrants. . . . Because relatively few recent immigrants are voters and immigrants do not have their own PACs, they are not widely feared or respected by liberals in the electoral arena. (Brugge 1995:209)

Immigration is not a U.S. problem, it is a global issue. Our perception of immigrants has dramatically changed since the "Statue of Liberty" days. Immigrants are no longer future citizens; they are economic drains.

Mark: I mean it is true they come here and then use up our water and stuff.

Joshua: It was different back then because there was enough land, there isn't a lot of land now.

Jacob: Sometimes they come here just to get welfare!

They and welfare mothers and single mothers are all stigmatized as the cause of the nation's problems. Deflecting and diverting attention from the root cause of the problem (Fine in Wollons 1993): the changes from an industrial base of production to a post-industrial order. Divide and conquer reigns supreme in dialectical doublespeak, we don't talk with each other, we fight among ourselves, categorizing in our boxes, and hating each other rather than uniting against the displacement of the work force by "automation, artificial intelligence and biotechnology." (Sklar 1995:117)

INGREDIENTS FOR A REVOLUTIONARY STEW—SIMMERED IN A CROCK POT

To paraphrase Baudrillard, topography precedes the geography. What is the topography of California that creates a situation where we all feel so precarious? Why do we feel so frightened? Who are our allies? Whom can we trust? We go underground.

Joshua: Did you guys see the Simpsons' *episode where the mom went underground? She wanted to stop Mr. Burns from viral warfare. The government rose against her, and she took a VW bus into the underground. She got caught because she was trying to help; she was being too nice.*

For Foucault, society maintains control by identifying part of the culture as pathological, dysfunctional, and anti-social. Our consciousness is to police and to be policed. To discipline and to be disciplined. For what? For whom?

> What we are aiming for is a period of recolonization. . . . We are already beginning to see it in journals such as *Foreign Affairs* the notion of "failed states"; that is Third World Nations which have had their experiment with self determination, sovereignty and democracy and failed in it. Now it is up to the United States to re-colonize and re-impose some level of what will be called in the press "civil society" . . . "Let's face it: some countries are just not fit to govern themselves." (Merrill 1993: 46)

Therefore, some people are not fit to govern themselves. The macro becomes the micro. Or did the micro inform the macro? Which came first the chicken or the egg? Any way you configure or reconfigure it, it is ultimately racism. Code it, package it, or re-package it: If it wags its tail it is still a dog! "Like paths in an M. C. Escher painting, the data can head off in opposite directions yet invariably lead to the same conclusion." (Tucker 1994:292)

Welcome to the world of dialectical doublespeak. In 1994, California passed Proposition 187. The next election presented Proposition 209 on the ballot, and much to our collective depression, oppression, and lingering migraines, the measure passed. One thing is certain: language remains obscured. The words are so vacuous they can be co-opted by any ideology for any purpose. The words are complex and contradictory, and constantly transpositioned. <u>Vote for Civil Rights by voting for Proposition 209!</u> Didn't it seem odd that David Duke appeared speaking at California State University—Northridge in favor of Proposition 209? Did the simulacra give away the ideology? It is impossible to believe that the language was so coded that people could not understand.

Xavier: I mean do you think a bunch of Chicanos in brown sheets dragged him off his burning cross to come to California?

Joshua: Mom, California always leads the nation. If it happens in California, it will happen in the rest of the country soon.

Indeed,

> Today's sunbelt represents a confluence of Social Darwinism, entrepreneurialism, high technology, nationalism, nostalgia and fundamentalist religion, and any Sun Belt hegemony over our politics has a unique potential . . . to accommodate a drift towards apple-pie authoritarianism. So wrote conservative strategist Kevin Phillips in his 1982 book, Post-Conservative America. The failed American dream can give way to a new American fairness or a neo-fascist nightmare. It can happen in Europe, it can happen here. (Sklar 1995:131)

In our kitchen/classroom conversations the students clearly understood. Maybe we have reached George Bush's kinder and gentler nation. In California we certainly have a kinder and gentler form of racism: (re)presenting and (re)configuring racism as equality. It is all a dead give away, and dead may be the operative word here. The doors have been slammed shut, and now we have added padlocks to them.

"How do we get to dead even if we can't get to the starting gate?" asked Xavier. "Don't they understand how racist the whole fucking thing is?" queried Mark. "Do they think if they close their eyes it will all go away?" questions Joshua. Tony inquires: "Who gives these jerks the power anyway?" "Wait a second," pleads Joshua. "Did anyone see Hoop Dreams? *How many kids make it in the NBA, and they want us to buy that hiring practices in the NBA has nothing to do with racism? How many white kids place their dreams in the NBA?"*

The students can see right through the varnished patina of David

Dukisms no matter how many coats of politesse are applied. These young people know how to listen for the keywords and the code words. They have developed a critical consciousness—an unanticipated critical consciousness—a cynical, sardonic, critical consciousness—often a nihilistic consciousness.

Joshua: Trust no one!

Jacob: It is all a conspiracy, like area 51.

Our horror at the notions of conspiracy theorizing is only modified by our fears and our sense of urgency. Conspiracy theorizing is part of the millenialist fantasies of the Christian Right Wing. If segments of the Christian Coalition claim that the AIDS epidemic is a plot conceived by gays, humanists, and (well, you can fill in the blanks), clearly, we have some viral warfare to combat as guerrilla teachers. "It is all pretty pointless, anyway," Mark proclaims. "There are shadows you know," says Jacob. "It all serves the state," Josh explains.

KNOCK KNOCK—WHO'S THERE

Evil is prosaic. It doesn't announce itself at your door. The postmodern shifts the alliances and configurations. Whom can we trust? What can we do? Is the *X-Files* our way of life where we can "trust no one?" It can not be so overly determined. It can not be so nihilistic.

Joshua: Is this what Germany felt like when Hitler took over?

> "Kick their ass and steal their gas," dominated right wing talk radio during the Gulf War. There never developed any public policy debate about U.S. foreign policy that took this bumper sticker sloganeering right to its political foundations. . . . Castoriadis uses the term "radical" in its literal Latin meaning, "root or foundation," not the ideological sense of someone who calls out for root or foundational changes in political structures. But the relation of the two uses of the term is crucial. Radical political changes can only occur after radical imaginary changes have occurred. (Merrill 1993: 27–9)

Mark: My mom's boss comes over, especially for holidays. Sort of like Scrooge after Christmas: filled with gifts. She sometimes takes us out to eat. For each time my mother has cried, for every time my mother has gotten sick, for every time we received a lecture from her about the value of this or that or some shit, I eat the most expen-

sive thing on the menu. I may not be able to give my family a life, but, at least, at least I can do this. It makes me feel in control of some part of our fates. She thinks she is helping out. I spend her money, as much of her money as I can. I have attacked her on the level she loves the most: her pocketbook and she doesn't even know it!

Karen: I see . . . So, you are radically changing the imagery.

David: The coolest thing driving back from San Diego or Tijuana are the signs. "Don't hit the illegals!"

Joshua: Yeah, those signs are great; they are really funny I mean they really say . . . look out for the illegals.

Karen: Where do the signs say that? The signs are just pictures, there aren't any words!

James: You've seen them. The picture of the family running. What do you think they are running across the border for: Taco Bell?

Karen's Note: Perhaps in the postmodern I should change my axiom from *"The ideology is in the adjectives"* to *"the ideology is in the street sign."* Pedestrian crossing signs are different in San Diego.

JOB SECURITY

In The *Los Angeles Times Magazine* (October 1996) there was a story about the border patrol:

> *Alto!* commands Herrera.
> *Alcen los manos y acuestense!* (Put your hands down and lie on your head)
> *No se mueven!*
> Nobody moves
>
> . . . and so it goes hour after hour, chase after chase, vanload after vanload.
>
> *"They just keep coming"* says Herrera.
> *"You can't beat this kind of job security. . . ."*

Proenca uses an air compressor to blow the dust off his clothes. "Tracking people is a lot easier than tracking animals. All animals behave differently. People always behave the same. . . . The U.S. Border Patrol's Imperial Beach Station know better . . . than any politician that these are real people, real people desperately seeking a better life for themselves and their families. Sometimes, says Herrera, "I look at them and see my grandmother, or my grandfather. I once apprehended a 72-year-old man. He had walked 500 miles. . . . " "I have to remind myself it is my country, not their country." (Dangard 1996:40)

What does it mean to learn to hate yourselves? We are the children of immigrants. The Right resurgence-emergence is both mean-spirited and horrifyingly reminiscent of Gestapo tactics. The mayor of Pomona was stopped by the INS and told to prove his citizenship. Indeed, " 'there already is a police state that has developed in the southwestern United States since the 1980s. No person is free to travel without the scrutiny of the border patrol,' " writes Leslie Marmon Silko of the Laguna Pueblo after describing her personal harassment at the hands of the Border Patrol in New Mexico (Brugge 1996:202). Scapegoating and fear beget more scapegoating and fear. Undocumented aliens renamed as illegals? The (re)positioning of the language part of the Orwellian idiom has driven us to take an activist stance:

> It is not far-fetched to see the seeds of ethnic cleansing—the widely adopted euphemism for genocide in the former Yugoslavia—in the widespread support given Proposition 187. Land plundered away from Mexico is called Texas, California, New Mexico and Arizona. . . . The anti–alien scapegoating is spreading rapidly to legal immigrants . . . How easy it's been to roll back civil liberties with the excuse of fighting the racially based "War on Drugs." How easy it's become to spend more money on prisons and less on education. How easy it's been to relabel millions of children as illegitimate. . . . A nation that committed genocide against Native Americans, enslaved blacks and imprisoned Japanese Americans should never doubt authoritarianism can happen here. (Sklar 1995:133)

CURRICULAR COLONIZATIONS

Lana: A missionary is far beyond arrogance. The missionary proselytizes. It is complete colonialization. It is superstition. It is the belief that you hold the truth. The colonizer sees no other model. The missionary believes that s/he holds the words of God. That s/he is a soldier of the truth. The missionary comes with benevolence. That benevolence is far, far more destructive.
Karen: Emma Goldman said: "I Want Freedom, the Right to self-expression, Everybody's Right to Beautiful Radiant Things" . . . Sometimes I think she meant

that everyone in the world has the right to shop at Neiman Marcus . . . But . . . in less supercilious moments I think she was speaking about an existential ethical politic . . .

Ron: There is always an aesthetic. For me when I was turned on to Maxine Greene everything began to make sense.

Karen: Why are you so dressed up? What's going on?

Ron: Monday. Mondays are administrative meetings. This is my uniforme politico. *It is my guerrilla outfit. It is my beautiful and radiant thing.*

Karen: Don't drip any sauce over that!

Ron: You have to fight the battle in disguise.

Karen: Don't tell me that you are in disguise. I know you love to dress up like that. Does being a revolutionary preclude you from wearing silk? You told me that you had a group of student revolutionaries in your office this afternoon, you know the "gang!" But they were in ROTC. Does being in ROTC preclude you from being a revolutionary?

Ron: No, no not at all.

Karen: How does one become a guerrilla? More importantly, how is one named as guerrilla?

Ron: Sometimes you just have no choice. Psychic pain can translate into physical pain which can translate into action.

Julio: Teachers don't care. Don't you get it. Why do you think so many people are going into teaching? Do you think it is because they suddenly have developed a love for us?

Jacob: No! They are scared, I think.
Joshua: No! The jobs dried up.

Jacob: It is a conspiracy!

Manifesto

Ron: At this point it isn't why you become a guerrilla. But how to be a guerrilla. We don't have time to sit around the table discussing this as if our children are not being attacked. We must become guerrillas because we care for and about the students.

74

I suggest the approach to attack is hit and run tactics. Let's face it, if you are going to safely negotiate and infiltrate your way into their territory you must be able to see life through their expectations and words. You navigate the terrain constructing and reconstructing language based on their interpretations of the meanings. Children have their own words. Adults, i.e., administration also have their own logic: BUT they also have their own esoteric language. Use their language. Use their language against them!

The way you use the words is part of the overall fundamental importance of planning your angle of attack. You must be able to use the code of the environment that you find yourself in. Being a chameleon can only be accomplished by the use of their weapons, their words. Otherwise you will find yourself a prisoner of the war you are trying to win.

Nurture and encourage alliances with key personnel in positions of influence. In fulfilling what they think is their agenda, you can succeed in subverting it as well. That is really a successful form of attack. Once initiated it is too late to stop. Once implemented it is too late to stop a war your allies chose to begin (and they really are not your allies, your allies always have to be the people). Therefore they are forced to compete and to win your battles for you.

All wars and battles are won by those who know the rules of the game, and how to use the weapons of war available to you.

Be informed. You must attack on your terms and territory only. You must choose your battles wisely. You must anticipate all possible action but especially in the current political climate, you must anticipate reaction! Stay cloaked and hidden moving at hit and run intervals. Remember a guerrilla war is won by those who can not be easily identified. When your adversary is off balance, they can only react to an attack. They can not plan one. Most importantly a true guerrilla does not give up until she or he has attained victory for the people.

In education the people you fight on behalf of are the armies of children that are losing the war of futility. The enemy is clearly defined. The enemy is privilege for the sake of exclusion, and the purpose of maintaining a status quo. This status quo: with its attendant divisions of ethnocentric and class based boundaries is morally . . .

Karen: Reprehensible . . .

Lana: But the question that remains is whom do we see as human?

We saw the Gulf War as a Nintendo game. Why not see students as collocations of objective characteristics? Why not see students as almost-but-not-quite-human? Of course, some humans have more potential than others.

Lana: I just want to know how many "of courses" do teachers take in the room with them. Of course, they have problems learning English, they are deaf. Of course, they have problems learning English, they are a minority. Of course, even able-bodied minorities have trouble in school. Of course, they have problems learning English, they get free lunch. Of course they have trouble learning English, they have limited life experiences. Of course they have trouble learning English, their parent's aren't [American] . . . well, all of you can fill in the rest of the blanks. Of course they have problems learning English, they have problems with abstract thinking they are so literal you know!

I refuse to believe that children cannot learn because they are poor, or have imperfect parents or think differently than I do. I was a good girl. Seventeen years later, given an opportunity to teach English, I felt that I had no choice but to go underground, to become a guerrilla fighter. I faded into the blackboard jungle. As a guerrilla fighter I don't have a massive supply line to back me up. I have to find ways to live off the land. Capitalist teachers live off the children—I live with the children.

GOOD-BYE MR. CHIPS

Tony: Got any chips?

Lana: What kind do you want?

Karen: It isn't a question of have . . . it is one of choice . . . Ron, you whined all the way to the car tonight . . . "I'm cold . . . This is such a long walk, if you parked any further away it would be Nevada. . . . " We have choice, we have the capital to have choice. Most people don't. We have cars, you don't even want to walk to the parking lot.

Ron: There is a morality to all of this.

Karen: I guess so. I hope so. I am getting tired of transcribing.

Ron: Transcendence, that's it! Beautiful and radiant things. There will always be those people whose ethics transcend the categories. There will always be those people who will stand and fight . . . the mist may be really thick.

Karen: The clearing obscured—the web tangled—but, we will somehow find a way to unravel this!

Lana: There will always be people who may seem like martyrs but remain committed wholly and completely to a moral and ethical purpose. Those who won't cross over the line to save themselves.

Karen: To take an ethical stand is to take a political stand. Want a slice of pizza? Try not to get it on your uniforme politico.

REFERENCES AND SUGGESTED READINGS

Ackland, R. *Youth, Spectacle and Violence.* Boulder, CO: Westview Press, 1995.

Anijar, K., and K. Casey. *Adolescents As Curriculum Theorists. Journal for a Just and Caring Education*, 3 (4)(1997): 381–98.

Apple, M. *Cultural Politics and Education.* New York: Teachers College, 1996.

Berlet, C., and M. Quily. "Theocracy and White Supremacy." *In Eyes Right: Challenging the Right Wing Backlash.* C. Bertlet, ed. Boston: South End Press, 1995. 15–43.

Broughton, J. "The Bombs Eye View." In *Techno Science and Cyber Culture.* S. Aronowitz, B. Martinson, and S. Menser, eds. New York: Routledge, 1995.

Brugge, D. "Pulling Up the Ladder." In *Eyes Right: Challenging the Right Wing Backlash.* C. Berlet, ed. Boston: South End Press, 1995. 191–209.

Casey, K. *I Answer with My Life.* New York: Routledge, 1993.

_____."New Narrative Research in Education." *Review of Research in Education* 21 (1995): 211–53.

Clarkson, F. "Christian Reconstructionism." In *Eyes Right: Challenging the Right Wing Backlash.* C. Berlet, ed. Boston: South End Press, 1995. 59–80.

Dangard, D. "The Real Spur Posse." *Los Angeles Times Magazine.* 41, 10, (1996).

Farell, E. "Giving Voice to High School Students: Pressure and Boredom, Ya Know What I'm Saying?" *American Education Research Journal*, 25, 4, (Winter 1988): 489–502.

Fine, M. "Making Controversy: Who's at Risk." In *Children at Risk in America*, C. Wollons, ed. Albany, NY: SUNY Press, 1993. 91–110.

Gates, H. "Why Not?" In *The Bell Curve Wars.* S. Frasher, ed. New York: Basic Books, 1995.

Gramsci, A. *Selections From the Prison Notebooks of Antonio Gramsci.* Q. Hoare and G. N. Smith, ed. and trans. New York: International Publishers, 1980.

Goodman, M. "The Warlord Amongst Us." *Los Angeles Times Magazine*, 1, 41, 10 (October 1996): 72–8.

Green, M. *Teacher as Stranger.* New York: Wadsworth, 1973.

Huebner, D. "Curricular Language and Classroom Meanings." In *Curriculum Theorizing: The Reconceptualists.* W. Pinar, ed. Berkeley, CA: McCutchan, 1975.

Jervis, K. "A Teacher's Quest for a Child's Questions" *Harvard Educational Review* 56, 2 (May 1986): 132–50.

Jones, P. "Posting Modernity." In *Postmodern Contentions.* P. Jones, W. Nattler, and T. Schatzki, eds. New York: Guilford, 1993.

Kellner, D. *Media Culture.* New York: Routledge, 1995.

Kincheloe, J., S. Steinberg, and A. Gresson, eds. *Measured Lies: The Bell Curve Examined.* New York: St. Martin's Press, 1996.

Lind, M. "Brave New Right." In *The Bell Curve Wars*, S. Frasher, ed. New York: Basic Books, 1995. 172–78.

Lyons, M. "What is Fascism?" In *Eyes Right: Challenging the Right Wing Backlash*, C. Berlet, ed. Boston: South End Press, 1995. 244–45.

Merrill, R. "Simulations and Terrors of Our Time." In *The Politics and Imagery of Terrorism*. D. Brown, and R. Merrill, eds. Seattle: Bay Press, 1995. 27–46.

Noblit, G. "Power and Caring." *American Educational Research Journal*, 30, 1, (Spring 1993): 22–38.

Paley, V. J. "On Listening to What Children Say" *Harvard Educational Review*. 56, 2 (May 1986): 122–31.

Pharr, S. " Divisions that Kill." In *Eyes Right: Challenging the Right Wing Backlash*, C. Berlet, ed. Boston: South End Press, 1995.

Ross, L. "White Supremacy in the 1990s," In *Eyes Right: Challenging the Right Wing Backlash*, C. Berlet, ed. Boston: South End Press, 1995. 166–81.

Sklar, H. "The Dying American Dream." In *Eyes Right: Challenging the Right Wing Backlash*. C. Berlet, ed. Boston: South End Press, 1995. 113–34.

Stallabrass, J. *Gargantua: Manufactured Mass Culture*. London: Verso, 1996.

Steinberg, S. and J. Kincheloe, eds. *Kinderculture: The Corporate Construction of Childhood*. Boulder, CO: Westview Press, 1997.

Tucker, W. *The Science and Politics of Racial Research*. Chicago:University of Illinois Press, 1994.

THE CRITICAL TRANSFORMATION OF A SPECIAL EDUCATION CLASSROOM:
A BEGINNING TEACHER PUTS THEORY INTO PRACTICE

Nina Zaragoza and Marge Scardina

Preservice teachers educated from a critically constructivist perspective encounter major struggles during their first years of teaching in traditional settings. Struggles related to collegial relationships and curriculum design are a powerful undercurrent as new teachers confront those seasoned by lockstep, mechanistic education. This chapter discusses the experiences of one special education teacher forced to confront the system as she implemented a constructivist curriculum in two behavioristic settings. Her struggles and successes over a two-year period emerged through personal diary entries and conversations between the teacher and her university professor. This story will strengthen the resolve of teachers determined to engender positive classroom transformation.

I think that it is time I start having a better relationship with my cooperating teacher. I asked her if she wanted to go have a drink after school and we did. I was able to get to know her a little bit more. She was previously an LD (learning disabilities) teacher and this is her second year of teaching emotionally handicapped students. I asked how she felt about what I was doing and she was giving me the old, "Yeah, it's going okay" routine. I asked her to be honest and said that I wanted and needed her input. Then she said, "I don't understand what you're doing."

I began by telling her about Zaragoza's program, not so much the academics, but how students need to be successful to learn and how we need to set up a safe environment so learning and success could happen. I told her that these students are faced with failures every day of their lives and that school should be the one place where they can succeed. She said "I am fighting a losing battle".

At the time of this entry Marge was in the middle of her student teaching experience. Because she majored in Special Education she was required to teach for sixteen weeks under the supervision of a classroom teacher in a special education setting. At this point she was desperate to get the classroom teacher to understand her beliefs about education and teaching. These beliefs differed from the teacher's and Marge was confronted daily with opposing views and behaviors. Her struggle and ultimate success is a testament that classrooms based on critical and constructivist theory (Freire 1993; Kincheloe and Steinberg 1993; Zaragoza 1997) can be maintained by reflective teachers educated to consciously connect philosophy to pedagogy (Giroux 1988).

MARGE'S BACKGROUND

Marge was in her early forties when she entered a teacher preparation program. She is a single mother of four children. Marge decided to major in special education with an emphasis on the emotionally handicapped because of the emotional stress her son underwent during her divorce.

Her beginning general teacher courses focused on creating classrooms that were structured in a behavioristic manner. This perspective was reinforced as she began taking courses specifically designed for emotionally handicapped majors. Marge was taught to use behavior level systems, token economies, and mechanistic curricula approaches (Colvin et. al., 1993; Binder et. al., 1990; Heward et. al., 1989).

During her last year of undergraduate work Marge enrolled in a required language arts course taught by me (Zaragoza)Students in this class were either special education or regular elementary education majors. The class was unique for Marge in a number of ways: First, I held all class sessions within a third grade elementary school classroom that she co-taught with the classroom teacher. The university students "learned by doing" as they were integrated into the children's community and engaged in all work: silent reading, writing, choral poetry, class discussions (Zaragoza and Slater 1996).

Second, Marge was given a view of a classroom clearly founded on critical theory. Here she saw a community based on individual and collective success as each learner was enabled to work through the reading and writing process in a safe environment that encouraged reflective thinking and risk-taking. The classroom was based on intrinsic motivation and void of any materialistic rewards for behavior or achievement (Zaragoza 1997).

Third, Marge was given the opportunity to see her professor teach in a diverse, urban public school. Indeed, she saw in a concrete way that theory learned at the university could be successfully practiced "out in the real world."

Fourth, all university students were expected to keep daily diaries and reading logs that were responded to weekly by myself, by the classroom teacher, or by their peers. Through the use of these writings and hourly discussion sessions philosophical and pedagogical connections were examined throughout the semester (Zaragoza 1994).

Finally, Marge could envision *her* future classroom community as she was pushed to continually discuss what she believed about children, teaching, and learning and how these beliefs would be evident in her educational decisions. Marge was given the time and opportunity to grow as a reflective practitioner.

Marge took this opportunity to develop as a teacher willing to confront many of the myths entrenched in traditional education. The vision she created for her classroom contained the major concepts she internalized in my class and included: a supportive environment, process instruction allowing children to make choices and to work within a full community at their own pace, and an assessment program based on individual growth.

STUDENT TEACHING SETTING

The last sixteen weeks of Marge's undergraduate career took place in an elementary school classroom for students labeled "emotionally handicapped." The school is part of the fourth largest district in the country situated in a culturally diverse urban neighborhood. After a week of observation Marge wrote in her diary:

I have learned so many strategies at the university but the one thing I know is that what these teachers do is ineffective. They group the children into three groups: the high group which is about fourth to fifth grade level, the middle group which is about second to third grade level and the low group which is pre-primer. Reading is strictly taught from basals and workbooks. The teacher asks a few low level questions and then students do workbook comprehension on their own. This is so boring and yet the students do it like robots. Math is pretty much grouped the same way. They use three different math books and students work at their seats from the book with little instruction given. In the morning they do writing but they have to write about whatever prompt the teacher gives them. Today I took home the teacher manuals. One decision has been made for today— NO BASALS!!

The decision to change the reading program forced Marge to look for her own materials since:

There were no reading materials for personal reading, no student work displayed, no literature displayed, no manipulatives, a computer that no one knew how to use, and one small bookshelf with old, torn books. My first step in teaching was

81

to fill the classroom with as many types of reading materials as I could get my hands on. When I told the librarian all the books were for the emotionally handicapped department she seemed very reluctant to release the books. I want them to acquire a love for literature and realize that books can be fun. If I don't have time to teach them everything, then at least I can teach them to love books.

You will see that Marge's strong convictions about the teaching and learning environment she wanted to create and her ability to hold on to these convictions carried her community to great success. From beginning to end though, she was harassed by colleagues who did not understand what she was doing or where she was going, even from the classroom aide who seemed to have much of the decision-making power in the classroom. Marge realized that the classroom teacher had relinquished all power to the aide. When Marge asked for direct help to "get around the aide," the teacher hesitated.

But Marge was determined not to give up. She introduced the literacy program almost immediately and encouraged student interaction during writing and reading. The aide had little understanding of Marges actions and openly attacked them:

The aide is furious with me and has told me that the reason the class is having behavior problems is because of me and my ignorant way of teaching. Well maybe she's right. But I don't think so. I don't think the way to control students is through physical restraint or threats—which is what this aide does.

As determined as Marge was to implement new things, so was the aide determined to keep things the same. She insisted on keeping in place the behavioristic level system that permeated all the special education classes in the school. This system contradicted the intrinsic motivation built into Marge's developing literacy program and inevitable clashes occurred.

The aide was quick to show me how the level system worked. The students have point sheets that are kept at their desks. Points are given or taken away according to inappropriate or appropriate behavior. If students make the required amount of points, then they progress to the next day on the level chart. To acquire a level four for 16 days entitles a child to begin mainstreaming in areas of lunch, phys ed, music, and art—not academics.

Marge attempted to explain and to model some of the fundamental principles of the program but:

The aide refused to help because according to her, she doesn't understand what I'm doing and why we don't have the students in groups. I've explained it to her over and over again.

Marge soon realized that it wasn't worth the energy to solicit the aide's understanding and help because the students would end up receiving the wrong messages anyway:

The aide refuses to help and the teacher is still not sure what I'm doing. I don't want someone helping them if they are going to say anything negative about a student's ideas or spelling.

Unfortunately, the behavioristic management system continued to be a thorn in Marge's side as she almost daily complained about its negative effects: "I want to throw the aide and this level system out the window!"

The battle became so intense that Marge even referred to it using boxing terms:

Well the aide has won this round. Why this woman has such authority is beyond me. Even though I have control of the class, without a contract to give me authority, there are only certain things that I have control over. But I will not give up. Now five of my students are either off level or on indoor suspension and not allowed to do any academic work. I have to figure out a way to get around this aide.

While at times Marge and the students had a respite ("I did let the off level students participate today, the aide wasn't there. It was a good day."), the war continued:

Because my activities include fun, the aide feels that students off level should not participate in them. I have tried to explain to her that when you put students off level and insist that they do nothing for the day this allows them to avoid responsibility to complete their work.

These types of interactions happened regularly and became even more ferocious as Marge became stronger in her conviction that students should not be removed from academics:

I am going to World War III with the aide. She is having a fit about students doing work while they are off level. In the meantime I allow the students to participate and she tries to belittle me in front of them. My stress level is at its max. Today Carl finished his short story. He was so excited about finishing his story and couldn't wait to put it into publication. Now he's also off level which means that he is not allowed to do any work but of course I just ignored that. I took Carl to the computer to design his story and begin his typing. A few minutes later, the aide screams across the room, "Mrs. S do you know that Carl is off level and should not be out of his seat?" I turned around and said, "Mrs. C I do know that Carl is off level, but he needs to finish his short story on the computer, which is academics not pleasure. When he is done he will return to his seat."

Finally, during a grade group meeting issues regarding the aide were brought to light and the special aide supervisor stepped in:

Meeting today. What came out of the meeting was that off level students do participate with academics including music and art. I was really shocked because my students have not been able to participate in music or art since I have been there. The rest of the teachers and aides couldn't believe what the aide was doing to some of the students, i.e., isolating students for extended periods of time, not allowing them to eat for an hour. Maybe now I can get some work done without someone questioning every move I make.

Marge was relieved to gain some ground and while she won the battle about the behavior system, she could not bring the aide or the classroom teacher to a closer understanding of her program:

The classroom teacher was not supportive of the play. She couldn't understand why I didn't write the play myself and have the students memorize the parts. I can't get her to see the importance of the students writing their own pieces and making their own decisions.

This constant struggle to help adults understand her classroom environment and the interactions and work she facilitated began to wear Marge down. She felt tired and overwhelmed as the end of her assignment neared:

I give up, three weeks left and I'm too tired of fighting for what I believe in when this is not even my class. The classroom teacher can see the advantage of the program but she is not secure enough or knowledgeable enough to do it on her own.

Marge's struggles were ultimately overshadowed by the incredible success she experienced with her students. It was initially difficult to undo many of the negative interactions that were reinforced by the competitive, behavioristic environment they were familiar with but Marge's determination, conviction, and persistence prevailed.

Marge introduced many of the concepts and activities she envisioned for her own classroom. She realized that the students and teacher were in for a drastic change from the passive environment they were accustomed to. Children started to work on choral poetry, a writing process that included topic choice and individual book publication, a reading process that enabled children to choose their own books to read and to participate in reading discussion groups, creation and performance of a drama production, and total immersion into varied forms of literature and literacy. Marge also exposed them to the view of teacher as co-learner as she began writing in her diary along with the rest of the community.

At first Marge attempted to run the spelling program in the traditional way but only two out of thirteen students passed the weekly test. She knew she needed to try something else to ensure success for all her students so the next week she used spelling words from the solar system unit but there was little improvement. Marge then decided to try individualized spelling (Zaragoza 1997):

I had each student pick out five words that they would like to know how to spell. One student was reading and came along the word "chief." He asked me what a chief was. I told him someone who was in charge. He said, "Oh I got to know how to spell that word." When I went around the room to check on everyone's words, I was very pleased to see that they had all chosen personally challenging words. We had our first individualized spelling test today and the results were very impressive. The students felt very confident going into the test and 85% of them scored an A.

With this success Marge became more confident and enthusiastic about her decisions and started to gather materials to support her program. Marge also noticed the excitement her students began to express about the changes she was beginning to implement:

When I brought all the books in from the library the students were shocked to see so many, then they began to ask,"Mrs. S what are you going to do with all those books?" I told them the books were for us to use in the classroom. "You mean that we are allowed to look at those books?" "Yes you are!" I had them pick a partner and a book and share with one another. It was wonderful—they were full of excitement and they were laying on the floor talking and helping each other read. There were no behavior problems either! I'm going to have to slip this reading in slowly because the teacher is still waiting for me to do BASALS!!

Marge remained adamant about not using basals and consistently allowed the students to choose their own books. She also gave them the opportunity to read and to share their books in small groups and their enthusiasm was evident:

These students have never read a whole book before. Now I catch them hiding books in their desks so no one can take the ones they like. Their love for books is beginning to show!

By the middle of March the competitiveness that seemed so entrenched in this classroom started to fade within both the academic and social arenas:

Today we did TAG ("T-tell what you like; A-ask questions; G-give ideas;" Zaragoza and Vaughn 1995; 1992). They were so kind with one another. I coudn't believe how well they took the suggestions and questions from their peers. That is one thing that they haven't done well before. I can see a definite change in their attitudes about each other and I think much of it has to do with the fact that they have all been successful in things that most of them didn't think was possible. There is no more making fun of kids who read slow and the competition of who is the best is rarely mentioned. Maybe it's also because I have taken away the stigma of grouping. The books they choose for their personal reading all look alike. Only when you look at them can you tell what level they are for.

When I first started and they were in groups the low readers would shut down because they didn't like having baby books. If I was eleven and had to read them I would shut down too.

Marge also reported powerful individual student progress during her weeks as a student teacher. Students became more positive, began to take more academic risks, and continued to be extremely engaged during classroom activities. For example, Andy and Marge struggled together initially but over time both triumphed:

Today was my first day of taking over the class for the whole day. My first quest was going to be Andy. I have talked until I'm blue in the face. I have refused to write the sentences for Andy this week. I have spent time talking to him about how diary writing belongs to him and he is allowed to make as many mistakes as he likes. But nothing works. They are all hung up on spelling, they spend so much time worrying about the spelling that they do very little writing. I can see it is going to take some time before I can get them to feel free to write and enjoy it.

Marge continued to grapple with Andy as he struggled with this new way of teaching and learning. That the teacher was not going to tell him exactly what to write was shocking. Marge was discouraged as she found herself resorting to methods of coercion that were totally alien to what she thought a good teacher should do:

This morning when it came time for diary writing, Andy would not even start. I asked him to just try. He still refused, so I told him he had to stand in the corner until he was ready to show me he was willing to try. He told me, "You're the teacher and you're suppose to do it for me." "Wrong, I am the teacher and I am here to help you but you have to try first." I kept asking him if he was ready to try and the answer was still no. Making Andy stand in the corner almost killed me, but I never expected him to stand there all day. I feel like such a failure, how could I have made him stand there all day?

Thankfully, things began to turn within the next few weeks when Andy wrote his first line:

This morning when Andy came into class he had this really mad look on his face. But when it was diary time, Andy took out his diary and wrote his first sentence. Yes, yes, yes! He wrote "I hop you com bak!!!!!" Not bad! His enthusiasm has done a turnaround. He told me today that he can't wait to read like everyone else.

Andy would go back and forth from active participation and engagement to total withdrawal from all literacy activities. By this point, though, Marge took this in stride as she noted the outside influences that surrounded Andy and swayed his interactions in the classroom:

Andy has shut down again, all he wants to do is draw, but then again the aide put him "off level" for fooling around at lunch. I expected Andy to fall back now and then, but I would rather it happened for any other reason than being off level. I'll get him back, I refuse to give up.

This refusal to give up and Marge's dedication to meaningful literacy activities pushed both Andy and classroom community to success. Marge helped students to feel safe and they began to take risks as they read:

Andy and four other students read their books out loud. When they came to a word they did not know, I told them to just say "I don't know." At first they were frustrated because they didn't know all the words. I kept assuring them that it was okay. Slowly they began not to be embarrassed when they didn't know the word.

Success and growing confidence were also evident in Andy's increased desire to share his own writing and the willingness of his peers to recognize him and his work in a positive way. By the end of Marge's student teaching assignment her students moved from feeling embarrassed and threatened to feeling like members of a connected community willing to listen and to respond to each other positively:

Andy wrote today and got up in front of the class and read what he wrote. It was the first time he has ever been able to read what he wrote!! I looked at the class and said,"Wow, do you know that this was the first time Andy has read his writing to us." Then the whole class began to clap!

During her last week as his student teacher, Marge talked about Andy's success. She reflected on how the creating of their community powerfully influenced his literacy development:

Andy got up in front of the class and thanked me for teaching him how to read and write. I think Andy has always known more than he realized. All I did was build his self-esteem and take away those rigid rules of perfection. Andy could be himself with me. I didn't isolate him by grouping; he was a part of his class. He felt comfortable to ask his classmates to help. He learned from me and his classmates.

When Marge went back to visit the students after her student teaching requirement ended, Andy told her that: "I didn't forget to believe in myself" and that he reads all kinds of books with his mom and in his class.

In only sixteen weeks Marge created a community that enabled Andy and his classmates to perceive themselves as writers and readers. Her determination to hold on to her beliefs in the face of strong resistance enabled to stand up to the prevailing mechanistic mentality. While on the one hand Marge was fighting battles with the aide, she was also feeling more confident about her teaching/learning decisions. Imagine what she could accomplish in her own classroom.

MARGE'S CLASSROOM

Setting

Marge now teaches in a middle school special education center for students labeled emotionally handicapped. She is a language arts teacher who sees a total of six classes for at least fifty minutes a day. One day a week she sees each class for a two hour block. While she has success-fully maintained a critically constructivist classroom community and has much more decision-making power in her own classroom she still confronts many of the same problems she encountered in student teaching. She continues to try to convince both adults and students that her way of teaching and learning is effective and powerful. But, as her students become confident with their success, adults actively try to sabotage Marge's program or turn an indifferent shoulder. Marge is persistent though, as she successfully creates a critically constructivist classroom within an overtly resistant environment. Marge includes the same major elements of my program that she attempted during her student teaching. She contextualizes all her lessons as she uses her students' writing and reading materials to teach skills and adamantly refuses to use teacher manuals.

Marge was required to have a peer teacher for guidance during her first year of teaching. Unfortunately, this peer teacher resisted her efforts throughout the entire year. Since this experience paralleled the difficult time she had with the classroom aide Marge knew how to han-dle the situation:

Today I met with my peer teacher. She asked me if I was nervous about teaching, I said, "No." I guess that wasn't the response she was looking for because she insist-ed that I must be and then she assured me that she understood how I felt. She also told me how she knew how I probably had no idea of how I was going to teach. I resented that and told her that I knew exactly what I was going to do—individual-ized spelling, the writing of stories, poetry, play writing, individualized reading. She told me she has plenty of basals in her room for the low readers I was going to have to deal with. It was just as if she never heard a word I was saying. I was so annoyed and blurted out "I don't use basals." She assured me that I would resort to basals.

The peer teacher did not support Marge emotionally or materially. At times Marge thought that the teacher was actively trying to block her success:

I've spent hours in this library that consists of classics and nothing else. I've asked my peer teacher who is the head of the language arts department to order me some high interest low readers but she's giving me the run-around. I can't wait any longer, I'll go buy the books myself.

Even during department meetings Marge felt the peer teacher's negativity but refused to let it influence her convictions about teaching and learning:

This week I had my first language arts meeting. My peer teacher is the one in charge. They all sit around talking about how useful it is teaching Winnie-the-Pooh *to seventh graders. We have barnyard kits for* Charlotte's Web *and journal prompts. After the meeting she got nasty and demeaning and yelled at me because I haven't gone to observe her. She keeps trying to threaten me about how a peer teacher has so much authority over new teachers. No one has that kind of authority over me. No longer do I teach in ways that I do not believe in. I wish she would come and see what I do!*

The peer teacher did observe Marge because it was her duty to give feedback that would provide assistance and guidance. No feedback was ever given:

Well she did come and observe me. The students were all working on their stories. They even came up to her and asked her to read their stories. Veronica who never talks to anyone asked her to read her story. My peer teacher watched us intently then she got up and left and hasn't said a word to me. How do you like that for feedback?

Perhaps the peer teacher was turned off by Marge's strong attitude and confident style. She could not fulfill her required role because this first year teacher seemed not to want or to need any help. Clearly this teacher felt threatened by Marge. Other adults were also threatened by Marge and attempted to sabotage her techniques:

Nobody wants you to tell them what you're doing. It seems they don't want to see success. For example, when I put on the play I was sabotaged right and left. I was accused of writing the play myself or allowing the children to copy it from a book. Then the librarian wouldn't give me microphones to use.

Negativity was also directly aimed at Marge:

I can't believe that the teacher next door actually went to Mr. Jay to complain about my showing a video every Friday during the month of Black History. I guess it annoys her because all she ever does with her students is give them math dittos and makes them sit at their seats and do the math by themselves.

Marge felt isolated within her grade group and struggled constantly with her intern but she was encouraged by the principal of the school:

There is one good thing about this school—Mr. Jay. He likes a noisy, busy classroom and he doesn't approve of the things that my peer teacher does. When I had my meeting with him after my observation he said that he was glad to see me teaching the classics instead of Disney characters.

Marge initially had some difficulty convincing her aide of her goals.

My aide is not sure what I'm doing. I've talked to her about what I need her to do but I can see she is used to just passing out worksheets. There is so much to undo!

At first the aide tried to tell Marge what to do:

My aide keeps telling me that we need dolch words. In a moment of despair, I gave in and gave her some dolch words because I still didn't have the appropriate reading material. That was a disaster! When she put the students in the group they all became resistant as they were forced to read words they didn't know in front of everyone.

Marge decided to turn this negative situation into a learning experience for herself and for her aide. She spoke to the aide about her program within the context of the community. The aide listened, followed Marge's advice, and was amazed at the progress the students made by the beginning of November. Marge was pleased with her aide's progress.

While Marge had mixed results with adults in her school setting, she worked hard to create a community where safety and success could become a reality for all. To begin the transformation of her classroom she needed to deal with the behavior management program required throughout the school. As in her student teaching situation, she found a way to work around the system:

I hate this point system with levels. I have to fill out the point sheets because the students carry them from class to class. But I refuse to tell students that they were responding in the correct way so they get a point. I tell the students that they have to do well because it makes them feel good and helps them to obtain their goals. At this school everybody thinks the only way a student can obtain their goals is get the right amount of points. In my class it's simple. Do the best that you can, stay on task, don't be afraid to try.

At the same time that Marge was getting around the behavior system she was laying the foundation of the program. Her students initially resisted her efforts. The program began with the introduction of diary writing:

First day of class. As the students walked through the door they were handed a blank diary. I explained that everyday they will get their diaries and begin writing. Most of them seemed shocked. We talked about how a diary can be your best friend to confide in. The students are confused because they have never been given the privilege to just write their own thoughts. Not having a prompt has left many of them staring and complaining they don't know what to write.

After about a week or so most students felt comfortable with the daily use of diaries:

Diary writing has finally become a part of everyone's daily routine. Some students are still not writing, maybe 5 out of 65, but it's going well. I still have to remind them to get their diaries but they do it with no problem.

Resistance was still apparent, though, during other aspects of writing and reading. Students were shocked and dismayed that they would be expected to pick their own spelling words:

This was a difficult week. I introduced individualized spelling. These students are so programmed to being handed a ditto, told to be quiet and just write anything to get credit. How dare I walk in and ask them to think. I was ready for the resistance but it wears you down. I had one student throw his paper and book across the room, fold his arms and tell me he ain't doing this stupid s—I said,"That's your choice that's fine, but I want you to know that you have another choice. You can sit with me and I can help you." He acted as if he didn't hear me and then got his book and we worked together reading and finding words that he wanted to know how to spell.

Conditions improved the following week as students became comfortable with their power:

They seem to be having a good time with it now and they enjoy the challenge. One day a week they work in pairs teaching each other their words and practicing. The results were about 90% of the children got A's.

It was difficult securing purposeful reading material. Marge was expected to use only basals and the required literature. She struggled with some of the required readings but used them to support her view of teaching and learning:

We're reading The Pearl. *It was difficult in the beginning to get them to answer my questions. Many were opinion questions and I had to keep saying this in an opinion question; there are no right or wrong answers. Then the real shock came when I asked them "why?" Most responded "I don't know." When I continued to push, though, everyone could defend their opinions.*

It took a while to gather material and books for the classroom and Marge was still trying to win over her aide. But with the inclusion of more reading material the students and the aide felt more comfortable with the reading in their community and broadened their definitions of reading success:

Everyday this week we read. When I read with Walt he refused until I assured him I didn't care if he didn't know the words because if he didn't know I would tell him. For the first time Walt read an entire preprimer book. When he was done, he looked at me and said, " I read the whole book." He then chose his spelling words by himself and was so confident he reread the book to his friend. Even the aide became tickled at how proud Walt was. It was not just that Walt could read—it was also that his learning environment was safe and free of embarrassment. When he didn't know a word I just simply told him the word and then we just casually talked like two friends would talk about what he was reading.

Walt, just as Andy during Marge's student teaching, needed added support to feel comfortable in this new teaching environment. During the first week of school the aide forced Walt to read isolated vocabulary words and he failed. To make sure that Walt was not placed in this type of situation again, Marge made sure the aide did not work with him until she understood the program more clearly. With positive support Walt began to read:

This week Walt couldn't wait to get a book and read it to me. He no longer has to be coaxed to read. It's my whole class. They are even doing process writing with such enthusiasm. The learning environment is safe, no one feels stupid and they all feel successful. There is a calmness and bond of respect that is developing in my classes that comes from content, successful learning.

By the middle of October this mutual respect helped push Walt to greater enthusiasm and success:

Walt has completed five books and has three A's on his spelling. He's also writing a story with a friend. Walt comes into class everyday and says, "I do diary first, right? Then I can read?" He even asked me if he could take a book home! He hid it so no one in the halls could see what level it was but he wanted to read!

Marge jumped easily into designing her reading program but hesitated with the writing process. She knew she would have to deal with negative reactions from students:

These students cannot say a nice thing to one another and introducing TAG is going to be really hard. How are they going to "Tell what you like?"

She knew, though, she needed to implement it quickly since it would be the foundation of the classroom community. During the second week she took the plunge:

We began the writing process. Most of the students were really excited about doing their own stories. Some of them were complaining they couldn't write a story but I'm not giving up and I'm not pushing them either. I also began TAG. I go through this whole thing about what TAG means and wouldn't you know that the first comment after someone reads is "That was really stupid!" We stop and I ask them if they like every book that they read? By the time I got to the 6th period class, I had it down pat. This student who wrote a really awesome story got up to read what he wrote. Before he started I reminded them that their turn would eventually come and they wouldn't want everyone talking so give this student the same respect that you would want. When John finished I again reminded them what TAG was. The first student John called on said in a very timid voice, "It was really good. I liked it a lot." After that comment came two more appropriate responses and questions and suggestions about how he might end the story.

Though the writing process got a little rough at times, once Marge started she never stopped. Her students responded in kind:

The editing is hard though they hate being told that they have to add something or anything that you have to say. I am so careful that I don't ever say that what they wrote is wrong. The most frustrating thing that I find is making time for TAG. I know that this is really important but with 50 minutes to a class, diary, silent reading the students never want to stop writing before the end of the period. They're upset when I don't do writing process every day. I've created monsters!

But at the same time Marge, too, voiced increased excitement:

Each week gets smoother and I can see light at the end of the tunnel. In process writing students are working well either independently or with a peer. They enjoy the freedom of being able to work and talk with another student or just get comfortable with writing by themselves.

Even though Marge was aware of her success she also knew its costs:

Dealing with 65 students, really knowing my students, and teaching has just worn me out. I'm so tired these days.

I've made so much progress with my students though. When I remember the beginning of the school year and then look at what they can do now it is amazing. But it is not just academics that have improved, it's their behavior. They've learned it's okay not to know everything and that they are capable of learning. There is a tremendous bond that I was not really aware of until this month. I hear students saying, Mrs. Scardina's class is the best class and we do our work here. I guess I should be feeling good but instead I feel tired.

She realizes though that it is the right way, the only way to teach. No matter how tired, she holds on to the success of her community:

I can see all this is possible with a lot of hard work and you can't give up just because it doesn't work the first time. You can't let the labels given to these students get in the way of doing what is right.

Marge and her students continue to struggle against the mainstream as they design and participate within a critically constructivist curriculum. Success is evident in the students, Marge, and the aide as they progress within this respectful environment. Student resistance to independent thinking and personal responsibility is quelled since they now feel safe about being themselves and taking both academic and social risks. And, once they feel secure they even help Marge construct the curriculum and ensure its continuance. Indeed, the students made sure the writing process happened. Some, like Walt, were so pleased with their progress they began to read at home—no matter what others would say about the books they had chosen!

Marge has shown great strength, courage, and perseverance during these first two years. Yes, she is tired. Educating students in a respectful and critical way within a nonsupportive, resistant system is difficult! Yet Marge's story illustrates, that, it is not impossible. Yes, the work was draining but she was energized by her students' success. As Marge enters her next year of teaching she is even more confident about her ability to maintain the classroom she and her students will design.

Presently, Marge is in her second year of teaching in this setting. Some who did not want to know about Marge's successful classroom are now soliciting her advice. Clearly, respectful, caring classrooms can survive and begin to flourish even within a system that supports mechanistic, behavioristic approaches to teaching and learning.

REFERENCES

Binder, C., E. Haughton, and D. Eyk. "Precision Teaching." *Teaching Exceptional Children*. (Spring 1990): 24–7.

Colvin, G., G. Sugai, and B. Patching. "Precorrection: An Instructional Approach for Managing Predictable Problem Behaviors." *Intervention in School and Clinic*. 28, 3 (1996): 143–50.

Freire, P. *Pedagogy of the Oppressed*. New York: Continuum, 1993.

Heward, W., F. Courson, and J. Naravan. "Using Choral Responding to Increase Active Student Response." *Teaching Exceptional Children*. (Spring 1989): 72–3.

Giroux, H. *Teachers as Intellectuals: Toward a Critical Pedagogy of Learning*. South Hadley, MA: Bergin & Garvey, 1988.

Kincheloe, J. and S. Steinberg, eds. *Thirteen Questions: Reframing Education's Conversation*. New York: Peter Lang, 1993.

Zaragoza, N. "Teaching and Learning as Human Community." In *Teaching as Enhancing Human Effectiveness*, E. Dottin, and L. Miller, eds. Lanham, MD: University Press, 1995. 79–87.

———. *Rethinking Language Arts: Passion and Practice*. New York: Garland, 1997.

———, and F. Slater. "Project FUSE: Connecting Theory and Practice in an Undergraduate Methods Course." *Educational Transitions*. 1, 1 (1996): 11-15.

———, and S. Vaughn. "The Effects of Process Writing Instruction on Three 2nd grade Students with Different Achievement Levels." *Learning Disabilities Research and Practice*. 7,4 (1992): 184–93.

———, and S. Vaughn. "Children Teach Us to Teach Writing," *The Reading Teacher*, 1995.

VI

A TEXTBOOK FOR EVERYONE:
BALANCING CANONS AND CULTURE IN ENGLISH TEXTBOOKS
Timothy A. Dohrer

How do we decide what to include in a course or in an anthology? Once we recognize that the answer to that question is not foreordained by God, the curriculum committee, or even the Norton Anthology, a spectacular and dangerous world of choice opens before us.

—Paul Lauter, Canons and Contexts

In an era fraught with debates over cultural literacy, canon formation, and multiculturalism, secondary school English teachers find themselves at the mercy of forces that sometime seem beyond their control. The debates rage on in theoretical and philosophical arenas with little practical relation to "the trenches," the classroom. English teachers in the nineties are being asked to do everything: teach the "classics" but include the voices of "others," be innovative with material but use only the state adopted textbook, teach students to read and to write of course, but don't forget speech, critical thinking, collaboration, listening skills, and word processing. While teachers are continually rising to the challenge, the burden of being society's solution to everything is over-loading the current system.

The irony of these debates is that they all come together in a very real way inside the classroom and that they all relate to content. Pedagogy aside, the question of "what to teach?" is at the heart of these three explosive debates and while this question has been raised constantly throughout history, the changing face of American schoolchildren today raises a more compelling question: "*Whom* to teach?" For decades, the constant has been curriculum and content from a white male perspective written for a white audience. Until the late 1960s the racial bias of curricular materials, textbooks, and teaching practices was seldom questioned. In the following decade changes were made and the multiculturalism movement attempted to answer racial bias. But today the current debates are once again questioning the issue of content.

As an English teacher, I find myself overwhelmed at times by the philosophical debates raging outside the classroom. Despite this furor, I continue to ask the same questions about the content I teach. Am I teaching too many works or not enough? Am I presenting a balance of voices? Did I ask the right questions in our discussion about *Huck Finn* or Gwendolyn Brooks's "We Real Cool?" Is it OK for me to stray away from the textbook and bring in another perspective? If I do, then which author will I leave out? Each of these questions deals with cultural literacy, canon formation, and multiculturalism. They also deserve more attention by educators who spend most of their time in the classroom rather than in the world of theory. These issues are the core of every English teacher's curriculum and, consequently, educators must begin to engage in these debates. In the end, the struggle over the curriculum is struggle over power. Educators, not pundits or critics, should be leading the discussions over the content and methodology of classroom instruction. However, without the proper "tools," educators cannot wrestle control of the curriculum away from these outside forces.

In an effort to understand these issues, I investigated the current state of content and curriculum available to English teachers by focusing on their primary content tool: the textbook. Today, the textbook forms the backbone of most English department curricula. It also provides an insight into the treatment of literature by publishing companies. While some broad studies have examined secondary education English textbooks, none have focused on the treatment of a single author. Such a focus could isolate and magnify the effect outside forces have on content material, especially in regard to selection and presentation. In this case, Langston Hughes was chosen because of his widespread inclusion in English textbooks. While the case study on Hughes reveals an increase in the quality of textbooks and a decrease in racial bias, it also clearly shows how the debates over the canon and culture have poisoned curricular material critical to students, teachers, and the community. While all three groups are essential in the process of American education, teachers are ultimately responsible for guiding and shaping education. It is the role of the professional educator to synthesize literary criticism, multiculturalism, and pedagogy. Yet, it is clear that the teacher must do more. It is time for teachers to reclaim control of the cultural debates and demand curricular material that is accessible, balanced, and honest.

These debates most recently began again in earnest with the publication of *A Nation at Risk* (1983) and the one-two punch of Allan Bloom's *The Closing of the American Mind* (1987) and E. D. Hirsch's *Cultural Literacy: What Every American Should Know* (1988). Plummeting SAT scores and fears of foreign competition forced the country to evaluate the performance of the schools. Conservatives trumpeted the move "back to basics" as the answer to all our problems. The call also left a lot of people asking, "what are the basics?" Bloom, Hirsch, and others suggest that there is an intrinsic American culture that is codified, and therefore learnable, by all members of society. According to Hirsch, "cultural literacy is the oxygen of social intercourse"(19). Without it, the culture and society break down, resulting in many of the social problems facing the country today. At fault, Hirsch contends, is the "cafeteria" style of education, in which choice is more important than quality, leading to fragmentation and a lack of shared knowledge (21). To prove he is not just all theory, Hirsch presents a list of "What Literate Americans Know" chosen by Hirsch and a few close friends delineating what is essential for cultural discourse.

Clearly, most will agree that a common language is needed for oral discourse and the same concept can be true for cultural discourse. If we use Hirsch's definition of culture, then we are talking about the common or shared language, knowledge, history, and stories that identify us as "American." This national knowledge allows us to communicate with each other. Yet, the opposition to Hirsch is equally compelling. First, which "culture" are we discussing? The United States of America, based as it is on the premise that "all men are created equal," is a society composed of many different cultures. Author Barbara Herrnstein Smith contends, "There is…no single, comprehensive macroculture in which all or even most of the citizens of this nation actually participate"(77). Second, who ultimately decides what is culture? In *Cultural Literacy*, a few academics have determined the list. Yet, critics such as Smith argue that this list is simply a reflection of white male culture and is not inclusive. Inevitably, this argument addresses the actual transmitters and artifacts of cultural literacy: literature, otherwise known as the "canon."

Generally, the term "canon" has taken on two meanings in this debate and has led to considerable confusion. In its strictest sense, a canon is an authoritative list in a particular area. In high school English, there is supposedly a canon of works that are taught in most schools across the country, though no one publishes a national list of works that all teachers must teach. One literary definition of the canon is: "those works considered to be literature, works for that reason preserved, taught, written about, and surrounded by the scholarly and critical activities that constitute literature as a field of study" (Johnson 111). But canon can also mean something much bigger and when it is coupled with "cultural literacy," it means all the "great works" by the "great authors." Once again, the questions of who exactly is "great" and who decides this have caused sometimes emotional reactions from all sides of the debate. At stake is something much greater than academic reputations. According to Jane Tompkins, the very definition of America hangs in the balance: "The struggle now being waged in the professoriate over which writers deserve canonical status is not just a struggle over the relative merits of literary geniuses; it is a struggle among contending factions for the right to be represented in the picture America draws of itself " (201).

On one side of the debate are many of the same individuals who endorse Hirsch's *Cultural Literacy*, including Allan Bloom and William Bennett. They believe that a return to the classics is in order so that students know the foundational works of American culture. In Robert Royal's essay, "Creative Intuition, Great Books, and Freedom of Intellect," the rationale for such a return to the classics seems quite sound: "All the misconceptions and exaggerated hopes about Great Books are understandable reactions to the cultural chaos in which we find ourselves. In current conditions, what could be more desirable than a manageable set of readings that define what an educated person should know?" (71). The Great Books are considered "great" because they have intrinsic literary merit and value. An individual must be exposed to these works to be culturally literate in our society. However, the main problem of the Great Books approach is deciding who is a "great" author. According to Tompkins, the choice between a major and minor author, indeed the creation of a "canon" is "never made in a vacuum, but from within a particular perspective that determines in advance which literary works will seem good"(193). This issue of perspective has become the key argument against Great Books.

If indeed literature is not a stable entity, as Tompkins suggests, but a "category whose outlines and contents are variable," then there can be no intrinsic canon (190). In fact, canon critics such as Paul Lauter, Barbara Herrnstein Smith, and Richard Ohmann believe in a pluralistic, relative canon based on the contingencies of value, and focus their attention on the ideological, social, and cultural functions any particular text serves (Cutter 119). A pluralistic canon places values on works that serve a particular purpose. In this way, a canon is recognized as changing along with the social and political life of the times. Proponents of multicultural education endorse this view because it allows all perspectives, even unpopular ones, at least to have a chance at the canon. This opportunity is absolutely essential, according to William Pinar, if Americans are to understand themselves honestly and completely. "If what we know about ourselves—our history, our culture, our national identity—is deformed by absences, denials, and incompleteness, then our identity—both as individuals and as Americans—is fragmented" (61). Clearly, African Americans have struggled with this problem longer than any other group and highlight the problems of canon formation.

In many ways, the inclusion of African Americans in the literary canon can be seen as the litmus test of canon formation. In literature and in history, African Americans have been ignored and misrepresented, rendering their identity as a cultural group vague and almost nonexistent. For example, Africans whose identity was Ibo, Yoruba, and Dahomeyan were rendered "black" by white authors, collapsing the diversity of Africans into a monolithic, racialized category (Pinar 61). The same has been done to Native Americans, Asians, and Hispanics. As a result, our students receive a warped view of reality through textbooks and curricular material. This denial of identity and knowledge will only cause further societal problems. Pinar writes, "In order to realize our national intelligence we need to remember…those denied and repressed elements of who we are. This means, in part, that we must incorporate African-American experience throughout the school curriculum"(69). Here is an example of this repression and its subsequent negative impact on individuals. In 1971, *Time* ran a cover story on a riot in Attica Prison. In one section of the story *Time* reported: "They (the prisoners) passed around clandestine writings of their own; among them was a poem written by an unknown prisoner, crude but touching in its would-be heroic style" (Burke 25). *Time* then quoted four lines from the poem. It was actually Claude McKay's "If We Must Die," a famous poem from the Harlem Renaissance, but the writers and editors could not identify it as such. These journalists must have received reputable educations to achieve their positions at this national magazine. It just happened that African-American literature was not a part of educational experience. Clearly, by denying our children exposure to varied cultural voices, we are creating gaps in their education and cultural literacy.

Literature is the core of the canon and cultural literacy debates and, not surprisingly, literature is an essential component of high school English. According to a 1987 study of English teachers, around 50%

of time in class is spent on literature instruction (Applebee 33). This amount has remained constant since the early 1960s. The study also asked teachers to estimate the amount of time students had spent on literature related activities in the previous five school days. They reported that 78% of class time and 52% of homework was somehow related to literature (Applebee 37). In a country where most secondary schools require four years of English to graduate, literature consequently becomes an essential element in the development of its citizens and, as a result, its culture. Through their interaction with literature, young people are given the opportunity to develop social skills, to understand themselves and others, to explore and to question the world, and to discuss the issues presented. While canons exist in the literary world, the canon of high school English is more crucial to this discussion since almost every student in the United States will be exposed to it. Since World War II, this particular canon has been defined by the high school English anthology.

An anthology is simply a collection of works, usually decided upon by an editor or group of editors. By bringing a cross-section of works together into one book, the anthology allows readers to access literature easily. It is also the means by which the canon reaches the broadest segment of society (Johnson 113). Studying the creation of an anthology is one way to study canon formation since anthologies necessarily have a selection of literature. For schools, anthologies offer a savings of time and money. Since a school year has a limited number of days and teaching opportunities, a single anthology can be the single text in a class for the year. Instead of purchasing a series of stand-alone texts, a district can purchase one book that offers a variety of literary forms. In fact, during Applebee's study of English classes, 63% of teachers reported using an anthology as the main source of selections (43). In a way, the anthology not only becomes the curriculum for the teacher but also, due to the large number of teachers using it, a kind of "national curriculum." Clearly, this powerful instructional tool merits further investigation.

Before beginning this investigation, we should note the difference between anthologies and textbooks. In the nonacademic world, an anthology is simply a collection of works. However, the moment it is used in a classroom—be it college, high school, or elementary—the anthology becomes much more. At the college level, where student attendance is voluntary and professors have more choice over teaching material, the anthology becomes a bridge between academia and the "real world." Glen Johnson, who studied the impact of the Norton American Literature anthology, notes that "the teaching anthology is one obvious place where the academic world intersects with the marketplace" (112). Indeed, the anthology can be viewed as both a cultural artifact and a commodity, carrying with it the pressures of academia and the marketplace. However, in elementary and secondary schools the anthology has been transformed over the years into something much more. Instead of simply presenting a work alone, publishers also supply questions for discussion after each selection, biographies of the authors, suggestions for activities, glossaries of words, and annotated teachers' editions filled with lesson plans and suggested responses to questions. Thus, the anthology is transformed into a textbook.

The two terms, anthology and textbook, are used interchangeably throughout this discussion, although the inherent meaning of both is that they are instructional tools. The National Association of Textbook Administrators' definition is widely accepted: "The term 'textbook' as used herein shall mean printed instructional material in bound form, the content of which is properly organized and intended for use in Elementary or High School curricula" (Warren 43). As early as 1913, studies have shown the role textbooks play in instruction (Woodward 178). According to researchers, textbooks are essential tools in the secondary English classroom and, because of the additional editorial support included by publishers, teachers rely on them to create the backbone of the curriculum. Applebee discovered that 92% of teachers surveyed rated the selected works in their textbooks as "adequate" and 42% rated them "excellent" (45). Their use has in turn strengthened the role of the literary canon in high schools (Applebee 69).

But textbooks also present problems, especially in matters of selection and representation. John Carr, who studied English textbooks in 1972, argues that these books have not lived up to the *Basic Aims for English Instruction* endorsed by the National Council of Teachers of English, especially in developing "a keen sense of permanent social values" and promoting "literature as a mirror of life" (123). It is up to the teacher to take more control over supplementary material and to reject inferior products from publishers. Daniel Boorstein, author and editor of several textbooks, agrees that teachers must stop accepting textbooks at face value and begin to question who is making these instructional decisions:

> The textbook generally is chosen by somebody else, by the professor or by the committee or commission in the state that selects the textbook. And these people are elected or appointed by elected governmental officials. This gives

another special significance to the textbook in our civilization because in a free economy, a free society, the textbook is a special test of freedom. Can we provide basic books, foundation books, which present the consensus of a subject…and yet preserve the freedom to grow and the freedom to dissent, the freedom to be free? (x)

Once we begin to question these decisions, critics like Carr raise questions about misrepresentation and racial bias in these textbooks, especially of African Americans, and the effect this may have on students: "The chances a student has for developing values relating to blacks and whites through reading anthologies is directly related to his opportunity to see each reading experience in a context which clearly indicated that all people are appropriate subjects for artistic expression and are equally capable of making artistic comment" (126). Yet, the people making these decisions concerning textbook content are not the teachers but the textbook publishers.

The textbook publishing industry is enormous. Each year, an estimated $1.7 billion is made in sales of instructional materials from only forty publishers, with the number of publishers shrinking every year (Squire 107). High school subjects alone represent $700 million, 12.5% of which are literature. The pressure on employees in these companies to create viable products is enormous. But these publishers also feel pressure from their consumers, the schools. Because textbooks have become so essential in the classroom, the publishers are essentially providing schools with their curriculum as well. According to Ian Westbury, the absence of a national system of curriculum control in American schools "has inevitably thrown a peculiar and paradoxical burden onto the textbook publishing industry: publishers not only provide textbooks but they provide (and create) the curriculum by embodying the curriculum in their texts" (8). Consequently, while Hirsch argues that the curriculum in America is fragmented, others contend that the publishers are in essence creating a type of "national curriculum."

The danger of this arrangement lies in the conflict between the goals of business and the goals of education. One critic put it bluntly: "Overall, the textbook development process in America has less to do with educating a nation than with selling a product" (DelFattore 10). This type of attitude produces in a litany of criticisms and problems. For example:

• books treated as assembly-line products which leads to insensitivity

- resources put into sales rather than the product
- general sloppiness
- "pedagogical stylishness" or trying to be all things to all people
- a penchant for trivial material
- resulting dullness in material and presentation (FitzGerald 51).

While much of this can be proven, the publishers can also argue that they spend time and money finding out what teachers and students want, suggesting that they aren't the only ones to blame (Applebee 85). A still greater force influencing the anthology curriculum is the purchasing power of large states. It is no secret that for a textbook series to be successful, it must be accepted for purchase in states like Texas, California, New York, and Florida. And to be accepted for purchase, the textbook must be deemed "acceptable" by these states' boards of education. In this billion dollar industry, 11% of sales come from California and 7.3% come from Texas (Squire 107). Based on this economic arrangement, the rest of the country, all forty-six other states, must follow. Finally, the biggest problem is the creation of the product itself. If educators are accepting instructional materials without question, then who at the publishing company is deciding what literature is included?

Interestingly, textbook publishers today are probably more attuned to the debates of canon formation and cultural literacy than anyone else since their livelihood is based upon the selection of literature for their respective anthologies. Yet, elementary and secondary editors face a much more difficult task than their college text counterparts due to the amount of editorial and instructional comment added to the K-12 books. Issues such as depth versus breadth become more complicated. Editors must be even more selective with literary works, consequently creating their own particular "vision of culture." This type of "selective tradition" has changed over the years in the publishing industry. In the past, editors would rely on what they deemed was important for inclusion, basing decisions on the "inherent worth" of a work. As a result, this vision tended to be white and male. The multicultural movement that began in the 1970s has resulted in editors polling educators for opinions about material and contents (Johnson 113). They have also begun to hire teachers as consultants on textbook series. While this process seems more democratic, one problem is that those polled are not necessarily the most innovative or even knowledgeable teachers, resulting in a presentation of the status quo. People interested in education must begin to critically question this decision-making process to ensure that teachers and students are receiving quality material. They must also question the vision of culture being presented, returning us to the questions of "what" and "whom" are we teaching.

Racial bias in textbooks has been an explosive issue since the 1960s. While the topic was unheard of during decades of publishing, the Civil Rights Movement of the late 1950s and 1960s raised awareness regarding the instructional material our teachers and students were using. It became clear, for example, that the exclusion of *The Adventures of Huckleberry Finn* and similar controversial works undermined the Civil Rights Movement and suggested that racism, sexism, and prejudice didn't exist in American history (DelFattore 132). The key word in textbook debates became "relevance" and some changes began to occur. Yet, inaccurate portrayals of African-American lifestyles and stereotypes furthered. As a result, activists and educators proposed changes during the 1970s in two important areas. First, teacher education programs and textbooks required more emphasis on racial diversity. Second, instructional material should be studied more carefully for racial bias, especially concerning omissions and distortions of African-American culture and authors.

There is clear evidence that publishers excluded and omitted African Americans and other minorities from their textbooks. Between 1962 and 1964, African-American subjects and authors were present in only 349 of the 5,206 textbooks published (Taxel 114). Many of the textbooks published before 1970 do not include photos or drawings of African Americans, even though they include photos and drawings of whites. According to William Pinar, "The absence of African-American knowledge in many school curricula in the United States is not a simple oversight. Its absence represents an academic instance of racism" (62). The exclusion of African Americans from textbooks negatively affects the self-image of African-American students and limits the education of all students. While this situation has improved, instances of exclusion continue.

A more subtle problem with textbooks is the distortion of African-American culture and accomplishments through misrepresentation. Until 1950, African Americans were portrayed in children's literature as "shuffling, lazy, shiftless, singing subhumans" (Taxel 115). They would also appear only in minor ways as characters in stories so the publisher could say that minority views were expressed. In a study of textbooks published between 1950 and 1980, Christine Sleeter discovered that as few as one textbook contained an African-American as the main character and none portrayed an African-American in an African-American cultural context (88). The greatest example of distortion occurs when African-American writers are "sanitized" so not to offend white readers. For example, several publishers try to increase minority representation by including Martin Luther King, Jr.'s "I Have a Dream" speech but only after removing references in the speechto racism in various states (DelFattore 123). In other instances, the works of African-American authors are presented without any reference to their ethnicity. Even biographies of the authors fail to mention that the author is black.

If we then turn our attention to the broad history of literature textbooks with the concepts of exclusion and distortion in mind, a clear pattern of racial bias begins to present itself. As far back as 1880, textbooks have displayed only the "virtues and achievements of an Anglo-Saxon United States founded by New England Puritans" (Jay 8). The Progressive Era temporarily removed the emphasis on a single basal reader and introduced an increased reliance on multiple texts, projects, charts, skits, and discussions, but the bias in the books continued. During the 1940s, racism continued in both history and literature textbooks. In fact, neither the Elson-Gray nor the Gates readers of the time listed the authors of the stories, an easy way for a publisher to avoid difficult decisions of inclusion (Foshay 27). Avoidance became the general practice during the 1950s. During this period, the American Textbook Publishers Institute published a pamphlet encouraging publishers to "avoid statements that might prove offensive to economic, religious, racial, or social groups or any civil, fraternal, patriotic, or philanthropic societies in the whole United States" (Franklin 9). Despite all this, changes began to occur in the 1960s when concern over misrepresentation and exclusion of minorities, especially African Americans, led publishers to rethink their presentation, photos, and literature selections. During the 1970s and 1980s, nationally organized campaigns made huge strides in changing the selection process in publishing houses (DelFattore 5).

Today, publishers are more aware of the issues of exclusion and distortion due to the campaigns of the 1970s, but unfortunately very few studies have been conducted on textbook content and racial bias to test this awareness. Generally, until recently, textbooks' effects on students, teachers, and the publishing industry were under-investigated. The National Society for the Study of Education, founded in 1901, has published two reports over the years in its annual yearbook, in 1931 and 1990, focusing on the textbook in American education. James Lynch and Bertrand Evans published *High School English Textbooks: A Critical Examination* in 1963, which is a comprehensive view of textbooks since World War II. Yet, their recommendations for change were to reduce the size of textbooks and to ensure that every work admitted be of high literary distinction. No suggestions are made as to how this should be done or by whom. John Carr looked at racial bias specifically in his 1972 essay" " My Brother's Keeper: A View of Blacks in Secondary School Literature Anthologies." Glen M. Johnson published an analysis of college level anthologies in 1991 with "The Teaching Anthology and the Canon of American Literature." Perhaps the most valuable recent study was published in 1993 by Arthur N. Applebee titled *Literature in the Secondary School: Studies of Curriculum and Instruction in the United States.* Applebee uses the Lynch and Evans study as a baseline to chart changes in publisher activity. Each of these studies attempts to address the complex issues of canon formation and textbook impact on high school English classes.

John Carr's essay "My Brother's Keeper: A View of Blacks in Secondary School Literature Anthologies" is the most comprehensive study of racial bias in textbooks from the important 1960s. Carr analyzes three essential areas of six popular literature textbook series: choice of literary selections, use of illustrations, and editorial comment (Carr 126). In doing so, Carr questions how these publishers have portrayed African-American authors and culture. Carr ranks the six textbook series from least successful to most successful: *Ginn Literature Series*, Ginn and Company (1964); *Themes and Writers Series*, McGraw-Hill Company (1967 and 1969); *Mainstream Series*, Charles Merrill Company (1967 and 1968); *America Reads Series*, Scott-Foresman and Company (1967 and 1968); *Impact Series*, Holt, Rinehart and Winston (1968); *Crossroads Series*, Noble and Noble (1969 and 1970). Carr found that several of the series contained very few African-American selections, especially in the earlier textbooks. These books were also weak in the area of illustrations, in some cases actually distorting or ignoring cultural messages in the literature. For example, in the *Themes and Writers Series*, one illustration of an African-American is subtitled "Minority #1" and a photo of Sidney Poitier is shown but he is not named in a section on film (Carr 129). Carr found the most unsettling evidence of subtle racial bias in the area of editorial comment. For example, the comments on Samuel Allen's poem "To Satch" in the *Themes* series don't acknowledge that the author is black, nor do they comment on the poet's use of colloquial language (Carr 128). In a biography section on James Baldwin, the *Ginn Series* notes that he "grew up in the Harlem section of New York City" but fails to mention that he is black or what Harlem is (Carr 128). Merrill's *Mainstream Series* presents more African-American authors but its editorial comments are "cautious and paternalistic," according to Carr, not revealing any kind of social unrest, dissatisfaction, or protest (131). The *Impact Series* is "a better melding of literature and social awareness" with more diverse authors; yet it lacks questions or activities (Carr 133). While this allows teachers the freedom to create their own questions, it also can be seen as avoiding editorial comment that could enhance the literature or possibly relate the poem to black experience (Carr 132). In the end, Carr believes that for us to understand the black experience we must be exposed to literature that speaks to that experience. Pretending as these texts do that the literature is devoid of racial commentary is simply distorting reality.

Glen Johnson's study of college anthologies is not as comprehensive as Carr's study and at first seems rather irrelevant to the subject of high school textbooks, but it does raise several interesting and helpful points. Johnson studied three editions of the *Norton Anthology of American Literature* (1979, 1985, 1989), no doubt the most widely taught American literature anthology in the country. Although the three editions were published within a ten year time frame, some changes occurred, most notably the addition of a female editor to the group of text editors. In regard to multiculturalism, Johnson recorded the total number of pages dedicated to African Americans and the number of African-American authors presented. The first edition contained only ten African-American authors totaling less than 3% of the book. The second edition increased the number of authors to fourteen, more than 3% of the book. The third edition presented twenty-one African-American authors, amounting to 6% of the book (Johnson 123). While the increase in authors is positive, the percentage of the book that presents African-American literature is still very small. Clearly, college publishers are facing the same difficulties as high school publishers. More importantly, the students at the college level who are reading this anthology are not being introduced to African-American authors. Some of them will no doubt become English teachers someday.

The most comprehensive study to date is Arthur Applebee's 1989 book, *Literature in the Secondary School*. Based out of the National Research Center on Literature Teaching and Learning at the State University of New York in Albany, Applebee surveyed 331 schools nationwide and studied over 38,500 textbook pages, including seven textbook series. After analyzing these textbooks, Applebee concluded that "rather than offering schools a choice of emphases, all seven of these 1989 series offered a very similar cross section of literary traditions" (97). While this conclusion makes it easy for Applebee to generalize about these particular textbooks, it also reveals how rigid the high school canon and, consequently, most high school curricula have become. Instead of diversifying the literary offerings and taking some chances in their presentation, these textbooks offered more of the same. Applebee also found that of the 917 pages in the average literature textbook, 450 pages are devoted to literature selections and 467 pages are given over to supporting material, including artwork, introductions, questions, biographies, appendices, and other editorial commentary (89). Fewer pages devoted to literature means more and more content must be excluded.

Applebee's most intriguing discoveries deal with gender and minority issues. Of the authors in the book-length study, 86% were male and 99% were white, prompting Applebee to write: "Recent attempts to broaden the curriculum seem to have had very little effect on the representation of women and minorities among the authors of required book-length texts" (60). In the anthologies, African Americans represent only a small percentage of authors presented. Out of the seven series, each with six textbook volumes covering grades 7–12, white writers represented 86.5% of the selections while African Americans represented 7.6% (Applebee 93). Even in American Literature textbooks, where one would expect to find writings from former slaves, the Harlem Renaissance, and the Civil Rights Movement, only 9.7% of the selections were from African Americans. Of the 122 most frequently anthologized authors, Langston Hughes is the only African-American in the top ten, appearing at number eight with fifty-three appearances. Overall, it seems that anthologies have also narrowed their focus, "presumably to place more emphasis on works of merit," although the term "work of merit" is never clearly defined (Applebee 114). While many textbooks boast to be "cutting edge" and include many "new" titles, Applebee found that there were 20% fewer selections from the twentieth century than there were thirty years ago (Applebee 91). Applebee contends that pressure from Great Books advocates, the conservative view of the canon, and teacher unfamiliarity with modern works are the cause of this dramatic change. It is not surprising then to also note that Applebee found that English textbooks "remain quite narrow in their representation of non-white authors" (114).

In all these studies, the authors looked at textbooks in broad terms and while the results are fascinating, especially in terms of racial bias, none have isolated a single author's inclusion and presentation. Such a study could reveal the minute intricacies of racial exclusion and distortion. Taking a cue from Applebee, the current study selected

Langston Hughes, the most anthologized author in the 1989 study, to accomplish this. In doing so, ten textbook series were selected from various years since the early 1960s through 1994 in an effort to both verify Carr and Applebee's findings and to chart the evolution of Hughes's presentation in textbooks. The majority of these textbooks represent popular series created by major publishing companies. In several cases, textbooks were selected because they appear in Applebee's study. Many also included annotated teachers' editions and supplementary material. The series include:

- *Ginn Literature Series*, Ginn and Company (1964, 1981)
- *America Reads Series*, Scott-Foresman and Company (1963, 1976, 1989)
- *Themes and Writers Series*, McGraw-Hill Book Company (1969, 1975)
- *McDougal*, Littell Literature (1989, 1994)
- *Elements of Literature*, Harcourt Brace Jovanovich (1993)
- Adventure in Literature, Harcourt Brace Jovanovich (1968, 1980, 1985)
- *Focus on Literature*, Houghton Mifflin Company (1978, 1981)
- *Houghton Mifflin Literature Series* (1968, 1975)
- *MacMillan Literature Series* (1984)
- *Prentice Hall Literature Program* (1991)

In addition to these, several textbook series that are no longer in print were analyzed to create a basis for comparison. They were published just prior to the textbooks of Applebee's study and before multicultural debates began in the textbook industry. These include *Ideas in Literature* from Charles E. Merrill Books (1966), *New Dimensions in Literature* from McCormick-Mathers Publishing Company (1966), and *Prose and Poetry Series* from L. W. Singer Company (1963). More recent editions of these series and new series being published were used as a tentative "end line" for purposes of comparison. Yet, since textbooks are being updated and published constantly, this should not be the final word. As we will see, educators must annually monitor, study, and critique textbooks as long as they are used in the classroom. In this study over 100 textbooks totaling 90,000 pages were analyzed. The textbooks were evaluated in the following four areas: first, the number of selections by Hughes included in the textbook; second, the merit of those choices based on appropriateness for the goals of the book, as well as the work's literary merit in the Hughes canon; third, the presentation of the work, including photos, drawings, and general layout; fourth, the accompanying editorial comment, including biography, discussion prompts, and teaching suggestions.

While the focus of attention in this study was the treatment of Langston Hughes, the treatment of other African-American authors was also noted. Yet, the rationale for choosing Hughes specifically must be justified before examining the texts. In a way making such a choice infers that Hughes is an important part of the literary canon, both generally and in high school English. In support of this, writer Edward Mullen has said: "No writer better exemplifies the issues of canon formation than Langston Hughes" (44). Born in 1920, his literary career took flight during the Harlem Renaissance, and in his life he published thirty-six books of poetry and prose. He is most famous for his poetry, publishing almost one thousand poems and earning the praise of literary critics and other writers. Robert Hayden and others have called Hughes "the poet laureate of the Black people." Ironically, Hughes wasn't well-recognized outside the African-American community until after his death in 1967, mainly because he never published a single major work (Mullen 45). But his poetry, soaked with the voices of African-American culture and dialect, garnered him praise and respect across the world. Adrian Oktenberg writes: "The poets of Africa and Latin America have long recognized Hughes as a master of political poetry and used his voice as a model for their own. It is past time for us in the United States to repair a myopic critical vision and, perhaps for the first time, read the work of Langston Hughes whole" (99). Even E. D. Hirsch places cultural relevance on Hughes by including him in his list of "what every American should know." These accolades make Hughes an important part of the literary canon generally and at the high school level. This combination of reputation, respect, and accessibility have helped Hughes's poems find their way into English textbooks and makes him a good choice for this type of study. The question is: How did these textbook editors portray him?

The three oldest series in the study represent the most racially unbalanced textbooks and serve as a good baseline by which to compare the others. These include *Ideas in Literature* from Charles E. Merrill Books (1966), *New Dimensions in Literature* from McCormick-Mathers Publishing Company (1966), and *Prose and Poetry Series* from L. W. Singer Company (1963). In all three series, a total of fifteen textbooks, only one major African-American writer appears. In the *Prose and Poetry Series* book on American Literature, a section titled "Diverse America" includes poems by Carl Sandburg, Sara Teasdale, Edna St. Vincent Millay, and Robert Frost. The lone African-American writer is Countee Cullen, represented by his poem "Yet Do

I Marvel." Clearly, these three series represent one extreme end of the multicultural spectrum and, as we will see, later series contain a more diverse selection of authors, including Langston Hughes.

The first area of the current study analyzed the number of selections by Hughes included in the textbooks. As in Applebee's study, Hughes appears more often in textbooks written for grades 7, 8, and 9. The most frequently anthologized works continue to be the short story "Thank You, M'am" and the poems "Mother to Son," "Dreams," and "The Negro Speaks of Rivers," although several others prove just as popular. In fact, Hughes has gained in popularity with textbook publishers over the years. Thirty poems and stories by Hughes are presented in these textbooks for a total of seventy-one appearances. None of the selections were altered in any way by the editors. The table below shows the top ten works and the number of appearances for each.

Title	Appearances
"I, Too"	6
"Mother to Son"	6
"Dream Variation"	5
"Harlem"	5
"Thank You, M'am"	5
"As I Grew Older"	4
"Dreams"	4
"Let America Be America Again"	3
"Motto"	3
"The Negro Speaks of Rivers"	3

Most of these works appear in the textbooks geared for Grades 10 and 11, especially "I, Too" and "Dream Variation." While the sixteen appearances of Hughes' works coincides with Applebee's finding of more diversity at the underclass levels, the Grades 10 and 11 textbooks contained more selections with seventeen and twenty-one works respectively. This seems to indicate more diversity in the upper-class books but it is more likely to be a reflection of textbook goals, especially in Grade 11 where every textbook in the study focused on American Literature. Clearly, though, Langston Hughes continues to be a popular author for textbook publishers, who present a wide variety of works from the Hughes canon.

But, in analyzing the literary merit of these selections, we find the editors have not agreed overall on which works of Hughes should be presented. The preponderant use of "Mother to Son" and "Thank You, M'am" in all the Grades 8 and 9 textbooks seems appropriate given their similar theme of young versus old at a time when adolescents are feeling the stress of the generation gap. The preponderant use of "Mother to Son" and "Thank You, M'am" in all the Grades 8 and 9 textbooks seems equally appropriate. "Theme for English B" and "As I Grew Older" are excellent selections for the American Literature textbook in Grade 11, coming as they do from the beginning and end of Hughes's career, and both clearly presenting an African-American voice. Looking back at the top ten selected works, the editors have chosen well overall. Most of Hughes's well-known poems are here. Some surprises are evident though. The "Simple Stories," for which Hughes was extremely popular in the fifties, no longer appear in current textbooks. Only two series from the early 1960s presented them. Another surprise is the lack of obvious blues poems even though Hughes's connection to the musical form is constantly mentioned in his biographies. Only "The Weary Blues" appears in two Grade 11 textbooks. Finally, a few editors chose poems that seem inappropriate for the audience. The 1981 *Ginn Literature Series* Grade 7 textbook presents "I, Too" but never mentions an African-American connection. It is unlikely that seventh grade students will fully grasp the implications about sending the speaker "to eat in the kitchen / When company comes," nor the lines "They'll see how beautiful I am / And be ashamed," without additional explanations of racial injustice and history.

Besides choosing works for a textbook, editors also control how they are presented. Textbook designers spend much of their time experimenting with layouts because they realize how important visual appearance is to the emphasis and merit of a literary work. For example, a single poem on a page seems more significant than three poems on a single page. Other considerations, such as complementary photographs and drawings, can have an impact as well. Overall, it appears that Hughes is given the respect he is due in terms of presentation. Almost all of his works are presented alone on a page and most are given two pages of space. The two-page layouts usually include a photograph of Hughes or a complementary piece of artwork, the work itself, and discussion questions. For example, McDougal, Littell's 1989 series offers "Mother to Son," "Troubled Woman," and "The Negro Speaks of Rivers" each with a two-page layout as well as a full page biography and a photograph of an older Hughes. In the 1994 Grade 11 textbook, four pages are dedicated to Hughes, including "I, Too" with a full page color illustration of 1920s

African Americans on the front step of a building. The layout creates a powerful impact. They also present a short excerpt from Hughes's "When the Negro was in Vogue" and a full page biography with photograph. But not every series handled Hughes this well. Scott-Foresman's 1976 *America Reads Series* Grade 10 textbook presented "Dream Variation" on a two-page layout with two other poems by other authors (226). As a result, the poem is lost a bit in the design. Similarly, Harcourt Brace Jovanovich's 1968 series presents "Kid in the Park" on a page where 75% of the space is devoted to discussion questions about poems from the previous pages (463). In this layout, the poem becomes secondary to the questions. However, the 1993 edition is filled with multipage presentations of poetry by Hughes, including a four-page section in the Grade 11 textbook dedicated to the author. Clearly, while some books remain weak in this area, the increase in space allotted to this author has resulted in creative and powerful designs, striking illustrations, and more photographs of the author himself.

The final section of this study analyzed the editorial comment that accompanied the literary works. The editors of earlier textbooks clearly tried to write biographies without mentioning the racial background of the author. Often, the author's photograph was omitted. In 1981, the *Ginn Literature Series* presented several biographies of Langston Hughes that fail to mention he is African-American. In the Grade 7 textbook, part of his biography says Hughes was "an outstanding writer of Harlem" (90). Students unfamiliar with Harlem would not realize their importance in the African-American community. In the Grade 10 textbook, no mention is made of his ethnicity (478). These types of omissions are clearly attempts to sanitize textbooks and to ignore the accomplishments of African Americans. Many of the biographies are better than this and try to present Hughes realistically and connected to his culture. One representative paragraph of these positive Hughes biographies comes from McDougal, Littell's 1989 Grade 11 textbook:

> In his poetry, fiction, and drama, and in his work as an editor, newspaper columnist, and champion of black art forms, Langston Hughes sought to affirm and celebrate the "deep soul" of the black masses. Hughes captured the beating pulse of urbanized black life, articulating its common sorrows, struggles, and triumphs. His life of passionate advocacy, as well as the many achievements of his own prolific art, amply justify Hughes's stature as a major

Biographies such as this also include information about his publications, often listing several of his books and the themes of his poetry. Several speak of his commitment to helping other writers in the African-American community. One of the best biographies appears in the 1976 Grade 11 textbook from Scott-Foresman's *America Reads Series*, where poet Robert Hayden has written excellent material about the Harlem Renaissance, Hughes, and other writers. Another is Harcourt Brace Jovanovich's 1993 *Elements of Literature Series*, no doubt due to Sandra Cisneros's well-written contributions. As with most of these textbooks, the biographies seem to improve in quality in later editions.

In most textbooks, each selection is traditionally followed by a series of questions for students to either think about or respond to in writing. The way a question is phrased can reveal whether or not a question is appropriate, given the literary work, topic, and audience. In the case of Langston Hughes, many of his poems, such as "I, Too" and "Harlem," deal with African-American cultural issues. These particular poems seem to require not only basic questions of plot and structure but also questions that will ask the student to recognize the cultural implications inherent in the poem. Doing so would allow students and teachers to engage in an honest dialogue and, ideally, real learning. It can be argued that editors who choose to remove the cultural implications simply wish to present Hughes as a *writer* rather than as a *black writer*. While this view may seem valid, Hughes himself has argued against this in his essay, "The Negro Artist and the Racial Mountain." He writes that he is ashamed of the black poet who wants to write like a white: "An artist must be free to choose what he does, certainly, but he must also never be afraid to do what he might choose" (309). Clearly, Hughes often chose to write what he knew best: African-American culture.

Unfortunately, exclusions and distortions continue to occur in some of the textbooks in the study. It is hard to understand how racially charged poems like "I, Too," "Harlem," "Dream Keeper," and "The Negro Speaks of Rivers" could be presented without any reference to African-American culture. Instead, the questions deal with the meanings of single lines, identifying simile and metaphor, or vocabulary. For example, Houghton Mifflin's 1981 *Focus on Literature Series* Grade 9 textbook presents "The Negro Speaks of Rivers" with only the two following questions: "What words suggest ancient times? How might the flow of rivers and the flow of time be similar?" (557). These questions are poorly written and extremely elementary. They certainly do not suggest the issues of racial pride evident in the poem. By excluding the racial issue the editors have not only avoided controversy but also distorted the themes of the poems. For example, in the 1976 Grade 10 textbook, Scott-Foresman's editors avoided any racial questions in "Harlem," opting to ask questions about the meaning of "deferred" dreaming, how the poem should be read aloud, and tone (235). Avoiding the racial implications in this case renders this powerful poem meaningless. But, there are certainly examples here of editors who have not avoided the themes and issues Hughes and other African-American writers thought were so important. For example, Houghton Mifflin's 1972 Grade 10 textbook presents three in-depth questions on "I, Too" that speak directly to the poem's theme. Question number three reads:

> Langston Hughes's great pride in being a black man comes
> through clearly in this poem. He knows who and what he
> is. His search for self is complete. To what extent do you
> feel that the change in attitude predicted in the poem, written
> long before the major civil rights gains of the 1960s,
> has come to pass? (505)

This goes beyond basic plot or structure and asks the students to evaluate both the poem's message and events in American history, a much more demanding task. Clearly, the more serious, in-depth questions suggest to the student that the poem is itself serious and in-depth. The relationship between the literary work and follow-up questions is a powerful one in school textbooks.

The results of this study clearly indicate that across the country Langston Hughes is an important part of high school English textbooks. We can also conclude that the presentation of Hughes's writing has improved over the past thirty years. With seventy one appearances across the textbook series studied and a wide selection of important works from the Hughes canon, the editors seem to understand the literary significance of this writer. They have also demonstrated creativity and energy in the visual presentation of those works. Problems, however persist in decisions concerning editorial comments. Many of the biographies of Hughes fail to mention he is African-American, an omission that hints at racial bias, either on the part of the editorial staff or public pressure groups. In addition, the questions posed to students following selections are not always well-written. More significantly, some of Hughes's most racially charged and best poems are not followed by questions concerning these issues. This exclusion saves the publishers from possibly being censored by state boards but it also results in a bland product that does not speak truthfully to students.

From this study we can conclude that the warnings from the Carr, Johnson, and Applebee studies are justified and relevant today. Despite the strong multicultural movement, racial bias continues to be a problem in education. While many are tempted to believe the textbook industry is eliminating racial bias, "textbooks continue to legitimate the status of white males, despite the inclusion of other groups" (Sleeter 98). As fewer overall works are presented in textbooks due to increasing editorial space, editors find it difficult to create a diverse and complete textbook. It is also fallacious to believe that a separate African-American anthology will solve the problem. While such collections benefit Black Studies courses and highlight the depth of African-American literature, such literary segregation could be easily "unadopted" by state school boards. The fight to present a true reflection of our society to the students of America continues today with the final outcome still hanging in the balance.

Beyond the classroom it is clear that the battle over textbooks is only one part of the cultural war being waged in broader society. As noted earlier, textbook creation is a great way to study the canon. In our current debate, liberal and conservative forces fight over issues of inclusion. Conservative action groups contend that because it is impossible to teach everything, education should start with the "Great Books." Yet, critics such as Paul Lauter view that approach as dangerous: "I think the literary canon as we have known it is a product in significant measure to our training in male, white, bourgeois cultural tradition, including in particular the formal techniques of literary analysis" (59). While the Great Books may help us feel more secure, they are not "salvation from our current cultural crisis" (Royal 69). But problems with the canon also come from the liberal side of the equation. As liberal activism groups demand an increase in the representation of women, minorities, and non-Western cultures, something must be excluded from the canon to do so. We cannot do it all. Henry Louis Gates sees the role of literary critics and educators in the future as bringing compromise to this debate: "Our task will be to bring together the 'essential' texts of the canon, the 'crucially central' authors, those whom we feel to be indispensable to an understanding of the shape, and shaping, of the tradition" (108).

While the debate of what to teach goes on, the question "Whom to teach?" is also crucial. The audience is clearly changing and, according to Applebee, "the changes that have taken place in the curriculum have hardly been sufficient to reflect the multicultural heritage of the United States" (193). In 1986, a reported 50 million people, 21%, of America's 240 million were of Hispanic, Asian, or black descent (Sesse 170). By the year 2020, that number will be 35%. Clearly, more work is needed in the canon, curriculum, and textbooks to reflect a diverse, rich American culture. In order to do this, we will need to abandon the traditional white canon but also the concept of a totally black literature program (Sesse 170). As Applebee concludes in his study: "Development of a successful multicultural curriculum in literature is unlikely to happen without some serious re-examination of the traditional organization of the curriculum as a whole in each of the middle and high school grades" (194). Which brings the debate back to the issue of choice.

The entire cultural debate is centered around who makes the ultimate choices in what we deem important, what we want our children to learn. E. D. Hirsch believes he can make those choices, fairly and equally. In fact, in his book *Cultural Literacy*, Hirsch writes: "To acknowledge the importance of minority and local cultures of all sorts, to insist on their protection and nurture . . . are traditional aims that should be stressed even when one is concerned, as I am, with national culture and literacy" (98). Yet, Hirsch's sixty-three page list of "What Literate Americans Know" includes only a handful of African-American figures, several of whom are sports figures. Of the authors, the African Americans included are Maya Angelou, Gwendolyn Brooks, Countee Cullen, W. E. B. Du Bois, Langston Hughes, and Richard Wright. It is this type of literary exclusion that most frightens Henry Louis Gates:

> The return of "the" canon, the high canon of Western masterpieces, represents the return of an order in which my people were the subjugated, the voiceless, the invisible, the unrepresented and the unrepresentable. Who would return us to that medieval never-never land? (111)

Obviously, the question of choice is the key to all these debates. Yet, while the larger world of canons and cultural literacy has difficulty giving the power of choice to one person, in the world of education there exists one individual who can and should make these decisions: the teacher.

Recent studies, however have shown that even teachers fall victim to the same problems facing our students. Paramount in this is their ability to understand a variety of ethnic and gender related issues. Unfortunately, the very textbooks that teachers-to-be read are oftentimes racially biased. Several recent studies by education professors and groups like the National Council of Teachers of

English have reported: "After a year of textbook analysis, we reached our conclusion: Our major teacher education textbooks are failing to include important issues related to women and minorities" (Sadker 42). As a result, many educators won't admit the presence of bias in their teaching materials because they can't recognize it (Miller 13). Teachers are also not familiar with multicultural literature, yet another reason to include it in high school and college texts. Virginia Burke said: "Young people, especially those who will teach, need cultural and literary pluralism, not a narrow ethnic tradition" (27). If we are going to empower teachers to make proper decisions about diverse cultures, then we must more vigorously teach them how to make those decisions. A report from the NCTE Standing Committee on Teacher Preparation and Certification makes a strong plea for changes in teacher education: "In a multicultural society, teachers must be able to help students achieve cross-cultural understanding and appreciation. Teachers must be willing to seek and to use materials which represent linguistic and artistic achievements from a variety of ethnic and cultural perspectives" (14). With more complete preservice and inservice education training focused on diversifying the classroom, in a nation that embraces diversity, there should be no hesitancy in giving teachers control over curricular choice.

In all these discussions concerning cultural literacy, canon formation, multiculturalism, and textbook publishing, the role of the professional educator in our schools has been lost. Clearly, curricular decisions should include all members of a school community, but we must also recognize the professional training and judgment of teachers. Each day educators make decisions concerning what to teach and what not to teach. They are faced with being experts in pedagogy, classroom management, literary criticism, cultural literacy, and multiculturalism. In many ways a teacher is an educational "Everyman" who makes decisions minute-by-minute concerning our children. Many of these decisions are made based on the immediate audience. How many teachers have left the safe path of textbook questions and curriculum plans to do what was appropriate for the particular students in the room? This type of creativity in the classroom must continue and be encouraged. While remaining accountable to students, parents, and taxpayers, teachers must be allowed the professional freedom to make these decisions. They must be given the power to create the curriculum. That is, after all, their job.

But this type of empowerment is not enough. The lessons of this study and others on textbooks clearly show that teachers must stop accepting narrowly confined material without question. Teachers must approach curricular material in a critical way and then select material that is appropriate for their students. That is the first step. Teachers must also break out of their position as passive or even oppressed servants of more powerful curricular forces. If we agree that textbooks are racially biased and we also agree that this is wrong, then how can any teacher possible agree to teach such a book? If we agree that education is based on the concept of truth and democracy, then it is the teacher, the active agent of education, who must defend its values. One critic noted that "educators have a major responsibility for the kind and quality of textbooks and other curriculum materials used in the learning-teaching process"(Rosenberg 44). The current cultural debates are a plea for leadership, for someone to make decisions. One of the reasons Hirsch's book is so compelling is that he at least tries to make these kinds of decisions. But the task is not for him, nor for the multitude of literary critics and pundits. Our teachers must quit sitting on the sidelines and take the lead in these decisions, serving as curricular visionaries. Otherwise, the essential material we use to teach the children will continue to be undermined by those who don't have the perspective or ability to properly teach them.

The task is not easy. The forces to be overcome are economically, politically, and socially strong. But clearly power can be used to liberate as well. As John Carr points out, "textbooks *are* commodities" and publishers will listen to the demands of teachers. Teachers must begin to influence textbook purchasing decisions, both within their school and district but also outside of it. Improved preservice and inservice training that raises awareness concerning publishing, multiculturalism, and curriculum design is one way to do this. Creating a dialogue with publishers is another. By asserting themselves in the area of publishing, teachers will begin to influence the way textbooks are designed. By becoming active audience members at school board meetings and state textbook adoption hearings, teachers will have a say in the purchasing of textbook. By conducting research and suggesting new instructional material and strategies, teachers will begin to shape the curriculum. Twenty-five years ago, John Carr encouraged teachers to take control of the curriculum:"It is time for him (the secondary school teacher) to leave his cocoon entirely, establishing his professional competency and asserting his right to academic freedom" (135). It is again time for teachers to do so.

REFERENCES

Applebee, Arthur N. *Literature in the Secondary School: Studies of Curriculum and Instruction in the United States*. Urbana, IL: National Council of Teachers of English, 1993.

Boorstien, Daniel J. "Introduction." *The Textbook in America Society*. Washington: The Library of Congress, 1981.

Burke, Virginia M. "Black Literature for Whom?" *Negro American Literature Forum*. 9, 1, (Spring 1975).

Carr, John C. "My Brother's Keeper: A View of Blacks in Secondary School Literature Anthologies." *Black Image: Education Copes with Color*. Dubuque, IA: W. C. Brown Company, 1972.

Cutter, Martha J. "If It's Monday This Must Be Melville: A 'Canon, Anti-canon' Approach to Redefining the American Survey." *The Canon in the Classroom: The Pedagogical Implications of Canon Revision in America Literature*. New York: Conrad Publishing, 1995.

DelFattore, Joan. *What Johnny Shouldn't Read: Textbook Censorship in America*. New Haven: Yale University Press, 1992.

FitzGerald, Frances G. "Textbook and the Publishers." *The Textbook in American Society*. Washington: The Library of Congress, 1981.

Foshay, Arthur W. "Textbooks and the Curriculum During the Progressive Era: 1930–1950." *Textbooks and Schooling in the United States*. Chicago: University of Chicago Press, 1990.

Franklin, Phyllis. "Storytellers and Gatekeepers." *Black Image: Education Copes with Color*. Dubuque, IA: W C. Brown Company, 1972.

Gates, Henry Louis. "The Master's Pieces: On Canon Formation and the African-American Tradition." *The Politics of Liberal Education*. Durham, NC: Duke University Press, 1992.

Hirsch, E. D. *Cultural Literacy*. New York: Vintage Books, 1988.

Hughes, Langston. "The Negro Artist and the Racial Mountain." *Voices from the Harlem Renaissance*. New York: Oxford University Press, 1976.

Jay, Gregory S. "The End of American Literature: Toward a Multicultural Practice." *The Canon in the Classroom: The Pedagogical Implications of Canon Revision in American Literature*. New York: Conrad Publishing, 1995.

Johnson, Glen M. "The Teaching Anthology and the Canon of American Literature." *The Hospitable Canon: Essays in Literary Play, Scholarly Choice, and Popular Pressures*. Philadelphia: J. Benjamins Publishing Company, 1991.

Lauter, Paul. "Caste, Class, and Canon." *A Gift of Tongues: Critical Challenges in Contemporary American Poetry*. Athens: University of Georgia Press, 1987.

Lynch, James Jeremiah. *High School English Textbooks: A Critical Examination*. Boston: Little, Brown, 1963.

Miller, LaMar P. "Evidence of Ethnic Bias in Instructional Materials." *Eliminating Ethnic Bias in Instructional Materials*. Washington: Association for Supervision and Curriculum Development, 1974.

Mullen, Edward J. "The Dilemma in Selecting Representative Scholarship on Langston Hughes." *The Langston Hughes Review.* 7, 2, (1988).

National Council of Teachers of English Standing Committee on Teacher Preparation and Certification. "Guidelines for the Preparation of Teachers of Language Arts." Urbana, IL, 1986.

Oktenberg, Adrian. "From the Bottom Up: Three Radicals of the Thirties." *A Gift of Tongues: Critical Challenges in Contemporary American Poetry.* Athens: University of Georgia Press, 1987.

Pinar, William F. "Notes on Understanding Curriculum as Racial Text." *Race, Identity, and Representation in Education.* New York: Routledge, 1993.

Rampersand, Arnold. *The Life of Langston Hughes: I, Too, Sing America.* Volume 1. New York: Oxford University Press, 1986.

Rosemberg, Max. "Evaluate Your Textbooks for Racism, Sexism." *Eliminating Ethnic Bias in Instructional Materials.* Washington: Association for Supervision and Curriculum Development, 1974.

Royal, Robert. "Creative Intuition, Great Books, and Freedom of Intellect." *The Hospitable Canon: Essays in Literary Play, Scholarly Choice, and Popular Pressures.* Philadelphia: J. Benjamins Publishing Company, 1991.

Sadker, Myra Pollack. "Diversity, Pluralism, and Textbooks." *The Textbook in American Society.* Washington: The Library of Congress, 1981.

Sesse, Mary Hawley. "Literature in a Multi-ethnic Culture." Literature in the *Classroom: Readers, Text, and Contexts.* Urbana, IL: National Council of Teachers of English, 1988.

Sleeter, Christine. "Race, Class, Gender and Disability in Current Textbooks." *The Politics of the Textbook.* New York: Routledge, 1991.

Smith, Barbara Herrnstein. "Cult-Lit: Hirsch, Literacy, and the 'National Culture.'" *The Politics of Liberal Education.* Durham, NC: Duke University Press, 1997.

Squire, James R. "The Elementary and High School Textbook Market Today." *Textbooks and Schooling in the United States.* Chicago: University of Chicago Press, 1990.

Taxel, Joel. "Reclaiming the Voice of Resistance: The Fiction of Mildred Taylor." *The Politics of the Textbook.* New York: Routledge, 1991.

Tompkins, Jane. *Sensational Designs.* New York: Oxford University Press, 1985.

Warren, Claude C. "Adopting Textbooks." *The Textbook in American Society.* Washington: The Library of Congress, 1981.

Westbury, Ian. "Textbooks, Textbook Publishers, and the Quality of Schooling." *Textbooks and Schooling in the United States.* Chicago: University of Chicago Press, 1990.

Woodward, Arthur. "Textbook Use and Teacher Professionalism." *Textbooks and Schooling in the United States.* Chicago: University of Chicago Press, 1990.

VII

DEEP VIEWING:
A CRITICAL LOOK AT VISUAL TEXTS
Ann Watts Pailliotet

VIEWING LITERACY THROUGH CRITICAL LENSES: THE NEED FOR CONNECTING CONTEXTS AND CREATING RELEVANT PEDAGOGY

Modern literacy involves much more than decoding print or developing literal understandings of written texts (Flood and Lapp 1995). Many contemporary media—including software, video, television, Hypertext, commercial advertising, and CD-roms—are rapidly evolving into dynamic, sophisticated blends of oral, print, and visual information. To be literate today means to actively engage with complex texts and to construct critical meanings through them.

Students with rich knowledge gained from modern communicational environments enter our classrooms, but much of literacy instruction is disconnected from their lived experiences. The average high school student has spent more time watching television than in school (Lutz 1989) and countless hours viewing films, magazines, computer games, comics, billboards, print advertisements, and electronic commercials. But students and teachers often see schools and society as distinct, separate worlds (Bianculli 1992; Pope 1993). Traditional, print-based instruction still dominates in most classrooms (Lusted 1991), and many educators resist using popular texts or teaching critical analysis of mass media (Witkin 1994).

Literacy development occurs across interdependent social systems that transcend classroom barriers (Emig 1983), and effective literacy instruction builds on students' background knowledge (Reutzel and Cooter 1992). Furthermore, individuals utilize interdependent literacy processes when they interact with oral, print, and electronic texts (Neuman 1991; Sinatra 1986). Postman (1985) points out that individuals are bombarded with information but have few ways to understand or to act on what they see. Prevailing social conditions and research require us to view literacy through broader, more critical lenses. We must develop pedagogy that enables students to actively make sense of their experiences in and out of classrooms.

Deep Viewing is a method that assists students to critically analyze and to make connections among contemporary media, texts, literacies, and contexts. It is a structured, social process through which individuals actively construct meaning using communal talk, images, and writing. It may be used for analysis of any visual medium—electronic, print, artistic, or situational—including film, television, video, books, magazines, comics, newspapers, advertisements, computer programs, illustrations, art work, and field observations. Here, I describe its theoretical premises, procedures, and some of its applications.

CONSTRUCTING CRITICAL VIEWS OF LITERACY THEORY

Deep Viewing's name comes from Himley's (1991) "Deep Talk," an analytic process through which children explore meanings in their writing. Yet, the method extends the definitions of texts to encompass any cultural or communicative event (Barthes 1957). I developed Deep Viewing's theoretical basis from premises shared among literacy researchers, media analysts, and critical theorists. These ideas serve as the foundation of the method as well as my own literacy instruction. They include:

- Texts are not only print books by a "recognized author" (Foucault 1986). Many forms of communication are worthy of study and analysis: visual (Considine and Haley 1992), oral (Goody 1978), electronic (Bianculli 1992) and student texts (Bissex 1980), as well as cultural events (Barthes 1957).
- The reader/viewer is not a passive recipient of information but actively engages in transactions with a text to create meaning (Barthes 1974; Rosenblatt 1978; McLuhan and Fiore 1967).
- Many meanings evolve as readers/viewers interact with texts and construct meaning from them (Barthes 1974; Derrida 1990). There are levels of understanding possible in every text from the explicit to the implicit (Derrida 1986; Herber and Herber 1993; Himley 1991).
- Constructing textual understandings is a recursive and ongoing process, not a linear or static one (Barthes 1974; Flower 1989; McLuhan 1964).
- Understandings are developed through past and present experiences (Bhaktin 1990; Considine and Haley 1992; Reutzel and Cooter 1992).

124

- Understandings are not developed in isolation, but are continually changing within social contexts (Althusser 1990; Emig 1983; McLuhan and McLuhan 1988; Vygotsky 1978).
- Textual understandings involve many types of human response including emotions, intellect and metacognitive awareness (Bruner 1990; Lusted 1991; Lipson and Wixson 1991).
- Strategies and understandings developed in one form of communication interact and support others. Reading, writing, speaking, listening and viewing are interdependent and interactive (Barthes 1971; Considine and Haley 1992; Dyson 1984; Elbow 1985; Sinatra 1986).
- Literacy environments of home, school and society are intimately linked and interdependent (Heath 1983; Lutz 1989; McLuhan and McLuhan 1988).
- All texts—whether print, electronic, or situational—share common elements, including genres, plots and structures (Frye 1957; Lusted 1991); metaphors (Lakoff and Johnson 1980); signs, symbols and signification (Barthes 1957; Bopry 1994; Saint-Martin 1990), images (Barthes 1971; Pettersson 1992); patterns and levels of meaning (Herber and Herber 1993; Kervin 1985); and rhetorical devices (Lusted 1991; Ohlgren and Berk 1977).
- All media and texts arise within specific cultures or ideologies (Althusser 1990; Giroux 1993).
- Critical analysis of texts promotes student empowerment, active learning, and multicultural awareness (Considine and Haley 1992; Sinatra 1990).

Deep Viewing provides a systematic process for critically analyzing, understanding, and interacting with information. It combines a heuristic framework (Lusted 1991), semiotic codes for understanding print and visual information (Barthes 1974; Saint-Martin 1990), and three leveled comprehension models (Herber and Herber 1993; Himley 1991) to help participants reach understandings. Its procedures are described next.

THE DEEP VIEWING METHODOLOGY: CONSTRUCTING A CRITICAL PEDAGOGY

General Guidelines

Deep Viewing is a three-leveled process. It may be done (a) individually (one person examines all codes); (b) partially (one person examines selected codes); (c) collaboratively (each member of the group examines one code); or (d) in a cooperative learning, Jigsaw II format (groups examine each code). Participants should write notes and/or draw diagrams as they view and talk. In an individual or partial format, participants discuss findings at the end of level three. In a collaborative format, after each level of discussion, groups share their observations with the whole group, thus creating a broad picture of understanding. Extension activities like prewriting, post-writing, artistic response, or reading enrichment may be used throughout the levels of inquiry. Responses may also utilize electronic media, like word processing or graphic design, as well as other printed texts, before, during, or after the process.

When analyzing longer texts, participants may determine stopping points for discussion and analysis; in an ongoing event like field work or an observation of a science experiment, participants should concentrate on Level One of the Deep Viewing process, and use Levels Two and Three at the conclusion of the observation. For an observational field text, individuals may share their observations subsequently with a whole group; in print, video, film, or artistic texts participants engage in the entire procedure. Deep Viewing may be adapted as needed to create a broad frame for understanding for all visual texts.

There are several points which are useful to remember in a Deep Viewing session:

1. Follow the stated progression to construct levels of understanding.

2. It is useful to designate a facilitator and a recorder in each group, especially when learning this technique. The facilitator keeps the group focused on the specific task of each level and makes sure each member is allowed to speak; the recorder takes notes about group comments.

3. For clarity, use "in the text" statements to describe the text. Use "I" statements to express your perceptions, ideas, observations, etc.

4. Prompts may be used. Possible prompts are included at the end of each code in the description of Level Two.

CODES FOR ANALYSIS

Form groups according to the following codes:

1. *Action/Sequence* This group notes events in text through oral discussion, written notes and/or visual devices like flow charts and time lines. They also note relationships of time. *They ask: What happens? When and how long do events take place?*

2. *Semes/Forms* Semes are units of visual meaning. This group notes forms in the text—both objects and people. They also examine characteristics of these forms: colors, textures, repeated, emphasized, and contrasted forms (i.e., objects that are paired with other objects like lightness with darkness), as well as the appearance, types of dress, and features of actors. Intersected lists are a good way to record information for this category. *They ask: What objects are seen? What are their traits?*

3. *Actors/Discourse* This group examines what the characters/actors say. They note words and phrases that may sum up main ideas or themes, repeated language, terms particular to a group, or language that seems out of place. This group also notes qualities of what is heard: the tone, rate, pitch of voices, and the lyrics of songs in a production. Use a Semantic feature analysis as a graphic organizer here. *They ask: What words are said? How are they heard?*

4. *Proximity/Movement* This group examines all movement, including gestures and movements of characters/actors and other forms. They note vectorality (where objects or actors move), relationships (how the forms move in relation to each other), and dimensions and relative sizes (does one form dominate by standing in front?) Use story boarding to record information here. *They ask: What sorts of movements occur?*

5. *Culture/Context* This group notes symbolic and discourse references to cultural knowledge like science, art, educational practice, or popular culture. Devices like Herringbone graphics, or character trait graphics should be used with this code. *They ask: What social knowledge is referred to and assumed? What is implied? What is missing? Where are the creators and actors in this text situated historically and culturally?*

6. *Effects/Process* In commercial texts, this group examines "Artistic devices": the use and repetition of techniques, quality of visual and sound effects and musical accompaniments, camera angles and technological enhancements, etc. In less sophisticated productions, viewers examine camera or observer angles, noting what is seen and missing, and posit how perspectives influence understanding. In print texts, they examine the devices used to structure the text, interest the audience, and further the author's purposes. In field work or naturalistic observations, they seek to understand how the observer's perspective and participation affects understanding and outcomes. This group should also focus on the quality of the text: e.g., how do factors like sound, angle of perception, and focus affect meaning? Cause effect graphics or decision making models are best here. *They ask: What production devices and elements are in the text?*

127

FIRST LEVEL: LITERAL—DESCRIBING AND SUMMARIZING

Groups are formed according to the codes. Facilitators, recorders, and reporters are selected. In a group setting, students focus on one category or code, using a variety of responses, including talk, writing, and pictures. For very small groups, ask participants to observe more than one code. For individual observations, create a paper with six vertical columns and record relevant observations under each heading as the observation proceeds.

Level One is *literal*. The purpose of Level One is to gain as much data as possible for subsequent analysis. *Describe only what you see and hear—do not interpret or evaluate.*

Procedure:

While viewing the text, take notes or draw pictures of aspects you notice. Record questions that puzzle you. Observe within your group's assigned focus or code.

During this level there is no cross-talk in groups.

1-1. After viewing, go around the table in your groups, each reading aloud your notes about what you have seen and heard in the text. This level is literal. Describe only what you perceive in the text—interpretation will come later. The recorder should record observations.

1-2. Summarize. Remain brief, but remain as true as possible to what each participant feels or perceives is the main point of his/her observation. Recorder underlines or summarizes main ideas.

1-3. Each group reports their findings to the whole group through oral, pictorial, and/or written means.

SECOND LEVEL: INTERPRETATION—RESPONDING AND EXPLORING MEANINGS

The purpose of Level Two is to explore a range of interpretations and responses to the data made explicit in Level One. There are no single "right answers," but a range of possible interpretations.

Strategies for response may be modelled before beginning this level (italized below). Any of the strategies may be used for any of the codes. These strategies may also be used for any text—print, situational, or electronic. Prompts may be created and used throughout Levels Two and Three as needed. Some examples of prompts are provided. Additional questions may direct or assist inquiry as desired (e.g., noting a particular strategy like persuasion, a specific issue like stereotypes, a theme stressed in readings, or guided inquiry into connections between the current text and others).

Often, some of the responses drawn from codes will begin to overlap at this level, as participants begin to discover relations between elements in the texts and their observations about them. This overlap is desirable, but in Level Two, focus on your category until all observations are completed.

During this level there is no cross-talk in groups until each participant has had a minimum of three uninterrupted turns to speak.

Procedure:

2-1. Go around the table in your groups again, but this time each viewer makes an observation. These observations should be based upon explicit aspects of the text. Note what is present in the text *and* what is missing. Begin with observations that are readily apparent and move to more inferential levels as you continue.

2-2. Talk at this level continues until readers agree that their observations are complete and are ready to move into the third level. Groups again stop and share their observations with the whole group.

EXAMPLES OF LEVEL TWO COMMENTS AND PROMPTS:

Action/Sequence - Conclusion: "The action continued longest during X scene—over three minutes. We must then posit that this is important for meaning."

Prompts: Is the time sequential or random? Does the action move around different time frames? What have we read that most closely parallels the time sequences in this text? How do we know what time it is? Why do you think the creators used this particular time development? How might the meanings in the text change if the time sequence were different?

Semes/Forms - *Observation:* "The symbol of X was repeated four times throughout the text." *Compare/Contrast* : "The image of Y was often paired with the image Z." *Questioning:* "What are the connotations of a symbol X?" "How do these two symbols convey possible antithetical meanings?" (e.g., of freedom versus entrapment, good versus evil, etc.)

Prompts: What symbols or objects were repeated most? Which ones were paired? Why? What feelings, memories, and thoughts do you associate with these symbols? In what other texts have you encountered these symbols? What might they mean to a person from a culture that is different than yours? What did you expect to see that was missing? Why do you think the creators used these particular symbols? Would you use the same ones? Why or why not?

Actors/Discourse - *Connecting:* "The characters repeat the phrases and words '........' When one reads repeated lines in poetry, these lines are often used to emphasize meaning." Identifying purposes: How do these repeated words further the purposes of the text?" *Noting what is missing*: "Why doesn't this text contain references or language about A, B, or C? I'd expect them to be there."

Prompts: What are the connotations of repeated words and phrases in the text? Why do you think the creators chose these words? What other words could they have used? How might using other words change meaning? What were the tone and mood of the characters and text? How do you know? How are tone and mood conveyed in a print text?

Proximity/Movement - *Noting context:* "In this scene, Character A stands between character(s) or object(s) B and C." *Forming hypotheses*: This relationship may foreshadow coming action; it may indicate how humans are always choosing between alternatives.

Prompts: What are the relations of objects and what do these relations suggest to you? Why are certain images closer to the viewer while others farther away? What does this suggest about their relative importance? What moves and what doesn't? What do ideas of movement and stillness suggest to you? How is movement or lack of movement used in this text to further plot, characterization, and mood? How are these devices used in literature or other texts you have encountered?

Culture/Context - *Observing*: "The text contains four references to science."

Remembering: "In the news last week they reported that this theory had been disproved."

Projecting: "If I were to make this text, I would . . ." *Locating Context*: "The characters refer to X historical event, are dressed in a particular style, and use several slang words that lead us to believe this film was made during the late 1950s." *Identifying perspectives*: Cultural allusions often convey hidden stereotypes and cultural biases. They also often reveal who is the perceived audience from the perspectives of the senders of a message. "The makers of this text seem to present women in submissive roles. How does this reflect the norms in 1950? Is this how people think today?"

Prompts: How do these references reflect the dominant views of U.S. culture? What assumptions are the senders of this message making about us and the greater society? Do we agree? How do they depict certain groups of people? Are these accurate portrayals? What sorts of words and images reveal stereotypes? How do you feel about these images?

Effects/Process - *Noting artistic devices and possible motivations:* e.g., "Why is this subject viewed from below? Does this connote respect or power? How do the special effects enhance or detract from the text? There are few reverse shots in this sequence. Why does this medium utilize the forms and processes it does?" *Noting visual devices:* "In the beginning of the text the camera is out of focus or pans in from a wide shot to a narrow shot of the main character. How is this like foreshadowing or development in a novel or poem?" *Personal observations and reactions:* "How aware am I of how devices are used? What responses do I have to them?"

Prompts: How many different angles and effects can you identify? How do these devices capture the viewer's interest? What sorts of devices were used to develop the story? How are they used? What devices are used to create feelings in the viewer like suspense or tension? What devices are used to create fast action? Slow action? How are these devices like those used by authors in print texts? How do they differ?

THIRD LEVEL: SYNTHESIS, EXTENSION, EVALUATION, AND APPLICATION

The purpose of this level is to synthesize, to evaluate, and to apply the information and interpretations made explicit in the first two levels. *During this level there is no cross talk until each participant has had two uninterrupted turns. Viewers may talk in any order and question each other. In this level, participants should start with their code focus, and then may progress to a discussion of the other codes.*

Procedure:

3-1. Groups now begin making broader inferences about the text's meanings. Besides making more speculative comments, participants now indicate their likes and dislikes about aspects of the text. They may compare or contrast this text with others, draw upon personal experiences, or express collective perceptions in their discussions about the text. Participants should also pose questions. Discuss these questions and responses in your groups. Be explicit about textual and personal connections. Say "I" when expressing an opinion or observation; say "in the text," when expressing perceptions of what you noted at the literal level.

At this level, the codes will overlap, as participants draw from the findings of other groups. Participants are now free to make connections between their own observations, those of their code group, and those within the classroom. Participants should relate the text to their own experiences, expectations, feelings, and knowledge. Often, at this stage, larger themes and connections are made. All participants should have ample opportunities to listen and to respond. There may be breaks in the group conversations. Facilitators should allow these reflective pauses in order for participants to assimilate and to formulate ideas. Questions and responses are discussed in the groups until members agree that the topic has been exhausted, and then groups report back to the whole group describing findings they see as particularly interesting or important.

Note: The Facilitator should be alert at this level, to keep participants on task.

3-2. Groups identify questions and general themes. Report findings back to whole group.

CONNECTING CONTEXTS AND CREATING CRITICAL PEDAGOGY: FURTHER APPLICATIONS OF DEEP VIEWING

Deep Viewing has been used by middle school students in California for analyses of films and newscasts, previews of textbooks, and examinations of persuasive strategies in commercials. In New Mexico, high school students Deep Viewed print advertisements and discovered that certain images, like colors and objects, are used by both authors of literature and sellers of consumer goods to hold audience interest and to further purposes. In New York, university English majors used the method to watch *The Wizard of Oz*. These sophomores, who often approached textual analysis with tepid responses, were engaged and on task throughout the session. They provided diverse interpretations and novel perspectives of this familiar classic: the existence of Jungian themes, its depiction of the monomyth or hero's quest, its contrast of Christian and pagan imagery, its depictions of cultural stereotypes, and issues of gender.

I have employed the method with teacher candidates to create anecdotal records and to analyze videotapes of instruction. Through examinations of what they say and do, as well as the objects and events in their classrooms, many are astounded to see cultural assumptions they make and the implicit biases they exhibit during lessons (Watts Pailliotet 1995). One of my preservice students implemented Deep Viewing as part of a math lesson. She used newspaper advertisements to teach students skills and to help them examine their beliefs about consumerism; another began with Deep Viewing, then developed a secondary art lesson involving animated video and story boarding to identify effective drawing techniques. I also teach my education students Deep Viewing to identify biases in textbooks and children's literature, to teach metacognitive literacy strategies needed to understand content reading texts and print advertisements like previewing and summarizing, and to examine their assumptions about diverse students. A colleague uses the method throughout her multicultural education course, inviting students to interrogate their own writing and popular texts as part of ongoing cross cultural analyses.

Experienced classroom teachers have Deep Viewed videotapes of their classrooms and college faculties have used the method when observing student teachers. These individuals reported value in the method because it enabled them to examine their own and others' practices in a systematic way and to notice aspects of their teaching they had overlooked in the past. For instance, a colleague viewed videos and deconstructed her students' behaviors during reading and writing consultations, as well as her own actions in a methods course, reflecting on how tacit power relations may result in cooperation or resistance (Briggs 1996). Reading teachers have used Deep Viewing for evaluating basals and textbooks, in order to select more relevant texts for students. It has also been utilized to examine films, print and televised commercials, picture books, computer software, and as an observational method in my dissertation fieldwork. A photographer recently used it as a way to analyze his pictures in order to explain them in a written narrative. Individuals have adapted it to develop visually effective software programs, to explore meanings in children's art, and to teach science students to observe experiments. I am currently Deep Viewing preservice teachers' ongoing drawings and narratives in order to better understand their perspectives, learning, and needs.

Deep Viewing provides a systematic method for students, teachers, and researchers to order, to construct, and to interrogate understandings. Because the method involves reading, writing, speaking, listening, thinking, and viewing, it connects literacy processes. It is also instructionally sound, because it fosters needed literacy skills and critical thinking. Deep Viewing promotes active participation, critical analysis, and awareness of culturally based assumptions. Perhaps most importantly, it empowers our students to connect, to extend, and to question their lived experiences. I have found that participants enjoy Deep Viewing, tend to stay on task during the process, and often exhibit increased academic or social skills that carry over from the examination of popular texts into traditional study. Deep Viewing is one move toward a modern, critical pedagogy. By using it, teachers may create powerful connections, teach all modern literacies, and help students to construct new views that are critical, meaningful, and cohesive.

REFERENCES

Althusser, L. "Ideology and Ideological State Apparatuses." In *Critical Theory since 1965*, H. Adams and L. Searle, eds. Tallahassee, FL: Florida State University Press, 1986. 239–51.

Bakhtin, M. M. "Intertexuality." In *Mikhail Bakhtin: The Dialogical Principle*, T. Todorov, ed. Minneapolis: University of Minnesota Press, 1988. 60–74.

Barthes, R. *Mythologies*, trans. Annette Lavers. New York: The Noonday Press. Farrar, Straus & Giroux, 1957.

———. *Image, Music, Text*, trans. Stephen Heath. New York: Hill and Wang, 1971.

———. *S/Z*, trans. Richard Miller. New York: Hill and Wang / The Noonday Press, 1974.

Bianculli, D. *Teleliteracy*. New York: Continuum, 1992.

Bissex, G. *Guys at Work*. Boston: Harvard University Press, 1980.

Bopry, J. "Visual Literacy in Education—A Semiotic Perspective." *Journal of Visual Literacy*, 14,1 (1994): 35–49.

Briggs, L. C. "Viewing Ourselves Through Critical Reflection: An Analysis of Literacy Instruction." Paper presented at International Reading Association 41st Annual Convention, New Orleans, 1996.

Bruner, J. *Acts of Meaning*. Cambridge, MA: Harvard University Press, 1990.

Considine, D. M., and G. E. Haley. 1992. *Visual Messages: Integrating Imagery into Instruction*. Englewood, CO: Teacher Ideas Press, 1990.

Derrida, J. "Structure, Sign, and Play in the Discourse of the Human Sciences"; "Of Grammatology"; "Differance." In *Critical Theory Since 1965*, H. Adams and L. Searle, eds. Tallahassee, FL: Florida State University Press, 1986. 83–137.

Dyson, A. H. "Reading, Writing, and Language : Young Children Solving the Written Language Puzzle." In *Composing and Comprehending* J. Jensen, ed. Urbana, IL: National Council of Teachers of English, 1984.

Elbow, P. "The Shifting Relationship between Speech and Writing." *College Composition and Communication*, 36,3 (1985): 283–301.

Emig, J. *The Web of Meaning*. Upper Montclair: Boynton / Cook Publishers, 1983.

Flood, J., and D. Lapp. "Broadening the Lens: Toward and Expanded Conceptualization of Literacy." In *Perspectives on Literacy Research and Practice: Forty-Fourth Yearbook of the National Reading Conference*, K. A. Hinchman, D. J. Leu, and C. K. Kinzer, eds. Chicago: National Reading

Conference, 1995: 1–16.

Flower, L. "Cognition, Context, and Theory Building." *College Composition and Communication*, 40, 3 (1985): 282-311.

Foucault, M. "What is an Author? / The Discourse on Language." In *Critical Theory Since 1965*. H. Adams and L. Searle, eds. Tallahassee, FL: Florida State University Press, 1986. 138-63.

Frye, N. *Anatomy of Criticism*. Princeton: Princeton University Press, 1957.

Giroux, H. A. "Reclaiming the Social: Pedagogy, Resistance and Politics in Celluloid Culture." In *Film Theory Goes to the Movies*. J. Collins, H. Radner, and A. P. Collins, eds. New York: Routledge, 1993. 37–55.

Goody, E. N. "Towards a Theory of Questions." In *Questions and Politenes: Strategies in Social Interaction*. E. N. Goody, ed. Cambridge: Cambridge University Press, 1978. 16-43.

Heath, S. B. *Ways with Words: Language, Life and Work in Communities and Classrooms*. Cambridge: Cambridge University Press, 1983.

Herber, H. L., and J. N. Herber. *Teaching in Content Areas with Reading, Writing, and Reasoning*. Boston: Allyn and Bacon, 1993.

Himley, M. *Shared Territory: Understanding Children's Writing as Works*. New York and Oxford: Oxford University Press, 1991.

Kervin, D. "Reading Images: Levels of Meaning in Television Commercials." In *Readings from the 16th Annual Conference of the International Visual Literacy Association*. N. Thayer and S. Clayton-Randolph, eds. Bloomington, IN: Western Sun, 1985. 36–43.

Lakoff, G., and M. Johnson. *Metaphors We Live By*. Chicago: Chicago University Press,1980.

Lipson, M.Y., and K. K. Wixson. *Assessment and Instruction of Reading Disability*. New York: Harper Collins,1991.

Lusted, D., ed. *The Media Studies Book: A Guide for Teachers*. London and New York: Routledge, 1991.

Lutz, W. *DoubleSpeak*. New York: HarperPerrenial, 1989.

McLuhan, M. *Understanding Media: The Extensions of Man*. New York and Toronto: McGraw-Hill, 1964.

———, and Q. Fiore. *The Medium is the Massage*. New York: Random House, 1967.

McLuhan, M., and E. McLuhan. *Laws of Media: The New Science*. Toronto: University of Toronto Press, 1988.

Neuman, S. B. *Literacy in the Television Age: The Myth of the TV Effect*. Norwood, N J: Ablex Publishing Corporation, 1991.

Ohlgren, T. H., and L. M. Berk. *The New Languages: A Rhetorical Approach to Mass Media and Popular Culture*. Englewood Cliffs, NJ: Prentice-Hall, Inc., 1977.

Pettersson, R. "Describing Picture Content." In *Visual Communication: Bridging Across Cultures*. J. Clark Baca, D. G. Beauchamp, and R. A. Braden, eds. Blacksburg, VA: International Visual Literacy Association, 1992. 153–60.

Pope, C. A. "Our Time Has Come: English for the Twenty-First Century."

English Journal, 82,3 (1993): 38–41.

Postman, N. *Amusing Ourselves to Death*. New York: Elizabeth Sifton Books: The Viking Press, 1985.

Reutzel, D. R., and R. B. Cooter. *Teaching Children to Read: From Basals to Books*. New York: Merrill, 1992.

Rosenblatt, L. *The Reader, the Text, the Poem: The Transactional Theory of the Literary Work*. Carbondale: Southern Illinois University Press, 1978.

Saint-Martin, F. *Semiotics of Visual Language*. Bloomington and Indianapolis, IN: Indiana University Press, 1990.

Sinatra, R. *Visual Literacy Connections to Thinking, Reading, and Writing*. Springfield, IL: Charles C. Thomas Publisher, 1986.

——. "Combining Visual Literacy, Text Understanding, and Writing for Culturally Diverse Students." *Journal of Reading*, 33,8 (1990): 612–17.

Vygotsky, L. S. *Mind in Society*. Cambridge, MA: Harvard University Press, 1978.

Watts Pailliotet, A. " 'I Never Saw that Before.' A Deeper View of Video Analysis in Teacher Education." *The Teacher Educator*, 31,2(1995): 138–56.

Witkin, M. "A Defense of Using Pop Media in the Middle School Classroom." *English Journal*, 83,1 (1994): 30–3.

VIII

STILL CRAZY AFTER ALL OF THESE YEARS:
TEACHING CRITICAL MEDIA LITERACY
Ladi Semali

Critical literacy is a contested educational ideal. Even though "critical" pedagogy has been en vogue for the past fifteen years, scholars continue to question what it means to be critical and how such a concept can be implemented across the curriculum. Grounded in the Freirian notions of emancipatory education, critical literacy has emerged as the most talked about alternative pedagogy. Critical literacy stands in contrast to the practice of teaching the classics and a canon of acceptable literary works far removed from the students' experiences for dry memorization exams. As a pedagogical tool, critical literacy draws its practice from "constructivist" approaches to teaching and to learning, from social theory studies of popular culture, and from the ideals of social justice. It draws from the media in its many forms, literature, the role of the state in struggles over race, class, and gender relations, national and international economic structures, and the cultural politics of imperialism, postcolonialism, and poststructuralism. These works of critical pedagogy are particularly useful in critical inquiry, the driving engine behind any critical literacy. They reassert the stance that discursive critical consciousness is necessary to critical education and to democratic public life (Fensham, Gunstone, and White 1994; Giroux 1987; Giroux and Simon 1989; Kellner 1995; McLaren, Hammer, Sholle, and Reilly 1995).

In the past ten years of controversy, critical theorists have been concerned with the centrality of politics and of power in our understanding of how schools work, and they have generated a debate that centers on the political economy of schooling, the state of education, the representation of texts, and the construction of student subjectivity. This chapter introduces five important elements of critical literacy that teachers and students might pursue in classroom practice to understand representation. In a step by step process, I will show that there are many ways in which coherent meanings for critical literacy might be constructed. I use these five concepts as a guide to critique and to examine film images of indigenous people in order to expose the oppressive spaces in the daily dose of media and visual messages designed to provide information and entertainment to credulous audiences. This chapter aims to be a model for teachers contemplating the use of such elements in their own classrooms to teach critical viewing, critical thinking, and critical reading skills. In the study of visual communication and media literacy, critical viewing is not used widely in American classrooms as a tool for deconstructing media images, particularly those images that represent people's culture, identity, or ethnicity. While this practice has begun to occur in schools in other countries, it is not yet happening in all U.S. schools.

With critical literacy, students learn to become critical consumers aware of visual manipulation and of stereotyping as important projects of education. Ira Shor (1993) defines critical literacy as:

> [a]nalytic habits of thinking, reading, speaking, or discussing which go beneath surface impressions, traditional myths, mere opinions, and routine clichés; understanding the social contexts and consequences of any subject matter; discovering the deep meaning of any event, text, technique, process, object, statements, image, or situation; applying the meaning to your own context. (32)

While reviewing recent works of Peter McLaren, Henry Giroux, Ira Shor, Alan Luke, and Norman Fairclough, Colin Lankshear (1994) elaborates critical literacy as a form of alternative pedagogy that examines the politics and sociolinguistic stances of text. Lankshear stresses that the adjective "critical" and its correlates, "criticism," "criticize," and "critique," convey the idea of judging, comparing, or evaluating on the basis of careful analysis.

In an attempt to design curricula that integrate critical literacy education, I established a media literacy course at the Pennsylvania State University for preservice teachers. Drawing on a range of concepts and techniques elaborated by theorists and by teachers working in various critical language studies, I developed activities around a simple media text, which has interesting possibilities for an interdisciplinary practice of critical literacy. I bring into the course the possibilities of working with media texts in conjunction with a set of different but relevant texts to address questions adapted from linguists and from literacy educators like Norman Fairclough, Allan Luke, Gunther Kress, and others. Offered every semester, this course calls for a context in which preservice teachers from several subjects—English, social studies, early childhood education, and science—work together to explore texts critically through their disciplines. Teachers often will immerse themselves in a media text or topic and take the time to explore the text in order to find questions that are significant to the learner and then systematically investigate those questions. One competency that students acquire in this course is the ability to apply the narrative analysis method to visual and other media representations. Student teachers are encouraged throughout this course to question the text, the context, and the subtext. They learn how to analyze what is in the text as well as what is omitted from the text, namely the context.

For preservice teachers therefore, media literacy becomes a competency to read, to interpret, and to understand how meaning is made and derived from print, photographs, and other electronic visuals. Media literacy consists of understanding connotative messages embedded in the text of the visual and media messages, as well as interaction of pictures to words, the context of the viewer, and relayed messages obtained from the maker of the image. For example, in the analysis of visuals used for advertising in various print media or textbook illustrations, students strive to uncover some of the narrative meaning by questioning: (1) the order of events depicted, (2) the actual history of visual production, circulation, and consumption, and (3) who produced the visual, under what circumstances, and for what possible reasons. Media literacy thus expands the notion of school literacy, principally the ability to read the printed text, to include a critical reading of all media texts. For teachers and for students, the classroom becomes a media literacy learning environment, where the learning process is not disconnected from the institutions that create knowledge and information, nor from the legal, cultural, political and economic contexts of texts whether they are books, films, or internet resources.

My experience in working with preservice teachers has been rewarding. It is particularly striking at the end of the semester to notice the extent to which preservice teachers' critical awareness has been raised. The level of awareness is especially visible in the rate of adoption of critical viewing, critical reading, and critical thinking skills they bring to their work and in the broad definition of "literacy" they eventually apply to a variety of projects embarked on long after completing the course. In preparing a lesson plan for an English class in high school, one graduate of media literacy wrote:

> Today's lesson addresses the fact that far too often oppressive
> events are packaged and phrased to take away any blame or

to remove any hint of ill-intent. Word choice and language are two techniques used by writers to shape readers' perception. [This lesson will] examine how writers present controversial issues and analyze what is and isn't included [in their narratives.]

Another student, while evaluating a teaching unit that included literature circles and reading, *The Lakota Woman* remarked:

> It is just shocking to discover how much discrimination goes on in present day America towards Native Americans! What is even more shocking is the fact that I had to come all the way to college to understand discrimination. I'm glad I found media literacy, the key to this understanding.

These two examples illustrate how students applied the critical literacy skills they learned to the English curriculum. By applying media literacy skills in questioning how a novel, a film, and other media texts represented Native Americans, students quickly realized the diverse layers of meanings, bias, distortion, manipulation, stereotyping, and multiple perspectives present in the media texts. Alternative critical pedagogy demanded that students look outside of, as well as at the representation of Native Americans: Who is the author/producer/artist? How was he/she placed in society? Which cultural forces of the author/producer/artist's society are raised? What is the message of the visual statement in terms of political and social import? How can we evaluate this message using the prevailing values of the culture of the artist rather than of the viewer?

At the core of the critical pedagogy movement are the needs (1) to develop an awareness of the constructed nature of representation in both print and visual media, (2) to provide knowledge about the social, cultural, economic, and political contexts in which media messages are produced by a variety of different institutions with specific objectives, and (3) to encourage renewed interest in learning about the ways in which individuals construct meaning from messages—that is about the processes of selecting, interpreting, and acting upon messages in various contexts.

In the pages that follow, I will illustrate the work that I and other university researchers in critical pedagogy have engaged in over the past ten years. This method of alternative pedagogy is based on two rationales: first, that teaching the classics and a canon of acceptable literary works far removed from the students' experiences to be memorized for exams runs contrary to the qualities that make up critical consciousness (Freire 1970); and second, that if we hope to create media and visual environments that will help us change oppressive literacy practices, we have to think critically about what kinds of learning we want in the classrooms and how literacy practices are projected or articulated with other social, political, and ideological forces.

FIVE CONCEPTS FOR CRITICAL PEDAGOGY ABOUT MEDIA REPRESENTATION

Visual representation refers to the way images and language actively construct meanings according to sets of conventions shared by and familiar to makers (producers) and audiences (viewers). As a visual representation of storytelling, films share much in common with the historical or fictional narrative, including plot, theme, character, setting, conflict, and resolution. Through the maneuvering of camera angles, cutting, and lighting, the manipulation of time and space is effectively accomplished to give the viewer a sense of realism. For this reason, visual representations of people demand a careful analysis to discover (1) what is at issue, (2) how the issue/event is defined, (3) who is involved, (4) what the arguments are, and (5) what is taken for granted, including cultural assumptions. In short, a systematic mode of inquiry will focus on the origins, the determinants, and the effects of media and visual constructions, all of which are carefully put together to influence the viewer in a certain way.

Adapted from Werner and Nixon's guide for teaching critical mindedness, and from Fairclough's for teaching critical language awareness, these five concepts provide an important starting point for critical pedagogy (Fairclough 1989; Werner and Nixon 1990). In this analysis, I introduce a discussion about the Sani. The Sani are the indigenous people of the Kalahari Desert in Southern Africa. These people have for many years been called the "bushmen," a derogatory name coined by early European settlers in the early 1900s. This name has been used until 1990, when Namibia obtained its independence. The culture, language, and social life of the Sani have been represented in the film *The Gods Must Be Crazy* (1984), now available on videotapes (*Gods I* and a sequel, *Gods II* [1990]) distributed all over the world. As the name "bushman" suggests, the Sani have been portrayed as creatures of The Stone Age that are obstacles to progress, civilization, and modernization.

In the study of visual representation in films, the complex issues surrounding culture, identity, and ethnicity are brought to bear. By

engaging critical viewing skills, viewers can recognize the social location of their interpretations, rather than believing those interpretations are somehow natural or idiosyncratic to the individual.   The
myth that the accepted conventions of film, video, and photographic
representation are mere neutral carriers devoid of content implications no longer holds ground. By posing questions that seek a deeper meaning and understanding, critical viewers avoid the inclination
to oversimplify their social identities into a collection of unified, discrete, and mutually exclusive territories that can be related only
through dichotomous opposition: good versus bad, hero versus vil-
lain, right versus wrong, moral versus immoral. This approach to
critical pedagogy provides students as audiences and viewers alternative ways of knowing, and gives room for multiple voices to be heard
in the interpretation of meaning(s). How might one apply such a critical pedagogy to visual representations of *The Gods Must Be Crazy*?

WHAT IS THE ISSUE?

We must first ask what context motivated the production of *The Gods*.
By questioning the production and construction of the meaning-making
processes in media representations, we will examine closely the visual
imagery and popular representation of people that help shape their
personal, social, and political worlds. In thinking about "what is the
issue," I direct attention towards the broader issues: (1) What sense do
representations make of the world? (2) What are the visuals representing to us and how? In other words, how do the individuals represented in the film become seen or how does the way we see them influence
how we treat them? (3) What are typical representations of groups in
society? (4) What does this example of visuals represent to me? (5)
What do the visuals mean to other people who see them?

To decipher *The Gods Must Be Crazy* as a visual representation of
culture, identity, and ethnicity, it is necessary to know something about
South Africa's past history, its present domestic and foreign policies,
and the singlemindedness with which South Africa, before majority
rule elections in 1994, used the system of apartheid to shape its future.
Within its borders, South Africa had for almost four decades been creating a new territorial and demographic entity. Although we tend to
hear only the pretty aspects of apartheid, its greatest manifestation was
the manipulation of people within a finite space. As several reviewers
of the film have acknowledged, *The Gods* is an expression of this aspect
of apartheid (Brown 1982, 42; Denby 1984, 47; Davis 1985, 51; Keneas
1984, 22). Accordingly, the film delves on this aspect of racist apartheid

by inversion.

In the comical, visual, and humorous images of *The Gods*, a South African writer-director, Jamie Uys makes jokes about the absurdities and discontinuities of African life. While the landscape of *The Gods* looks very much like South Africa, it is set in what some film critics call the mythical country of Botswana. Because Uys's Botswana does not exist, except in his imagination; features of the landscape, dress, and custom are not to be found in real Botswana. Uys's Botswana is instead a dream of a happy-go-lucky *bantustan*, those equally fictitious homelands that the South African government tried to create all over South Africa, literally out of dust, for the dumping of African people. Clearly, the central issue is the value questions defined by the filmmaker's goals, ideals, and hopes. As always, the contention or challenge therefore is to recognize that many of the things of value to us are not necessarily valued to the same degree by other people.

HOW IS THE ISSUE/EVENT DEFINED?

As we consider how the event is defined, several questions come to mind: (1) What is the source of the information? (2) What form does the event take? (3) How does the form shape my understanding of the event? (4) How does the form serve or not serve my purposes? (5) What information is left out?

The first ten minutes of the film address the relationship between illusion and reality. The imposing voice of the narrator intones: "It looks like a paradise, but it is in fact the most treacherous desert in the world, the Kalahari." After a series of cutaways and short narrative bits that set the stage for a childlike character, we see footage of the placid Kalahari "bushmen" searching for water. In this desert we meet the "dainty, small, and graceful Sani ('bushmen')." Suspecting satire, we're unsure of the filmmaker's intent, but the sequence turns out to be a fairly predictable documentary with dry, straight-faced narration about a peaceful, "primitive" tribe of tiny "bushmen" who live in a gracious, simple world digging for roots and foraging for berries, without any knowledge of crime or violence. A Coke bottle drops from a great silver bird in the heavens and into the orderly lives of the nomadic "Bushman" Xi and his family. The bottle, as it soon turns out, is a gift from the gods. You can blow on it and make a windy music, you can roll it and crush millet. Pretty soon comes arguing over the bottle's possession followed by acrimony, anger, and fights. When one of the "bushmen" decides to return the bottle to the gods by throwing it off the end of the earth, his search for the earth's edge forces him to enter

143

urban society for the first time, so the story goes. The story about the Sani is narrated by an outsider who does not include the point of view of those whose story is being told. In this narration, the culture of the Sani and that of other African societies is presumed to be a quaint relic of the past rather than a vibrant contemporary culture.

One might ask: Who are these "gods" who are crazy? They are the technologically advanced whites whose very garbage is a source of wonder to most of the developing world! In their indigenous wisdom, the Sani come to reject what white society has to offer, symbolized in the discarded bottle. This very rejection is a sop of white angst, because it means that the Sani do not covet the white standard of living, and so cannot be considered rivals—for South Africans, the ideal state of affairs. However admirable, the kind of decision this rejection represents is completely absent from the everyday lives of the indigenous peoples of South Africa. If there is one overwhelming fact of the dispossessed Tswanas, Zulus, Xhosas, and Sani, as it is for many Africans, it is that they have no control whatsoever over what they can accept or reject. For most Africans, the decision continues to be made by outsiders and that decision has never concerned itself in the least with what the African wants.

It would be curious to know how much Xi was paid for acting in the movie. Did he ever see the movie? What did he think of it? Has he read some of the raving reviews about his movie? Will he read this article? These rhetorical questions illustrate the predicament in which the continent of Africa lies in relation to the rest of the world. Unfortunately, a set of ethics that bind those who exploit indigenous knowledge systems for our own advantage does not seem to exist. For many Africans, the media are still out of reach and will be so for many years to come. Poverty is rampant; amenities of the modern world like telephones, electricity, plumbing, or permanent housing is a dream for many indigenous peoples who live in remote areas and out of the urban circle. Why is it this way? The context within which *Gods* was made is not explained anywhere in the production of this film. It is egregiously missing.

WHO IS INVOLVED?

As we explore "what groups are involved," our attention is drawn to two important questions: (1) What point of view is present? (2) Who is the target audience? The idea of whose interest or point of view prevails helps us to be critical of how a particular representation, issue, or event may be biased. Less obvious than identifying the filmmaker may be realizing that his reasons or arguments could be self-serving, designed largely to protect or to enhance the invested interest or dominant perspective in some way. A vested interest includes any privilege that a group enjoys and considers their "right." Arguments may be designed to protect or to enhance this interest—whether position, benefit, status, or credibility—perhaps at the expense of an opponent who is made to look foolish, selfish, stupid, immoral, uninformed, or downright perverse.

The film *The Gods Must Be Crazy*, employs a narrator to guide the viewers and to intone who and what is important. Some people are cast as victims, others as heroes. An ethnocultural bias runs throughout the plot. This bias portrays Africans as childlike, incompetent, and unscientific. This bias reinforces a long-standing myth about Africa—the Dark Continent. Even though the theme of this film may pretend to portray a simplistic tale of the search for the tranquil life and to satirize white urban living, beneath that tranquil life lies a parable about white South Africa with its basic values—those values of the privileged, for it is only those content with the world's goods who can afford to poke fun at them!

Who is in the film? The film's story is made up of a number of intertwining plots. The first story involves Xi, the so-called "Bushman." As Uys shows it, the life of the "bushmen" is idyllic, completely in harmony with their environment, living communally, until a careless aviator throws a Coke bottle into their midst. In another subplot, set in a neighboring African-governed country, a revolutionary Sam Boga attempts a coup. He is unsuccessful, and together with his followers flees into Botswana. A third subplot involves a white teacher who suddenly gets bored with her meaningless job in a city office and takes a job as a teacher in an African school in Botswana. There she meets up with Andrew Steyn, a shy, awkward biologist who eventually wins her. These three plots fuse at the resolution, when the African revolutionaries seize the white schoolteacher and her African pupils as hostages, and they are rescued by the biologist and Xi working as a team.

For many people, Africa is not a place but a state of mind, the heart of darkness. Africa has never been dark, however, to those who live there. It is ignorance on the part of the outsiders that was, and continues to be, dark. The great tradition that *Gods* draws on is the journey through Africa—not the sort of expedition where you hunt for animals, but the missionary journey where you hunt for the souls of human beings. When applied to white South Africa before independence, the notion of "missionary," someone with a mission, derives new meaning! This "mission" is essential to the white man's view of Africa. Europe sent its missionaries, including its fanatics, to Africa. The Afrikaner, the white man in that part of Africa we now call South Africa, decided early on that his mission was to bring the Word of God to the wilderness. Unlike Dr. Livingstone's ambition to bring the Word of God to the people of Central Africa, the Afrikaner had no desire to share that Word with the *kaffir*, the unbelievers, for Afrikaners were God's Chosen People, and the Chosen do not share with the unchosen, for then how would He tell the difference (Davis 1985, 51)? In the middle of this century, the Afrikaners' mission came to mean the protection of White Christian Civilization (against the Africans and Communism). In Uys's film, these two—the Africans and Communism—are personified by Sam Boga and his guerrillas.

A figurative interpretation of the plot, then, reveals that Africans are like children who are easily led astray by outside agitators (i.e., African liberationists). When this happens, the threat is not only to Africans but also to the white race personified by the heroine. To save Africans and Europeans alike, white organizational skills must mobilize all indigenous peoples and even African nature itself (in the shape of a poisonous bush). As the film illustrates, Andrew Steyn, the pacific, unworldly scientist—the personification of a technologically advance but nonaggressive South African—beats all the odds.

WHAT ARE THE ARGUMENTS?

This question drives the inquiry. Besides looking at what groups are involved in the film, an examination of the arguments postulated in the film reveals that *The Gods* has a strong point of view! What arguments enhance the interests of its dominant side and what arguments detract from the credibility of the other side? More specifically, students and teachers must ask the following critical questions: (1) Why was a particular visual image selected? (2) What information presented in the visual image is factual? (3) What portion of content is inaccurate? (4) Why are shots/camera work arranged that way? (5) Do visual images match narration? (6) How does sound affect visual images? (7) How is repetition of visual images, and text used? (8) How do graphics affect the message? (9) How does stillness or motion aid the message? (10) What is left out? (11) How is the message affected by what is left out?

Readers may be troubled in two contrasting ways: on the one hand, some who are shocked by the obvious racism of the film may wonder why I worry about basic principles of media representation; on the other hand, many may wish that the questions I pose could just be ignored, simply because, in their opinion, the film was only a piece of art and entertainment—why not just follow one's pleasures and savor the riches that the world of narrative provides? Unfortunately, there are many sides to any piece of art! Because all media and visual productions are produced from a variety of social locations and motivations, such underlying positions and motives need to be questioned. Perhaps if we can find a responsible way of defending the ethical criticism of narrative, we will encourage similar probing in the other arts or texts that I must neglect here.

It is important to look at how the visuals are manipulated in this film. For example, after about six minutes the film cuts to a big city, where we are introduced to "civilized man." Civilized humans, we are told, managed to make their lives more complicated by trying to make them easier. By contrast, the "bushmen" have a very simple life—until the Western world intrudes upon it. The mission of Andrew Steyn, the biologist, is scientific discovery, in the innocuous form of examination of elephant droppings. Xi's mission, however, is the preservation of the way of life of the "bushman."

The arguments are made through anecdotal stories of the way the people in the film go about doing their everyday work. As it is shown, the white scientist comes to the aid of the kidnapped children. Here, the underlying platitude by which most South Africans rationalize their relationship with Africans comes to the surface: "Africans are like children." In the film, they *are* children. By introducing the guerrilla fighters, the film shows that their own government, being African, cannot be relied upon to protect them. They must be rescued by the ingenuity of a white man *in collaboration with Xi the "Bushman."*

All these people scurrying around the landscape of southern Africa, colliding in pratfalls, constitute a distorted microcosm of the class of peoples and ideologies that is in reality deeply tragic. What Uys has done in the film, in fact (albeit a fact disguised by humor), is to create the never-never land that the architects of apartheid would have us believe in, in which South Africa's intentions are the good for everyone. In this land of make-believe, entire villages drop their work and turn out to sing a hymn of welcome to a white teacher. This gesture depicts the relationship of Africans towards white people as gratitude for the help being given, of whites towards Africans, as protective paternalism. This peaceful, dependent relationship would continue forever were it not for the advance of the guerrillas.

WHAT IS TAKEN FOR GRANTED?

To examine the assumptions or what is taken for granted several questions come to mind: What attitudes are assumed? Whose voice is heard? Whose points of view are assumed? Implied in these questions are the cultural assumptions. The ways in which media constructions are read or received by their audiences are often not questioned enough. For example, different disciplines of science measure Africa in different ways: Geographers point to a climate that ranges from the burning Sahara, to the steamy rainforests of Zaire, to the dry savannas of Kenya. Biologists note the astonishing abundance and variety of the continent's wildlife, with a particular mention of Tanzania's Serengeti and the Ngorongoro Crater. Epidemiologists speak with horror of deadly viruses like HIV and Ebola that are presumed to have come out of the jungle, and countless undiscovered microbes waiting to emerge. For anthropologists, Africa's most impressive statistics are the ones that measure the enormous diversity of its indigenous people. The diversity of the different African societies, from Ashanti to Zulu, and their customs provide a rich heritage rather than a deficit culture. With varying histories, cultures, and lifestyles, these indigenous peoples have lived on the continent for centuries and are spread over fifty independent countries. A majority of the indigenous people includes pastoralists, agro-pastoralists, hunters, and gatherers. Some 1,300 languages are spoken on the continent, about a third of the world's total. Each language represents a distinct indigenous group with its own beliefs and its own rituals and ceremonies— some of which have been performed for hundreds of years.

Africa is often misunderstood, however, because of the Western media's dismissal of the continent as backward and therefore unworthy of coverage, until disaster strikes, like in the case of the recent famine in Ethiopia, Somalia, and Rwanda. The media does not portray Africa as a diverse continent, of reemerging democracies and of troubled areas with leftover vestiges of colonialism, made up of many countries, climates, geographies, histories, and peoples.

By now it is common knowledge that Africa overflows with indigenous forms of communication: theater, drumming, dancing, traditional storytelling, and village meetings that have informed and entertained for centuries. And yet, in the past thirty years, the continent has been inundated with radios, televisions, VCRs, and other Western products at the expense of dislodging these indigenous artforms, practices, and knowledge systems. This persistent state of affairs makes African communities "knowledge colonies" of outside powers. Most African economies, apart from South Africa, are too poor to compete with European and American economies in terms of media production and dissemination. The reliance on the West for all but local news results in reduced and distorted coverage of Africa, consistent with the legacy of colonialism as portrayed in *The Gods*.

Tanzanians, for instance, get news about their neighbors, the Kenyans, from the Western media. Nigerians learn about Tanzanian events from the British Broadcasting Corporation (BBC). All over Africa the pattern is the same. The image we see in the United States, the corrupt, incompetent, starving, dependent, hopeless Africa, is the image manufactured in the West and transmitted to Africa, (although there are pockets of resistance to this inundation). Raised on a diet of Westernized history, Tarzan books and films, and sensationalized news media, many students in the United States believe Africa to be a primitive land of hot, steamy jungles inhabited by wild animals and savages. This myth is normalized and reinforced by *The Gods Must Be Crazy*.

Even though present day technological changes have brought far reaching structural changes in industrialized countries, particularly in the area of production and distribution of information and literacy materials, the situation in Africa and in much of the developing world remains a challenge. Communities in metropolitan cities like Dar es Salaam, Johannesburg, Lagos, and Nairobi look to the communities of Los Angeles and New York with awe and wonder, imitating their music and fashion, and craving the instant gratification and escape that movie entertainment has to offer.

Non-Africans have distorted the reality about Africa. For centuries, starting with perceptions of the remote "Dark Continent," the worldview of many non-Africans, particularly Europeans, was clouded over with myths and stereotypes. Some of the simplest myths are most common: lions in the jungles, the isolated Dark Continent, inferior savages, a race of Negroes (heathens developed only by the grace of God and the white man), and a land of turmoil, incapable of self-government. Because these myths and stereotypes are alive today in schools' curriculum (however unintentional the distortions and omissions may be), in the hands of unaware and unskilled teachers, the curriculum continues to feed the racist doctrines and practices of white superiority and privilege.

CONCLUSION

In this analysis, I have employed critical inquiry as an alternative pedagogy to unravel a discourse of ethnic bias and denigration of indigenous peoples disguised in humor as clear-cut realism. I encourage teachers to unmask such disguises embedded in media representations of everyday life. The five concepts for critical pedagogy about media representation outlined in this chapter cannot claim to substitute for or to uproot the century-old myths, fears, and stereotypes about Africa and the African people. These five concepts, however, provide a framework to question such myths and stereotypes, which have to a large extent been created in storybooks, literature, media, and cinema. By posing these questions, we investigate and critically evaluate the various assumptions underlying the production values of dominant news, pictures, and entertainment media. In fact, by using these concepts in critical pedagogy, we also examine the ways in which the language of media is socially and historically produced. We need to encourage students as well to question the clarity and strength of reasoning, to identify assumptions and values, to recognize points of view and attitudes, and to evaluate conclusions and actions provided by all narratives across the curriculum whether they be short stories, poems, plays, picture books, film, or pieces of nonfiction.

REFERENCES

Bordwell, D., J. Staiger, and K. Thompson. *The Classical Hollywood Cinema: Film Style and Mode of Production to 1960*. New York: Columbia University Press, 1985.
Brown, R. *Monthly Film Bulletin* 3 (1982): 42.
Canby, V. "Sequel to South Africa's 'Gods Must Be Crazy'." *The New York Times*. C (1990): 14.
Davis, P. *Cineaste*, XIV, 1 (1985): 51.
Denby, D. *New York* 7 (1984): 47.
Dyer, R. "Taking Popular Television Seriously." In *TV and Schooling*. David Lusted and Phillip Drummond, eds. London: BFI (1985): 44–5.
Fairclough, N., ed. *Critical Language Awareness*. Harlow: Longman, 1992.
Fensham, P., R. Gunstone, and R. White, eds. *The Content of Science: A Constructivist Approach to Teaching and Learning*. London: The Falmer Press, 1994.
Freire, P. *Pedagogy of the Oppressed*. Harmondsworth: Penguin, 1970.
———, and H. Giroux. "Pedagogy, Popular Culture and Public Life. An Introduction." In *Popular Culture: Schooling and Everyday Life*. H. Giroux and R. Simon, eds. New York: Bergin & Garvey (1989): 199-212.
Giroux, H. "Critical Literacy and Student Experience: Donald Graves' Approach to Literacy." *Language Arts*, 64 (1987): 175–81.
———, and R. Simon. "Popular Culture as Pedagogy of Pleasure and Meaning." In *Popular Culture: Schooling and Everyday Life*. H. Giroux and R. Simon, eds. New York: Bergin & Garvey (1989): 1–29.
Kellner, D. *Media Culture: Cultural Studies, Identity and Politics Between the*

Modern and the Postmodern. New York: Routledge, 1995.

Keneas, A. *Newday 9*, Part 11 (1984): 45–6.

Lankshear, C. *Critical Literacy*. Occasional Paper No. 3. Australian Curriculum Studies Association, (May 1994): 4–26.

Lankshear, C., and P. McLaren, eds. *Critical Literacy. Politics, Praxis, and the Postmodern*. Albany, NY: SUNY Press, 1993.

McLaren, P., R. Hammer, D. Sholle, and S. Reilly. *Rethinking Media Literacy: A Critical Pedagogy of Representation*. New York: Peter Lang. 1995. 25-35.

Shor, I. "Education is Politics: Paulo Freire's Critical Pedagogy." In *Paulo Freire: A Critical Encounter*. P. McLaren and P. Leornard, eds. London: Routledge, 1993.

Werner W., and K. Nixon. *The Media and Public Issues: A Guide for Teaching Critical Mindedness*. London, Ontario: The Althouse Press, 1990.

IX

BILINGUAL EDUCATION IN AMERICA:
IN SEARCH OF EQUITY AND SOCIAL JUSTICE
Lourdes Diaz Soto

I used to get whacks on my head for not spelling my name the way they wanted it spelled. After all they would say, "You're an American." But the next person would say, "You are Puerto Rican." The system is failing the kids, and it's not just one child.

—Luz, Steel Town, PA

This chapter discusses how the political mood of a nation can influence the linguistic human rights of children thereby disregarding a moral imperative to implement an education that promotes equity and social justice and IS bilingual and bicultural. Recent events show how privileged English-only voices in America are eliminating the possibilities of an education that is equitable and just for language minority and monolingual children. The conservative right wing and certain political elements of our nation are encouraging a tongue–tied and racist America. Language minority children are being effectively foreclosed from their home language while monolingual children are deprived of enriching linguistic and cultural experiences.

HOW ARE ENGLISH-ONLY FORCES POLITICIZING BILINGUAL EDUCATION?

The following examples will help the reader begin to analyze how the English-only politicians have disregarded the needs of children and of families. These powerful elements have access to the media and to the legislation, and have silenced the voices of children, families, and educators.

The basic appeal by U.S. English advocates in the popular media is a fear campaign wrapped under the guise of nationalism. One full-page advertisement disseminated to nationally prominent magazines this year asks, "Will it come to this?" The picture shows two children standing in front of an American flag with their right hands over their chests while the following letters are typed over the entire picture: "I pledge allegiance to the bandera de los Estados Unidos de Amerika und der republik. . . . " Underneath this picture the caption reads, "Will it come to this? We hope not. But it doesn't look good. . . . " This advertisement goes on to ask the readers to "Join us . . . fight with us . . . call 1-800 . . . "

The same organization, U.S. English, previously placed full page ads in a variety of newspapers including the *New York Times* depicting a dishwasher swamped with dirty dishes and stating, "If some NY educators get their way this is the kind of future many of our children will face" (*New York Times*, July 15, 1989).

The English-only media campaign and legislation has been very effective. Twenty-three states have passed official English legislation, at least eight states have bills pending, and two states are considering bills making their present official English statutes more restrictive. Hawaii is the only state that has approved official language legislation recognizing both English and Native Hawaiian (*Hispanic Link* 1996).

In 1996 the English-only arguments reached the Supreme Court. Lower courts struck down the English-only amendment adopted in 1988 in Arizona on the grounds that it "obstructs the free flow of information and adversely affects the rights of many private persons." The amendment was challenged by Maria-Kelly Yniquez, a state employee who assisted with medical malpractice claims. The amendment stated in part that "English . . . is the language of the ballot, the public schools and all government functions and actions." While Arizona attorney Stephen Montoya argued that official English legislation constitutes racism and is unconstitutional, the head of the U.S. English group stated, "You're in America now, so speak English, learn English (*CDT* 1996)." It is possible that the case may be seen as legally irrelevant since Ms. Yniquez left her job. The decision is expected in July 1996 (*CNN, Associated Press*, December 4, 1996).

James Crawford (1988) uncovered the fear of a loss of power expressed by a former leader of the U.S. English movement. Dr. John Taton stated:

> Gobernar es poblar translates to govern is to populate. In this society, where the majority rules, does this hold? Will the present majority peaceably hand over its political

power to a group that is simply more fertile? (Crawford 1988: 57)

In addition, Crawford documents contributions to the organization by advocates of eugenic sterilization. I bring this up because I think it's important for teachers and educators to understand the origins, goals, intent, and often not so hidden agenda of the English-only movement.

The world wide web site proclaims that "All contributions to the Leadership Institute are tax deductible . . . ." Contributions go not only to English-only goals, but towards other conservative projects as well. "As a former president of U.S. English, the organization fighting to make English the official language of the U.S., Ms. Chavez fought against multiculturalism and bilingualism." Ms. Chavez is a frequent guest on a variety of nationally disseminated television stations including CNN (*Home Speaker's Bureau* 1996).

Former Presidential Candidate Bob Dole declared that English should be made the "the official language of the United States" (*New York Times*, September 10, 1995). Politicians are working hard to ensure that children in America receive an English-only education (National Association for Bilingual Education 1995).

In an Amarillo, Texas courtroom the language issue also became a child custody issue. Judge Kiser told Ms. Laureano, "You're abusing that child and you're relegating her to the position of housemaid. Now, get this straight. You start speaking English to this child because if she doesn't do good in school, then I can remove her because it's not in her best interest to be ignorant. The child will only hear English" (*New York Times*, August 30, 1995).

HOW DOES THIS POLITICAL CLIMATE IMPACT CHILDREN'S EDUCATION?

An article in *The Wall Street Journal* (April 10, 1996) shows how bilingual education programs are being dismantled by the English-only proponents. The article is written by the vice president of the Center for Equal Opportunity, and refers to a school district superintendent as a "bilingual education abolitionist." Mr. Doluisio's role in dismantling a bilingual education program is lauded as the author states: "Bethlehem, PA, provides a stirring example of how other school districts can challenge the bilingual education orthodoxy—and win." The school superintendent in this article relays that ". . . meetings were very heated. I had to have cops in the back of the room to make sure that there was no trouble." Mr. Miller goes on to say, "At one point, a group of Latino activists physically surrounded the school board and led by a priest from out of town, engaged in a prayer to save Bethlehem's bilingual-education program." While the English-only fear based forces provided armed police guards, the bilingual education proponents were escorted by a priest and peacefully prayed before the school board! The use of "bilingual education abolitionist" is itself rather ironic as the conservative English-only forces attempt to align themselves with the notion of emancipation, even though their activities are earmarked at dismantling programs beneficial to children.

These events exemplify how a national climate is created that allows language domination, cultural invasion, and linguicism. These methods have the ultimate effect of totally disregarding children's linguistic human rights (LHRs). At the *individual* human rights level, children have the LHRs to learn their mother tongue ("the first language you learn and identify with," Skutnabb-Kangas 1984) and at least one of the official languages of the nation. It makes sense to think that it would be in our country's best interest to encourage teachers to become bilingual in order to protect children's LHRs and to encourage second language learning. At the *collective* human rights level, LHRs implies: a) the right to establish and to maintain schools that include home language, home culture, and second language learning; b) the guarantees of representation in political affairs, and c) autonomy with regard to issues of culture, religion, education, information, and social affairs.

> Often individuals and groups are treated unjustly and suppressed by means of language. People who are deprived of LHRs may thereby be prevented from enjoying other human rights, including fair political representation, a fair trial, access to education, access to information, freedom of speech, and maintenance of cultural heritage. (Phillipson, Rammut, and Skutnabb-Kangas 1995: 2)

The political reality of unequal access to power can be largely attributed to two myths generated by English-only proponents. First, that monolingualism is somehow helpful to economic growth and second, that minority rights pose a threat to the nation. But, international evidence shows that not granting rights to minorities is more likely to lead to secession (we think of French Canadians), while second language learning actually enhances economic possibilities.

Schools are the major agency that impose assimilation of the dominant language and the dominant culture. The forced inclusion into a monolingual and monocultural system physically, psychologically, and economically punishes children throughout the world for speaking their mother tongue (Skutnabb-Kangas 1984, Skutnabb-Kangas and Phillipson 1995).

> In fact, formal education through the medium of majority languages has extremely often forced minority children to assimilate and change identity. We are reminded of the definition of cultural genocide. . . . (Skutnabb-Kangas and Phillipson 1995, p. 72–73)

The international community views the English language amendments of the United States of America and the treatment of the Kurds in Turkey as the most extremely assimilation-oriented (Skutnabb-Kangas and Phillipson 1995). Activities earmarked at punishing children for speaking their native language still persist in contemporary America. In Louisiana, for example, children have been asked to kneel for speaking in a language other than English. In Pennsylvania, children have been retained a grade for speaking a language other than English. In California, children are expected to "prove" their national origin.

Even though many countries provide more protection to minority languages (Finland, South Africa, India), a variety of international documents begin to provide guidance for the protection of linguistic human rights, for example:

a) The Charter of the United Nations (1945) commits its member nations to promoting "universal respect for . . . human rights and fundamental freedoms for all without distinction as to race, sex, language, or religion" (paragraph 6.11, 55);

b) The Universal Declaration of Human Rights (1948) states in the second paragraph, "Everyone is entitled to all the rights and freedoms set forth . . . without distinction . . . such as race, colour, sex, language, religion, political or other opinion . . ." This document also calls for the "full development of the human personality" and the right of parents to "choose the kind of education that shall be given to their children."

c) The International Covenant on Civil and Political Rights (1966) in Article 27 states, "persons belonging to such minorities shall not be denied the right . . . to enjoy their own culture, to profess and practice their own religion, or to use their own language."

d) The U.N. Convention on the Rights of the Child (1989) emphasizes the importance of the "development of respect for the child's
parents, his or her own cultural identity, language and values"
(Art. 29.c) and "due regard shall be paid to the desirability of con-
tinuity in a child's upbringing to the child's ethnic, religious, cultural and linguistic background" (Art. 20.3).

In the United States the *Lau v. Nichols* (1974) Supreme Court
decision states that:

> there is no equality of treatment merely by providing stu-
> dents with the same facilities, textbooks, teachers and
> curriculum; for students who do not understand English
> are effectively foreclosed from any meaningful education.

The political aspects of bilingual education have shown that litigation is
the means for educational reform in America. The advent of English-
only policies clearly shows "considerable confusion as to what constitu-
tional rights to language are guaranteed, and . . . little understanding of
bilingualism on the bench" (Skutnabb-Kangas and Phillipson 1995, 87).

Issues of equity, justice, power, and cultural democracy continue
to plague educational institutions in America. The idea that "an
individual can be bicultural and still be loyal to American ideals"
(Ramirez and Castaneda 1974, 23) is one that may elude schools in
light of the increasingly conservative agenda being promulgated by
politicians and by selected media personalities. Language and cultural educational issues must be conceived with an additive (English-
plus) philosophy and not mandated by politically motivated personalities who are neither well versed on these issues nor on the needs
of America's children. Too many linguists in America are not concerned about children losing their English language skills but rather
about the issue of home language preservation.

Research reported elsewhere (Soto 1997) illuminates how issues
of power obscure the very voices representing children's best interests. Bilingual families I interviewed in Steel Town, as in many communities across our nation, defy stereotypical notions that families
do not care about their children's educational future. I saw families
initiate a prayer of petitions before their school district and school
superintendent. These families were passionate in their pursuit of a
quality education. The children whose voices rang out in community meetings were also attempting to preserve an exemplary bilingual
education program. The more powerful elements in Steel Town,

however, dismantled the bilingual education program. As an English-only program was being implemented, Margarita whispered that in her school children were not allowed to speak in Spanish ("En esta escuela no se habla español"), while Juan said he felt that he was walking into a "cage with lions and then you put in a little goat." It was evident that schools and policy makers in Steel Town eliminated bilingual programs and support without taking a careful and close look at what bilingual children are experiencing in schools, and what children need in order to become cultural participants in a diverse society. As a contemporary researcher living and conducting research in Steel Town, I struggled with ethical issues and found it impossible to maintain the traditional stance of a detached, passionless scholar. Such issues have a rich history.

James Crawford (1989, 1992) relates the historical and political context of bilingual education in America. He notes that German language schools prevailed until the twentieth century and that historically significant documents such as the Articles of Confederation were published in German and in French. When the U.S. entered World War I, however, anti-German sentiments created language restrictionism. Several states banned German speech charging with at least 18,000 persons of breaking this law by 1921 (Crawford 1989). Public attitudes toward languages changed as English-only speech became associated more and more with patriotism. In spite of the Supreme Court's ruling in *Meyer v. Nebraska* (1923) against restrictive language laws, the nation devalued minority languages. Public schools responded to the climate and to the politics of the times.

Native Americans were also mandated by the federal government to teach in English only. The U.S. Senate documented that in the 1850s the Oklahoma Cherokees attained English literacy levels higher than the white populations in Texas or in Arkansas. In 1879, however, Native American children were being separated from their families and sent to military boarding schools. U.S. Representative Ben Nighthorse Campbell retells that "Both my grandparents were forcibly removed from their homes and placed in boarding schools. One of the first English words Indian students learned was soap, because their mouths were constantly being washed out for using their native language" (Crawford 1989).

Mexican-American and Asian-American children have been punished under the guise of patriotic English-only speech. An early childhood educator and former migrant worker in California (Lopez 1994) recently relayed a common accepted practice in the local public school: "When our teacher caught us speaking our language, she would lock us in the closet. Sometimes there would be three of us in that tiny space. It was dark and pretty frightening for us. Sometimes it was even hard to breathe in there. Other teachers punished the Spanish speakers at recess, lunch, or with after school 'Spanish detention.'"

The dissemination of information capable of inciting fear and divisiveness has created a climate that devalues children's bilingualism and biculturalism. Jim Cummins (1994) refers to the "new enemy within" exemplified by groups and individuals who continue to spread xenophobic perspectives. He compares our nation to the *Titanic*, headed for destruction when dealing with issues of bilingualism. Isolated programs of excellence are shedding light on best practices; yet these programs appear to be the exception and face tremendous barriers from agencies and from the public at large.

The sociopolitical context of the nation contributes to crusades earmarked at eliminating bilingualism and institutionalizing linguistic repression. Language minority populations understand the need to communicate in English . . . so much so that the loss of home languages in America is a documented concern by linguists (Fishman 1995; Wong Fillmore 1991a, 1991b). Intergenerational communication is a vital part of child-rearing patterns that fosters young children's social, emotional, and cognitive well-being. It is vital that children are encouraged outside of their homes to express themselves in their native tongue. The loss of language and loss of intergenerational communication is bound to continue when reports indicate that as of 1990, 6.3 million children ages 5 to 17 do not speak English at home but are forced to at school. This figure represents a 38 percent increase over the last decade and indicates that the number of school-age children who do not speak English at home continues to rise (NABE NEWS 1992). The U.S. Census Bureau data (1991) shows that 31.8 million people or 14 percent of the population indicated that they spoke a language other than English at home. Spanish speakers represent 54 percent of the language minority population.

Data from the National Clearinghouse for Bilingual Education (1995), also reports an upward trend in the "limited English proficient student population (LEP)" in the last eight years. LEP students are younger, more than two out of three are in grades K-6, and three out of four LEP reveal Spanish as the native home language.

Most nations of the world have included second language learning possibilities for children. Second and multiple language learning is common in African, Danish, English, French, German, Greek, Italian, Latin American, Luxembourg, Scottish, and Swedish schools, which integrate multilingualism in the curriculum (Peck 1993).

WHAT DOES THE RESEARCH SAY ABOUT BILINGUAL EDUCATION?

One of the myths perpetrated by English-only proponents is that there is insufficient or inadequate research in the field of bilingual education. The question to ask is "Who benefits from this myth?" since extensive and clear evidence has been provided for decades by researchers in the field. But stronger, more powerful political and racist elements have dominated the discourse, sometimes loudly proclaiming, "when my grandparents came to this country . . . " 'Conventional wisdoms' have also generated the linguistic mismatch hypothesis and the insufficient exposure hypothesis. The mismatch hypothesis suggests that the home and school language shift causes children's educational underachievement. Researchers have actually shown that the unfair power relations, including the persistence of racism and oppression, constitute an educational "disabling process" (Cummins 1984, 1985, 1995, 1996; Ogbu 1978; Paulston 1980; Soto 1997). The insufficient exposure hypothesis intent on "immersion" and sink or swim programs, disregards the research evidence that documents that a strong home language base actually facilitates second language learning (Cummins 1979, 1984, 1986; Hakuta 1986; Krashen 1988; Soto 1993; Wong Fillmore 1991):

> It is perhaps naive to expect the policy debate on bilingual education to be any more rational than debates on other politically volatile issues. Nevertheless, it is sobering to realize the extent to which two patently inadequate 'conventional wisdoms' have dominated the debate for almost 15 years despite the fact that each is clearly refuted by massive amounts of research evidence. (Cummins 1995, 66)

Decades of educational research that have documented best practices for the field include, but are not limited to, the following studies: Ambert, A., 1991; Au, K. and Jordan, C., 1981; Crawford, J., 1989: Collier, V., 1989; Cummins, J., 1993; Delgado-Gaitan, C. 1990; Hakuta, K., 1986; Heath, S., 1983; Krashen, S. 1988; Lucas, T., Henze, R. and Donato, R., 1991; Macias, J., 1987; McLaughlin, B. 1984; Mehan, H., Hubbarb, L. and Villanueva, I. 1994; Moll, L., and Diaz, E., 1987; Ogbu, J., 1978; Peal, E. and Lambert, W., 1962; Philips, S., 1972; Swain, M., 1987; Soto, L. D., 1991, 1997; Spindler, G., and Spindler, L., 1997; Trueba, H.,1987; Trueba, H. and Jacobs, L. and Kirton, E., 1990; Willig, A., 1985; Wong Fillmore, L., 1991a.

I have found it helpful to organize the bilingual education research studies into eras: a) the bilingual "handicap" era; b) the positive findings' era; c) the era of newly evolving paradigms; and d) the era with a futuristic vision that critically analyzes issues of power.

First, the bilingual "handicap" era denotes findings in keeping with the notion that bilingualism was synonymous with deficiency. The initial research is responsible for creating what Cummins (1989) refers to as the "myth of the bilingual handicap." A biased philosophy permeated the literature by pointing to inherent deficiencies and pathologies. Major reviews (Darcy 1953; Jensen 1962; Weinreich 1959) of this era document not only the flawed research methodology but also the accompanying negative and biased results. Peal and Lambert (1962) and Cummins (1976) have relayed the severe methodological flaws of the era including careless sampling procedures, classifying bilinguals by surname, comparisons of students labeled as "monolingual or bilingual," and reliance on intelligence testing.

Jesen captured the attitude of this earlier work (1969) in his review of more than two hundred studies relating the "disadvantages" of childhood bilingualism including handicaps in speech development, emotional and intellectual difficulties, impaired originality of thought, handicapped intelligence, loss of self-confidence, schizophrenia, and contempt and hatred towards one's parents, to name a few.

Hakuta (1986) notes that it is important to view this early literature in light of historical context. The problem with the research era of the 1920s through the early 1960s (the bilingual "handicap" era) is that in spite of additional contemporary research, it continues to drive existing programs employing subtractive (Lambert 1975) strategies that replace children's home language.

The positive findings' era was initiated by Peal and Lambert's (1962) classic study of bilingual learners in Montreal. "The picture that emerges . . . is that of a youngster whose wider experiences in two cultures have given him advantages which a monolingual does not enjoy. Intellectually his experiences with two other systems seems to have left him with a mental flexibility, a superiority in concept formation, a more diverse field set of mental abilities"(20). For the first time, a brighter, more positive view of bilingualism began to emerge. The St. Lambert Project, a field study (Lambert and Tucker 1972) led the way for additional work by researchers in the U.S. and by other countries. Examples of these studies showed that children raised bilingually were more attentive to semantic relationships, indicated superiority in awareness of linguistic rules and structures, out performed monolinguals on a variety of measures of metalinguistic awareness, demonstrated divergent thinking and creativity, showed positive effects of bilingualism on a variety of cognitive performance measures (such as concept formation) indicated positive effects on Piagetian conservation and field independence, demonstrated an ability to monitor cognitive performance, showed a significant contribution to cognitive measures including the Raven Progressive Matrices, and that learning concepts in the native language will transfer and enhance second language learning (Bain 1974; Bain and Yu 1980; Ben Zeev 1977; Cummins and Gulutsan 1974; Cummins 1978; Cummins 1979; Duncan and DeAvila 1979; Hakuta and Diaz 1985; Ianco-Worrall 1972; Liedtke and Nelson 1968; Torrance, Wu, Gowan, and Alliotti 1970).

The era of newly evolving paradigms benefited the field by providing it with broader conceptual frameworks. These studies relied, to a greater extent, on qualitative methods, and initiated ways of viewing issues of language and culture as related domains. Findings from this era have helped us to understand: the value of changing classroom interactions so that they are compatible with the home (Hawaiian Keep Project; Au and Jordan 1981); how communities within the same setting can be both similar and different in their contributions to the home and community language learning environment (Heath 1993); the effects of teacher assumptions of children's English language proficiency on the quality of instruction (Moll and Diaz 1985); the importance of the distinction between social language skills and the more complex academic skills (Cummins 1989); why the loss of the primary language can be costly to children, families, and society as a whole (Wong Fillmore 1992); the long-term benefits of bilingual education programs on children's attitudes (Collier 1991, 1996); successful aspects of the learning context for bilingual literacy (Hornberger 1990); the need to incorporate 'funds of knowledge' in the bilingual education classroom (Moll 1992); the benefits of untracking high school programs for Latino and African American students' academic success (Mehan, Hubbard, and Villanueva 1994); how proponents of English-only were successful in dismantling a twenty-year-old award-winning bilingual education program in Steel Town (Soto 1997).

Home language preservation has been documented as beneficial in a variety of ways. Cummins notes that native language instruction develops pride in one's identity, which in turn has been linked to school achievement (see Cummins 1979, for a review of these studies). Hakuta (1986) indicates that bilingual children have certain advantages that monolingual children do not have, one of the most important being "cognitive flexibility" or divergent thinking.

Lily Wong Fillmore (1991a), in the NABE No-Cost Study, examined the effects of English-only early educational programs. These programs result in the loss of the child's native language and prove damaging to families: "What about the cost to the family and children? When what is lost is the means of communication in a family, the children lose access to all the things that parents can teach them" (Wong Fillmore 1991, 42).

Or, we can view home language maintenance as a part of a critical analysis of existing educational practices. The bilingual education research has shown the benefits of native language to both academic school success and to the enhancement of family communication (Cummins 1979; Hakuta 1986; Krashen 1988; Wong Fillmore 1991a).

These studies have added a tremendous amount of knowledge to the field of educational practices. The field will continue to build upon this knowledge base and evolve, explore, and experiment with research methods, theoretical frameworks, and alternative paradigms (Soto 1992 a,b). We also note the need for social-science research in general, to redirect itself from deficient stereotypical paradigms to exploratory and creative paradigms capable of meeting the needs of teachers, learners, and families (Ernst and Statzner 1994). The research studies conducted by Ada (1986), Cummins (1996), Soto (1997), and Walsh (1991) can be viewed as initiating an era that includes a futuristic vision by critically analyzing issues of power in bilingual education. This constitutes an exciting era for the field where experimentation and exploration will include additional research methods as well as collaborative opportunities for teachers, researchers, and learners.

WHAT CAN TEACHERS DO?

The search for social justice and equity in schools (and in the nation) includes the critical analysis of issues of power as they relate to bilingual education. A recent conversation with a graduate student reminded me of the courage and wisdom that educators will need in order to navigate against the prevailing political winds that are denying children their linguistic human rights. "What's the use?" she asked me, "After all, bilingual education is 'dead' now. I want to help bilingual children but I can't share my feelings with prospective employers. You know they just won't hire me." These statements were enlightening and I began to wonder if even students knowledgeable about the issues and the needs of second language speakers are willing to distance themselves from the field and from what they know to constitute optimal practices. Do educators in a postmodern era find they have the courage to voice and to implement programs that will benefit children? Will the conservative English-only and bilingual education abolitionists continue their sweep across the nation ensuring a monolingual, monocultural, tongue-tied nation?

I would like to challenge educators in America to think about this issue as a moral imperative. A local schoolteacher recently told me that I was an inspiration to her and that I helped her to think about a variety of issues. My heart sank, however, when she added, "But you know I can't become 'political' because of my religious beliefs." I'm not quite sure what she meant but I know we are in an extremely political era in which one way of looking at the world, one major monolingual, monocultural voice continues to have its way. Doesn't the long history of linguicism, racism, and oppression testify to the need for educators to become more courageous than ever? Are educators willing to promulgate "business as usual" with their silence? Is the fear of conservative forces creeping into the hearts of our teachers? Teachers, bilingual families, monolingual parents, learners, and communities have much to share and can in solidarity support courageous work, work that will benefit children.

A critical bicultural pedagogy "holds the possibility for a discourse of hope in light of the tensions, conflicts, and contradictions that students must face in the process of their bicultural development" (Darder 1991, 96). An education that is built on a theory of cultural democracy and acknowledges the issue of power in society and the political nature of schooling provides a space for optimism and possibility for our nation. "An education that is bilingual and bicultural becomes effective only when it becomes anti-racist education" (Cummins 1995, 66).

Only when educators begin to collaborate with expert voices, "the insiders who know what oppression is and feels like" (Walsh 1991, 93), will issues of linguicism and racism begin to be ameliorated. Moraes (1996) proposes a theory of voice that incorporates both Bakhtin's and Freire's work in what she refers to as a "dialogic-critical pedagogy": *"Through the lenses of both theories, emerges a dialogic-critical pedagogy that makes the possibility for voices to be heard within a dialogic social awareness in which the voice of the oppressed reaches the oppressor (who is another oppressed) and both agents must engage toward a reciprocal social freedom "* (118). Moraes's notion of dialogic-critical pedagogy provides additional space for "possibility." The national rhetoric about bilingualism and children of color has taken on a "mean-spirited" tone making it crucial for multiple voices to powerfully impact educational reform.

Cummins (1994, 1996) distinguishes between collaborative power and coercive power. Coercive power imposes oppression, abuse, inequity, totalitarianism, and violates human rights and freedoms while collaborative power affords democratic expression, human rights, and freedom.

The oppressive elements systematically silence children and families, forcing them to struggle with disrespect for their bilingualism and biculturalism:

> Experience has shown that where no bilingual program exists, parents are less likely to approach the school and talk with teachers, that children are neglected by their teachers and tend to drop out, and that little effort is made to teach them English, preferring instead to classify them as slow learners or retarded. These and other evils provided the impetus for bilingual education in the first place. (Otheguy 1991, 419)

Teachers will need to conduct a critical examination of educational programs in order to implement programs that reflect the needs of their own community. The Steel Town families (1997) shared advice that they feel is important for educators including the need for schools to collaborate in preserving languages and cultures. Darner also underscores the need for collaborative power models that include teachers, students, and families:

> "[schools]must work in collaboration with bicultural educators, students, parents, and their communities. Anything short of this effort suggests an educational process that is in danger of oppressing and disempowering students of color." (1991, 121)

In our busy lives we forget that there is inherent wisdom in all the people who touch our lives—families, students, colleagues, and members of our respective communities. When so many families in America pin their hopes on educational equity and freedom for their children, it is up to each one of us to maintain a vision of equity and social justice because we are all important to the future lives of children.

I used to get whacks on my head for not spelling my name the way they wanted it spelled. After all they would say, "You're an American." But the next person would say, "You are Puerto Rican." The system is failing the kids, and it's not just one child.

—Luz, Steel Town, PA

REFERENCES

Ada, A. F. "Creative Education for Bilingual Teachers." *Harvard Educational Review*. 56 (1986): 386–94.

Ambert, A. *Bilingual Education and English as a Second Language*. New York: Garland, 1991.

Aronowitz, S., and H. Giroux. *Education Under Siege*. South Hadley, MA: Bergin & Garvey, 1985.

Au, K., and C. Jordan. "Teaching Reading to Hawaiian Children: Finding a Culturally Appropriate Solution." In *Culture and the Bilingual Classroom: Studies in Classroom Ethnography*. H. T. Trueba and G. P. Guthrie, eds. Cambridge, MA: Newbury House, 1981.

Bain, B. "Bilingualism and Cognition: Toward a General Theory." In *Bilingualism, Biculturalism, and Education*. S. Carey, ed. Edmonton: University of Alberta, 1974.

Bain, B., and Yu, A. "Cognitive Consequences of Raising Children Bilingually: One Parent One Language." *Canadian Journal of Psychology*. 34 (1980): 304–13.

Ben-Zeev, S. "The Influence of Bilingualism on Cognitive Strategy and Cognitive Development." *Child Development*, 48 (1977): 1009–18.

Collier, V. "How Long?: A Synthesis of Research on Academic Achievement in a Second Language." *TESOL Quarterly*. 23(3)(1989): 509–31.

———."A Synthesis of Studies Examining Long-Term Language Minority Student Data on Academic Achievement." *Bilingual Research Journal*, 16 (1&2) (1992): 187–212.

Crawford, J. *Bilingual Education: History, Politics, Theory and Practice*. Trenton, NJ: Crane, 1989.

———. *Hold Your Tongue*. New York: Addison-Wesley, 1992.

Cummins, J. "The Influence of Bilingualism on Cognitive Growth: A Synthesis of Research Findings and Explanatory Hypotheses." *Working Papers on Bilingualism*, 9 (1976): 1–43.

———. *Negotiating Identities: Education for Empowerment in a Diverse Society*. California Association for Bilingual Education, 1996.

———. "Bilingual Education and Anti-racist Education." In *Policy and Practice in Bilingual Education*. O. Garcia and C. Baker, eds. Bristol, PA: Multilingual Matters, 1995.

———. Keynote speech at the National Association for Bilingual Education, Los Angeles, 1994.

———."Empowering Minority Students: A Framework for Intervention." In *Beyond Silenced Voices*. L. Weis and M. Fine, eds. Albany: SUNY, 1993.

———. *Empowering Minority Students*. Sacramento: California Association for Bilingual Education, 1989.

———. *Bilingualism and Special Education: Issues in Assessment and Pedagogy*. Clevedon, Avon, England: Multilingual Matters, 1984.

———. "Linguistic Interdependence and the Educational Development of Bilingual Children." *Review of Educational Research*, 49(2) (1979): 222–51.

———."Bilingualism and The Development of Metalinguistic Awareness." *Journal of Cross-Cultural Psychology*, 9(2) (1978): 131–49.

Cummins, J., and M. Gulutson. "Some Effects of Bilingualism on Cognitive Functioning." In *Bilingualism, Biculturalism and Education*. S. Carey, ed. Edmonton: University of Alberta, 1974.

Darcy, N. T. "A Review of the Literature on the Effects of Bilingualism on the Measurement of Intelligence." *Joumal of Genetic Psychology*, 82 (1953): 21–57.

Darder, A. *Culture and Power in the Classroom*. Westport, CT: Bergin & Garvey, 1991.

De Avila, E. "Bilingualism, Cognitive Function, and Language Minority Group Membership." In *Childhood Bilingualism: Aspects of Linguistic, Cognitive, and Social Development*. P. Homel, M. Palij, and D. Aaronson, eds. Hillsdale, NJ: Erlbaum, 1987.

Delgado-Gaitan, C. *Literacy for Empowerment: The Role of Parents in Children's Education*. New York: Falmer, 1990.

Delgado-Gaitan, C., and H. Trueba. *Crossing Cultural Borders: Education for Immigrant Families in America*. New York: Falmer, 1991.

Duncan, S., and E. De Avila. "Bilingualism and Cognition. Some Recent Findings." *NABE Journal*, 4 (1979): 15–50.

Ernst, G., and E. Statzner. "Alternative Visions of Schooling an Introduction." *Anthropology and Education Quarterly*, 25(3) (1994): 200–7.

Ferdman, B. "Literacy and Cultural Identity." In *Language Issues in Literacy and Bilingual/Multicultural Education.* Cambridge. M. Minami and B. Kennedy, eds. Harvard Educational Review, Reprint series No. 22, (1991): 347–71.

Fishman, J. "On the Limits of Ethnolinguistic Democracy." In *Linguistic Human Rights: Overcoming Linguistic Discrimination.* T. Skutnabb-Kangas, New York: Mouton de Gruyter, 1995. 49–61.

Freire, P. *Pedagogy of the Oppressed.* New York: Seabury, 1970.

———. *The Politics of Education: Culture, Power, and Liberation.* South Hadley, MA: Bergin & Garvey, 1985.

———. *Pedagogy of the City.* New York: Continuum, 1993.

Freire, P., and D. Macedo. *Literacy: Reading the Word and the World.* New York: Bergin & Garvey, 1987.

Giroux, H. "National Identity and the Politics of Multiculturalism." *College Literature,* 22 (2) (1995): 42–57.

Hakuta, K. *Mirror of Language: The Debate of Bilingualism.* New York: Basic Books, 1986.

Hakuta, K., and R. Diaz. "The Relationship Between Degree of Bilingualism and Cognitive Ability." In *Children's Language.* K. E. Nelson, ed. Hillsdale, NJ: Erlbaum, 1985.

Heath, S. Brice. *Ways with Words: Language, Life, and Work in Communities and Classrooms.* Cambridge: Cambridge University Press, 1983.

Ianco-Worral, A. "Bilingualism and Cognitive Development." *Child Development,* 43 (1972) 1390–1400.

Jensen, V. "Effects of Childhood Bilingualism, 1." *Elementary English,* 39 (1962): 132–43.

Krashen, S. *On Course.* Sacramento: California Association for Bilingual Education, 1988.

Lambert, W. "Culture and Language as Factors in Learning and Education." In *Education of Immigrant Students.* A.Wolfgang, ed. Toronto: Ontario Institute for Studies in Education, 1975.

Lambert, W. E., and G. R. Tucker. *Bilingual Education of Children: The St. Lambert Experiment.* Rowley, MA: Newbury House, 1972.

Liedtke, W., and L. Nelson. "Concept Formation in Bilingualism." *Alberta Journal of Educational Research,* 14 (1968): 225–32.

Lopez, A. "Personal Communication." *National Council of La Raza.* Washington, DC, 1994.

Lucas, T., Henze, R., and R. Donato. "Promoting the Success of Latino Language-Minority Students: An Exploratory Study of Six High Schools." In *Language Issues in Literacy and Bilingual/Multicultural Education*. M. Minami and B. Kennedy, eds. Cambridge: Harvard Educational Review, Reprint series No.22 (1990), 456–82.

Macias, J. "The Hidden Curriculum of Papago Teachers." In *Interpretive Ethnography of Education*. G. and L. Spindler, eds. Hillsdale, NJ (1987): 363–80.

McLaughlin, B. *Second-Language Acquisition in Childhood*. Hillsdale, NJ: Erlbaum, 1984.

Mehan, H. "The Role of Discourse in Learning, Schooling, and Reform." In *Language and Learning Educating Linguistically Diverse Students*. B. McLeod, ed. Albany, NY: SUNY Press (1994): 71–96.

Mehan, H., L. Hubbard, and L. Villanueva. "Forming Academic Identities: Accommodation without Assimilation among Involuntary Minorities." *Anthropology and Education Quarterly*, 25(2) (1994): 91–117.

Moll, L., and S. Diaz. "Change as a Goal of Educational Research." *Anthropology and Education Quarterly*, 18 (1987): 300–11.

Moraes, M. *Bilingual Education: A Design with the Bakhtin Circle*. Albany, NY: SUNY Press, 1996.

Ogbu, J. *Minority Education and Caste*. New York: Academic, 1978.

Otheguy, R. "Thinking About Bilingual Education: A Critical Appraisal." In *Language Issues in Literacy and Bilingual/Multicultural Education*. M. Minami and B. Kennedy, eds. Cambridge: Harvard Educational Review, Reprint Series No. 22 (1991): 409–23.

Paulston, C. B. *Bilingual Education: Theories and Issues*. Rowley, MA: Newbury House, 1980.

Peal, E., and W. Lambert. "The Relation of Bilingualism to Intelligence." *Psychological Monographs: General and Applied*, 76 (27, whole no. 546) (1962): 1–23.

Peck, B. "The Language Explosion: Europe Starts It Early." *Phi Delta Kappan*, 9 (1993): 91–2.

Philips, S. *The Invisible Culture. Communication in Classroom and Community on the Warm Springs Reservation*. New York: Longman, 1983.

Phillipson, R. M. Rannut, and T. Skutnabb-Kangas. "Introduction." In *Linguistic Human Rights: Overcoming Linguistic Discrimination.* T. Skutnabb-Kangas, New York: Mouton de Gruyter (1995): 1–22.

President's Commission on Foreign Languages and International Studies. *Strength Through Wisdom: A Critique of U.S. Capability.* Washington, DC: U.S. Government Printing Office, 1980.

Ramirez, M., and A. Castañeda. *Cultural Democracy: Bicognitive Development and Education.* New York: Academic, 1974.

Skutnabb-Kangas, T. *Bilingualism or Not: The Education of Minorities.* Clevedon, England: Multilingual Matters, Ltd., 1989.

———. *Linguistic Human Rights: Overcoming Linguistic Discrimination.* New York: Mouton de Gruyter, 1995.

———, and R. Phillipson. "Linguistic Human Rights, Past and Present." In *Linguistic Human Rights: Overcoming Linguistic Discrimination.* T. Skutnabb-Kangas. New York: Mouton de Gruyter (1995): 71–110.

Sleeter, C. E., and C. A. Grant. *Making Choices for Multicultural Education.* 2nd ed. Columbus, OH: Merrill, 1992.

Soto, L. D. "Success Stories." In *Research and Multicultural Education.* C. Grant, ed. London: Falmer Press (1992a): 153–64.

———. *Language, Culture, and Power. Bilingual Families and the Struggle for Quality Education.* Albany, NY: SUNY, 1997.

———. *The Early Education of Linguistically and Culturally Diverse Children.* Boston: National Coalition of Advocates for Students, 1994.

———. "Native Language for School Success." *Bilingual Research Journal,* 17(1&2) (1993): 83–97.

Soto, L. D. "Alternate Paradigms in Bilingual Education Research." In *Critical Perspectives on Bilingual Education Research.* R. Padilla and A. Benavides, eds. Tempe, AZ: Bilingual Press/Editorial Bilingue (1992b): 93–109.

Spindler, G., and L. Spindler, eds. *Interpretive Ethnography of Education.* Hillsdale, NJ: Erlbaum, 1987.

Swain, M. "Bilingual Education: Research and Its Implications." In *Methodology TESOL.* M. Long and J. Richards, eds. Cambridge, MA: Newbury House (1987): 61–71.

Torrance, E., J. Wu, and N. Alliotti. "Creating Functioning of Monolingual and Bilingual Children in Singapore." *Journal of*

Educational Psychology, 61 (1970): 72–5.

Trueba, H. T., ed. *Success and Failure: Learning and the Linguistic Minority Student*. Cambridge, MA: Newbury House, 1987.

Trueba, H. T., L. Jacobs, and E. Kirton. *Cultural Conflict and Adaptation: The Case of Among Children in American Society*. New York: Falmer, 1990.

Willig, A. "A Meta-Analysis of Selected Studies on the Effectiveness of Bilingual Education." *Review of Educational Research*. 55(3) (1985): 269–317.

Wong Fillmore, L. "When Learning a Second Language Means Losing the First." *Early Childhood Research Quarterly*, 6 (1991): 323–46.

————. "Language and Cultural Issues in Early Education." In *The Care and Education of America's Young Children*. L. Kagan, ed. The 90th Yearbook of the National Society for the Study of Education. Chicago: National Society for the Study of Education (1992): 30–49.

X

INNOVATIVE PEDAGOGY IN ART EDUCATION
Dennis E. Fehr

Students enter to the sounds of "Little Red Riding Hood," by Sam the Sham and the Pharoahs. Projected onto the screen is a slide of *Puberty*, Edward Munch's 1895 painting of a frightened, unclothed, adolescent female. By the time the song is over, most or all of the students have arrived. The lights go up. I welcome the students to the class, and then guide the following discussion.

Let's make a list of ten famous figures from history. I'll write the names as you call them out.

George Washington. Plato. Jesus. Einstein. John Kennedy. Adolf Hitler. Clara Barton. Julius Caesar. Elvis Presley. William Shakespeare.

I have asked this question of countless audiences over the years and, regardless of the audience's demographics—its ethnicity, gender makeup, educational levels, career choices—the lists typically consist either of ten men, or nine men and one woman. Usually all are of European ethnicity.

Now let's make a list of ten famous artists.

Picasso. Van Gogh. Michelangelo. Da Vinci. Rembrandt. Georgia O'Keeffe. Jacob Lawrence. Andrew Wyeth. Norman Rockwell. Andy Warhol.

This list most typically consists of nine men and one woman, nine whites and one person of color.

Because the largest oppressed group throughout Western civilization has been women, I use the lists to initiate a discussion of sexism; yet, one can use such lists to create awareness of the absence of any oppressed group from Western history. During this 3-credit, semester-long course, the students and I revise the established art canon to include work by artists of color, both Eastern and Western; by artists who are women; by people of alternate abilities and of all sexual orientations; and by artists schooled inside as well as outside the academy. Since this introductory lesson is about deconstructing the sexism within the Western canon, the works of art cited in this lesson reflect a Western emphasis. Eastern art is of course equally important and deserves equal emphasis in art teacher preparation programs.

Why is it that what women have done is considered unworthy of our attention? Why have women's accomplishments been erased from history? Is it true that women simply cannot paint as well as men? That they cannot write as well? That they cannot think as well? That they cannot lead as well?

It is not true.

I wish to make a few introductory observations. Because I cannot be certain that I speak truth, I am less interested in "converting" you than you may think. I at times will issue polemics to which you are encouraged to respond either pro or con. As indicated by the lists you offered me, the period in history called modernism is characterized in part by a subordinated place for women. This attitude so permeates modern thinking that traditionally it has been accepted by both men and women. We will challenge this "sacred text" of culture, and a number of other such "sacred texts" as well. It is appropriate that challenges such as these emerge from a university setting. You paid your money in good fatih; you deserve to have the university test your most sacred beliefs by exposing them to a diversity of views. Any institution of higher education, so called, that arrogates a monocular view, an 'immaculate conception,' of truth is an affront to the free marketplace of ideas. Universitites bankrolled by religious organizations are at times guilty of this. These moral gatekeepers rob their students in the worst way universities can—they not only deny their students the opportunity to test their prejudices, they seek to entrench them. Such lack of faith speaks ill of philosophies thus sheltered. It dictates that if professors espouse views contrary to those philosophies—no matter how brilliant those scholars might be, no matter how respected—their voices will not be heard within those institutions. Such policy is born of the fear that one's philosophy cannot withstand critical examination, that one's students will "fall away," seduced by the Pied Piper of Paralogisms. The result is a body of alumni who may know the "how" within their fields of studies, but prescious little "why." They are worse for it.

While the university itself must strive to be ideology-free, professors within the university should openly espouse biases—so long as you, the students feel safe to rebut them openly and, preferably although not necessarily, through scholarly argumentation. If the university has done its job, it has obtained a thoughtful faculty who represent an ideological cross section. Such a faculty will expose students to a variety of views. When the students then construct their adult ideologies, those ideologies will be informed.

In this course oppression will be gauged from an art historical database and viewed through the lens of art education. Art education encompasses both the visual and verbal records of Western civilization from prehistory to this afternoon. Humans made art for tens of thousands of years before they wrote and, following the advent of writing, the visual image continued to function as a societal mirror revealing truths that defy the printed word. At the same time, the power of the printed word is self-evident. So the lens of art education is wide.

The line separating art from art education meanders at will across the cultural landscape, presenting us with a recurrung problem of demarcation. Where the art education record is scant (this is particularly true of prehistory), we will examine oppression as it appears in the history of visual art per se. *Often we will discuss oppression in its many guises without mentioning art or art education directly. We will start and end with art education but, to make our inquiry meaningful, we must paint an extensive backdrop. We will undertake, for example, to balance the utopian* yang *of Western culture with its dystopian* yin. *By thus contextualizing art education, instead of studying it in a cultural vacuum, we can understand what it means. The pieces of this history form a sprawling cultural patchwork that was quilted with the thread of art education.*

A heartening number of works have been published in the last two decades that analyze the contributions of oppressed groups to the West's visual art heritage. This is not the case in art education (under which label I include training programs for adults as well as programs for students in the public schools). We are only now beginning to see literature—still in articles more than in books—in which art education's potential as a cultural force is linked with the dismantling of oppression. I suggest that the two most important periods of the human story to study, if one wishes to remediate oppression, are the dawn of history and the present. It is the dawn of history that oppression began, and its undergirding has changed remarkably little from then to now. To remediate oppression, one must dismantle this undergirding as it exists today. Consequently, most of this course is devoted to the present.

If one chooses to remediate oppression through art education, one must redefine art education. Immured for too long in a cultural closet, art education must shake itself free of the bonds of banality that have banished it to the outer reaches of the public school curriculum. Until it defines itself as more than merely a vehicle for 'aesthetic experience,' in the closet is where it belongs. Art education programs must resonate to the lived experiences of all *students by providing them a visual language through which they can express themselves with images that demand society's attention, images that jolt cultural preconceptions. If our artists and teachers join to change the world, the world will change.*

The institutionalization of oppression occurs mainly along the following dimensions: gender, class, race, and religion. Our prejudices run so deep that unflinching adherence to democratic principles is today's radicalism. I have anticipated the efforts of critics to neutralize my voice by categorizing me as, oh, an agnostic, anti-family-values, anti-

moral, ACLU freedom freak; or a bleeding-heart-liberal, lecherous, bookreading, baby-killing, devil-worshipping dopefiend; or maybe a longhaired, leftist, nigger-loving, pro-death, pro-thought, pro-sex nutzoid. I hypothesize this conversation:

"You know, Fehr says something interesting about that—"

"Fehr? Don't you know he's an anti-electric chair, gay-blubbering, gun-hating, femi-nazi, sicko/atheist/commie/pervert?"

"You're kidding! No, I had no idea. Well, forget it."

I must confess that the above descriptions of me are close, but the fact remains that I also am a white, middle-class, middle-aged, middle-income male of European ethnicity and Protestant background—a member of today's least fashionable (not to mention most boring) demographic group. I am not even gay—for which I feel compelled to apologize.

On that note let's look at some more art and listen to more music.

"Venus in Blue Jeans" by Jimmy Clanton begins. On this cue, and to the beat of the song, I rotate through the following slides of works of nude women taken from the Western canon. As the slide list demonstrates, each work was created by a man.

01. The Birth of Venus	c 1480	Sandro Botticelli, Italy	
02. Bathers France	c 1765	Jean Honore Fragonard,	
03. Andromeda	c 1852	Eugene Delacroix, France	
04. Olympia	1862	Edouard Manet, France	
05. The Birth of Venus	1876	William Bouguereau, France	
06. And the Gold of Their Bodies	1901	Paul Gauguin, France	
07. Danae	1908	Gustav Klimt, Austria	
08. Child Lying on Her Belly	1911	Egon Schiele, Austria	
09. The Great Bathers	1918	August Renoir, France	
10. The Rape	1934	Rene Magritte, France	
11. Rolling Stones album cover			
12. The Judgment of Paris	1939	Ivo Saliger, Germany	
13. Where the City Begins	1940	Paul Delvaux, Belgium	
14. Ode to Ang	1972	Mel Ramos, United States	
15. La Source		Jean Auguste-DominiqueIngres, France	
16. Yves Klein with model	1960		

17. Anthropometry of the Blue Period	1960	Yves Klein, France
18. Great American Nude No. 99	1968	Tom Wesselman, United States
19. Girl Table	1969	Allen Jones, Britain
20. Girl Sculpture (Gold and Orange)	1970	Anthony Donaldson, Britain
21. Bronze Pinball Machine with Woman Affixed Also	1980	Ed Keinholz, United States
22. *Penthouse* Pet of the Month	1992	Bob Guccione (publisher), United States

The song and the slides end. The lights are raised and the discussion continues.

Let's deconstruct the messages of these two art forms, the musical and the visual. What did you just see?

A historical survey of the female figure in Western art.

Painted by whom?

Men.

Did you recognize any of the images?

Yes.

Do you think it is fair to say that the nude woman constitutes a theme within Western art history?

Yes.

This is particularly true since the Renaissance. We will talk later in the course about how the Renaissance was not necessarily a step forward for civilization. Now, what did you just hear?

A piece of popular music that defines women as artistic and sexual objects.

The song was performed by whom?

A man.

Do the verbal message of the song and the visual message of the artworks agree on how men are to view women?

Yes.

Historians suggest that we in the late twentieth century are experiencing a change in how humans live, a change significant enough to call for a label other than modernism. What is that label?

Postmodernism.

The term "postmodern" refers to today, a time characterized in part by the questioning of modern notions. Consequently, we find ourselves surrounded by conflicting messages. Let's view some more slides, this time of artwork that depicts women differently from what we saw a moment ago. As we view the slides, let's listen to music—this time by women—and decide if the music sends messages that agree or conflict with the messages of the art.

As the students listen to "My Boyfriend's Back" by the Angels, "I Will Follow Him" by Little Peggy March, I rotate through the following slides. Slides 1–9 depict the Cosmic Goddess prior to patriarchy. Slides 10–12 depict the Goddess redefined by patriarchy. Slides 13–20 depict work by women from the Baroque into the early twentieth century. Slides 21–49 depict work that has emerged since the current wave of feminism began in the 1960s.

01. Goddess of Willendorf	c 25,000 BCE	
02. Goddess of Laussel	c 20,000 BCE	
03. Bird-faced Goddess brings energy of sun to earth	c 3500 BCE	Egypt
04. Goddess-shaped floorplan of Ggantija temple	c 3300 BCE	Malta
05. Violin Goddess	c 3000 BCE	Greece
06. Female Idol	c 3000 BCE	Mesopotamia
07. Snake Goddess	c 1000 BCE	Minoa
08. Durga overcomes water buffalo demon	c 700 BCE	India
09. Gorgon, Goddess of Destruction	c 600 BCE	Meso-America
10. Mary, Queen of Heaven	c 1100	France
11. Madonna and Child	before 1405	Master of the Strauss Madonna, Italy
12. Virgin and Child	after 1454	Rogier van der Weyden, The Netherlands
13. Judith Beheading Holofernes	nd	Artemesia Gentileschi, Italy
14. The Proposition	1631	Judith Leyster, The Netherlands
15. Sor Juana Inez de la Cruz	after 1714	Juan de Miranda, Mexico
16. Nameless and Friendless	1857	Emily Osborne, Great Britain
17. The Cradle	1873	Berthe Morisot, France
18. Mother and Child	c 1905	Mary Cassatt, United States
19. Red Canna	1923	Georgia O'Keeffe, United States

20. The Broken Column	1944	Frida Kahlo, Mexico
21. Earth Birth	1963	Judy Chicago, United States
22. Eye Body	1963	Carolee Schneeman, United States
23. Hon	1966	Nike de Saint-Phalle, France
24. Weeping Women # 2	1973	Faith Ringgold, United States
25. The Turkish Bath	1973	Sylvia Sleigh, United States
26. Woman Rising with Spirit		Mary Beth Edelson, United States
27. Technology/Transformation: Wonder Woman	1978	Dara Birnbaum, United States
28. untitled	1979	Cindy Sherman, United States
29. SOS-Starification Object Series	1974–1982	Hannah Wilke, United States
30. In Mourning and in Rage	1977	Suzanne Lacy & Leslie Labowitz United States
31. Woman-living Earth	1977	Clara Meneres, Portugal
32. Arbol de la Vida	1977	Ana Mendieta, Cuba/ United States
33.Vital Statistics of a Citizen Simply Obtained	1977	Martha Rosler, United States
34. Portrait of the Artist as Virgin of Guadalupe	1977	Yolanda Lopez, Mexico
35. Curandera Barriendo de Susto (Healing Woman Chases Away Ghosts)	1986	Carmen Lomas Garza, United States
36. Margaret Evans Pregnant	1978	Alice Neel, United States
37. Garden	1980	Meinrad Craighead
38. We Have Received Orders Not to Move	1982	Barbara Kruger, United States
39. Inflammatory Essays (detail)	1984	Jenny Holzer, United States
40. Goddess on Day after Nuclear Holocaust (still photograph from performance)	1985	Susan Maberry
41. Prehistoric Goddess Resacralizing the Planet (still photo from performance)	1987	Vilaji
42. photograph of Guerilla Girls		SoHo, New York City

43. Guerilla Girls poster	c 1987	SoHo, New York City
44. House Dress	1990	Beverly Semmes
45. D.A.A.D.B.		
(Dumb as a Dallas Banker)	1992	Rachel Hecker, United States
46. Red not Blue		
(still from performance)	1992	Rachel Lachowicz, United States
47. Paper Dolls for a		
Post-Columbian World	1991	Jaune Quick-to-See Smith, United States
48. photograph of WAC (Women's Action Coalition) Attack at Metropolitan Museum during Democratic National Convention	1992	New York City
49. WAC Attack during Republican National Convention	1992	Houston

The music and slides end. The lights come up.

What kinds of messages did you get from the slides?

Originally the deity was female. Women have been oppressed. Women are becoming empowered.

What messages did you get from the music?

Women need men to save them. Women should follow their men.

Remember that the first presentation was modernist. The visual and auditory messages agreed that women are to be objectified. The second presentation was more postmodern. The postmodern age is defined in part by the simultaneous presentation of conflicting messages, often from seemingly similar sources. Specifically how did this occur in the second presentation?

We received two messages simultaneously, but—although both were by women—they conflicted. One called for empowerment, one for submission.

During the writing of the text for this course, I was asked if such a book should be written by a White male. Am I the appropriate one to answer that?

As the author you are entitled to your opinion, but the readers will have the final say.

I agree. My answer begins with the observation that I do not anoint myself a spokesperson for women or minorities. After all, as Henry Giroux notes, "When freedom is defined by the privileged, the oppressed are victimized not only by labor

180

exploitation, racism, and patriarchy, but by liberal arrogance." Patti Lather adds, "Too often [liberatory] pedagogies fail to probe the degree to which 'empowerment' becomes something done 'by' liberated pedagogues 'to'. . . the as-yet-unliberated, the 'other.'"

Then what business have I, a member of the dominant group, saying the things I say? Is it enough to be aware of what Foucault labels the indignity of speaking for the oppressed? As Joe Kincheloe points out, we walk a tightrope between issuing our analyses (which I will strive to do in this course) and refraining from speaking for the victims of hegemonic forces (which I will also strive to do). I believe, however, that the demonizing of the heretofore-deified White male is not the answer; it tilts the ship of culture too far the other way. Lather continues, "To write 'postmodern' is to write paradoxically aware of one's complicity in that which one critiques." The alternative is, of course, not to write at all. Lather concludes, "In an era of rampant reflexivity, just getting on with it may be the most radical action one can make." I believe that my views contribute to postmodern dialectics against oppression, and I opt for just getting on with it. Dogs Playing Cards, *and this course, are not destinations; they are two more steps on the journey to a free world. My thesis, quite simply, is that the oppression of one group by another is bad for both. So, in terms of action, what are my options?*

You can act against oppression, or you can be the oppressor, or you can abet the oppressor by remaining silent.

I believe that I, a White male, can contribute to the struggle for emancipation, and that this option is preferable to the other two. I choose to voice my disagreement with certain aspects of modernism, and in so doing, I implicate myself within Lather's postmodern paradox.

I wear my anger openly. Not only am I tired of the oppression to which other groups are subjected; I am tired of my fellow men dropping dead eight years earlier than women from the stress of oppressing them. In adopting a subjective, angry voice, I undermine the pseudo-stance of the objective, muted voice. The myth of the muted voice, heralded for so long as the only appropriate academic voice, is no voice at all. It ill serves the radical emancipatory axis. The objective voice is simply another means by which H. L. Mencken's "booboisie" have made us shut up. I do not wish to assume the role of spokescreature for demographic groups, either marginalized or mainstream, but rather to contribute to the emancipation of us all.

Given that much needs to be done to achieve a world of peace and freedom, is there room for hope?

Yes, humanity is driven to survive, to improve its condition.

I agree. Riding shotgun with my anger, careening on this bouncing buckboard of civilization, is my hope. If hominids emerged three million years ago, and fully developed humans 100,000 years ago, then civilization, at only 6000 years old, is an infant. One could argue that we have done well in such short time. So my anger is contextualized to the present. I think we're going to make it.

Let us turn to art education. The subtleties of oppression are found throughout aesthetic philosophy. One view of aesthetic study could be called cultural literacy: it means familiarity with those books, works of music, and objects of art which society has deemed 'masterpieces.' This is a form of social adaptation—the embracing of elitist values in order to fit in. An example occurred in 1874 when Harvard University offered the firts art history class in the United States. Open only to wealthy White males, its purpose was to place them on a cultural level equal to that of their European counterparts.

A second approach might be called philosophical literacy. It involves studying the ideas of individuals our culture has christened 'great thinkers.' Does this view conform or challenge? It too is a form of social adaptation. The sheep are told by the wolves which exemplars to memorize if they wish to run with the pack, pretending that they too are wolves. The fantasy lasts as long as the wolves are amused. It ends when the wolves get hungry.

Another approach is that of critical theory—the study of value systems underlying sociological assumptions. In the case of art, this includes identifying which group magistrates the line separating 'fine' and 'popular' art, which determines what 'good' art is, who is excluded from these processes, and how the dominant value system is maintained. I have seen oppression deny so many their right to participate in the American experiment; to serve as dog catcher or president; to make, to teach, or to view whatever art they choose. Because of this, we all—oppressors as well as oppressed—inherit a diminished legacy. How is this so?

By denying certain groups the opportunity to make art, the world's art heritage is smaller. There is less art available for anyone—oppressor or oppressed.

Extend that point beyond art to the rest of society.

The result of oppression is slower scientific, philosophical, political and religious development.

What does art have to do with this? Art is a priest to many gods. At various times, art has been justified or attacked on grounds that it improves morals or destroys them, develops emotional health or breeds raving lunacy, elevates or pollutes society, increases intelligence or dulls the brain, stimulates problem-solving skills or deadens creativity, offers investment opportunities or dupes a gullible public, teaches patriotism or undermines a nation's values, instills respect for our siblings on spaceship earth or breeds cultural elitism, teaches other school subjects or teaches nothing of consequence, offers spiritual enlightenment or leads to idolatry, provides diversion for the leisure class as it improves the taste of the working class, and keeps women out of trouble as it imparts marketable skills to men.

Arthur Efland suggests that a three-fingered-fist—patronage, education, and censorship—has been used to control the arts throughout Western history. The rationales for art education that predominate in a given culture at a given time are determined by that culture's power conflicts. If we envisage a continuum with freedom on the left, indifference in the center, and censorship on the right, we find that powerbrokers gravitate leftward when they feel secure. Romantic rationales emerge. Under stable conditions art is not needed to acquire power, so overt agendas disappear. Powerbrokers become champions of culture. Governmental and private endowments appear. Censorship abates, patronage diversifies, and art educators are free to teach as they choose. Leaders praise the arts as central to a well-rounded education. Because they feel secure, they tolerate critical voices, creative thought, expressive freedom, and heightened connoisseurship. Art can thrive in such a setting.

Yet, when powerbrokers may choose the middle ground—indifference—such patronage may be elusive. Indifference results in an artistically unschooled populace which in turn results in a visually illiterate culture. Since art is not perceived to serve utilitarian ends, it is deemed unimportant. As art is ignored, so is art education. It becomes a caricature of itself. An example of this occurred in the mid-twentieth century. Modernism flourished within the art community but was popularly ignored. Meanwhile, sentiment in art education was to decry 'adult-imposed' standards such as art history or social criticism. The public, unschooled in connoisseurship, failed to grasp the innovations of modernism. "Why should we pony up the time and money to view art we don't understand?" the public reasonably asked. Had school art curricula been robust at mid-century, the public may have kept pace with the art of its time. The gap between artist and public would have narrowed rather than widened. A telling measure of the result of this approach is that so few artists who grew up during this time credit their public school art educations for helping them. Policymakers who came of age during this period occupy seats of power today. Visually ignorant, they by definition do not know what they are missing; consequently they do not value it. Under such leadership, it is not surprising that visual illiteracy is commonplace.

In troubled times, powerbrokers move to the right. Giftwrapping their tactics in the rhetoric of God and of country, they co-opt art education, and art itself, to serve their ends. If power lies with the state, technicians often are trained to produce state propaganda, or to develop economically exploitable skills. During the United States' revolutionary period, for example, as the infant nation struggled for economic self-sufficiency, industrialists implemented art education programs intended to produce able designers and to improve craftsmanship. It was hoped that this would make colonial products more competitive with those of Europe. If a culture's power is concentrated in the church, as it was in the Middle Ages, art education is often used to train technicians to disseminate dogma. In such circumstances a culture's leaders impose their own visions. The sound of silence echoes across the land as the visions of artists go slip slidin' away. Patronage shrinks, education ossifies, and censorship revives. Creativity dies.

Such circumstances are never inevitable. In a democracy, powerbrokers are helpless to push society without its consent. I call your attention to the untapped political potential of art education, one of our culture's most under-utilized means of enlightenment. Its network is already in place. Let us use it.

To summarize, in this course we will use the art record to help us define which groups have shaped civilization, and which have been silenced. We will become familiar with the machinery by which this hegemony has perpetuated. From there, we will establish links to the art education curriculum, and determine how both art and art education have been tools for various agendas. Finally, we will develop a mission for the art curriculum of today.

See you on Thursday.

FOR ADDITIONAL READING:

Fehr, D. *Dogs Playing Cards*. New York: Peter Lang, 1997.

XI

TEACHER SAYS, SIMON SAYS:
DUALISM IN SCIENCE LEARNING
David B. Pushkin

I.

Jack is a student of mine, the father of three children. His eldest daughter is a high school freshman and has the same science teacher that Jack had nearly twenty-five years ago. On a recent test, she solved a problem and determined the "correct" answer, but she was penalized points for not having solved the problem correctly. Her answer was not determined by dumb luck, a miscalculation, forgetting units, or even forgetting specific steps in the problem solving process; she was penalized for not having solved the problem her *teacher's way*.

Jack was obviously disappointed and frustrated for his daughter; it was not the first time teachers penalized her for employing alternative problem solving methods, or for providing additional information in her answers.

> Consider a student in the "Physics and Society" course. His first assignment grade was mediocre, reflecting his superficial answer to an essay question. During office hours, he stopped by to discuss the assignment. No complaints regarding the grade; he considered the grade justified. He, a junior majoring in history, mentioned that this experience was hardly unique; his grades were mediocre in all of his recent classes. *I don't get it; why am I doing poorly? I answer the question; what does everybody want from me?* His problem: answering the question, the whole question, and nothing but the question—every assignment, every test—as if under oath on the witness stand. *Just answer the question. Be precise; get to the point. Short and sweet; nothing more, nothing less. Do not say anything to precipitate an objection.*

Take no chances; play it safe. This is what he did; he took the approach of failure avoidance. Anyone who has ever played or watched sports knows one cannot play not to lose; a prevent defense does not guarantee a win. (Pushkin 1995a, 173–74)

A father's frustration: *Why is my kid being taught that thinking and creativity are bad?* Jack is not alone in his frustration. Many years ago while I was working on my master's in biochemistry, one of my professors vented his frustrations with my alternative problems solving. There was nothing wrong with my use of calculus, or my answers, but because he had to invest extra time to examine my methods, he would penalize me a considerable number of points to teach me to be a serious graduate student. He was teaching me to improve what Shelia Tobias calls my *obedience quotient.*

What Jack is beginning to realize fully is that the products of his daughter's high school will be the 18- and 19-year-old classmates he is currently attending college with. It is sad to hear college sophomores tell me "I'm so set in my ways . . . do you object to my using the same physics equations that I learned in high school?" "I get nervous when you rearrange those equations (algebraically) when doing problems. My (high school) teacher always told us to put the numbers in for the letters and calculate." "Are you sure you're teaching us right? That's not the way we did it in high school!" Adults so young. Adults so dualistic. Adults so programmed and conditioned to following orders, unable to adjust or to observe the similarities in problem-solving methods. Adults so eager to pursue higher education, but so well-learned in Pavlovian and Skinneresque behaviorism.

II.

Are my observations new? Are they limited only to my current geography? Unfortunately, they are not. Many years ago, while I was a high school student, our class read Hemingway's *The Sun Also Rises,* a very interesting book for a variety of perspectives. Being in eleventh grade, I found the sexual tension between Jake Barnes and Lady Brett Ashley very intriguing (I still do). Why would an impotent man relentlessly pursue a desirable woman he could not have? (Of course, these days when one reflects on *The Big Chill,* anything is possible!)

At any rate, I proceeded to write my assigned essay on this particular insight and submitted it to my teacher, Mr. Rick. Unfortunately, Mr. Rick let me and my entire class know just how foolish and wasteful my essay was—not for its grammar, not for its validity, but for its lack of importance; it did not correlate with what *he* thought was the most important theme of the novel. To this day, I still think of Mr. Rick's ridicule every time I write something to share with others.

Why share such distant and ancient history with people I do not know? Are we part of a "I had a rotten educational experience" support group? If we truly believe in the value of social constructivism, then we should be willing to share our experiences so that we can learn from each other and make teaching and learning more meaningful and enriching. We learn from our exchanges and dialogue (Greene 1992); we can learn a great deal using Pinar's method of *currere*.

What role in this biography do my evolving intellectual interests play? In what ways do they contribute to an understanding of the dominant themes of this biography? In what ways have they permitted biographic movement, that is, freed one from interests whose life has gone out of them, and drawn one on into areas that excite? What is the relation of these interests and concomitant professional activities to one's private life?

. . . The biographic past? It is usually ignored. Ignored but not absent. The biographic past exists presently, complexity contributive to the biographic present. While we say it cannot be held accountable for the present, the extent to which it is ignored is probably the extent it does account for what is present.

. . . What is the contribution of my scholarly and professional work to my present? Do they illuminate the present? Obscure it? Are one's intellectual interests biographically freeing, that is, do they permit, in fact encourage, movement?

Do they point to increased conceptual sophistication and refinement, deeper knowledge and understanding, of both one's field of study and that field's symbolic relation to one's evolving biography? Do they move to enter new, higher levels of being? (Pinar 1994, 20–7)

III.

Obedience still seems to be a highly valued commodity in education. Students are still taught work skills (Giroux 1992), be they college-bound or not; cultural capital, homogeneity, and the curriculum are not always distinguishable (Greene 1992; Pinar 1992). One must wonder if "critical thinking" is disseminated to students as "thinking to avoid criticism." To be "good" is still a social norm in our schools (Lewis 1992); students who embrace the great tradition will know of success and of rewards (Kincheloe 1992).

> *Well, we're waiting here in Allentown*
> *For the Pennsylvania we never found,*
> *For the promises our teachers gave*
> *If we worked hard, if we behaved.*
> *So the graduations hang on the wall,*
> *But they never really helped us at all.*
> *No they never taught us what was real,*
> *Iron and coke and chromium steel,*
> *And we're waiting here in Allentown.*

Billy Joel's song "Allentown" rings hauntingly true in northeastern Pennsylvania, where a diploma and a union card are still honored symbols despite a dead mining industry and a depressed economy. As Joe Kincheloe states: "Schools are the guardians . . . to institutionalize the attitudes necessary for the industrial discipline which leads to increased productivity" (1992, 228). When we discuss "functional literacy," how do the powers of a school system define it? Has the context changed with the times (McLaren 1992)?

> Student knowledge is based on the notion of replication rather than interpretation, as students are deemed "to know" only when they can display a fragment of data at a teacher's bidding. Schools reflect positivist assumptions when they affirm that the most significant aspects of school can be measured. In their positivist tunnel-vision objective tests deny students a chance to transcend the reductionism of measurability, they cannot in this context respond creatively, develop a relationship between their lived experience and the information, or learn intrapersonally by establishing a personal position on the issue. Such an approach encourages a stimulus-response reflex, erasing the totality of the person from the learning process. In the

positivistically defined school, student subjectivity is viewed with suspicion if not hostility. (Kincheloe 1991, 64–5)

In *Toward a Critical Politics of Teacher Thinking*, Kincheloe states: "Students of modernism's one-truth epistemology are treated like one-trick ponies, rewarded only for short-term retention of certified truths" (3), and "When behavioral psychology was added to the pedagogical recipe, teachers began to be seen more as entities to be controlled and manipulated" (7). Why are learners taught obedience? Perhaps it is because their teachers do not know any better. In colleges of education, students at all levels are proselytized to the methods of their teacher preparation programs. Upon entering their first professional position, novice teachers are indoctrinated to the state standards for efficient and effective teaching, as well as for minimal competency. At workshops, in-services, and other developmental meetings, teachers continue to learn the mantra of their superiors—*we run your life, be a team player, do as you are told, and watch your step.* No matter how we look at it, teachers and students are brainwashed with the agendas of teacher education and certification programs, of school and district administrators, as well as of prominent members of the community.

> Teachers are wimps—passive creatures who do what they are told, who feverishly avoid any challenge to mainstream values or perceived injustice. Attempts to teach higher levels of thinking, new ways of seeing, more sophisticated consciousness are repudiated by reformers fearful of any form of experimentation . . . creative pedagogy has been rendered evil . . . Education cannot be reformed by decree. (Kincheloe 1992, 230)

When I was a high school teacher in Bradenton, Florida, I too was caught in the machine of obedience and efficiency. Our principal, Mr. Bob, a former football coach and driver education instructor, was a firm believer in team philosophy. Individuality and autonomy were frowned upon, and deviating too much from the way things were done was feared since it would encourage all the other teachers to "do their own thing," possibly leading to an irreversible breakdown in structure. Teamwork applied to students as well. No student, regardless of academic standing, academic load, or reputation among the faculty, was permitted more than two years of study hall—if one student received special treatment, then everyone should receive the same treatment; everyone was an equal pawn in Mr. Bob's provincial view. Teachers and students alike were expected to conform to the "cookie–cutter" mentality that forcefully homogenized the school.

I chose to be different, daring students to think and to give a damn about themselves as learners. Many students despised this approach; they were accustomed to the administratively mandated apathy practiced at our school. They, and their parents, complained; Mr. Bob did not like to hear complaints, and was intent on letting me know this on numerous occasions. With each reprimand I received, I was reminded of how dangerous I was for education; I was an enigma: intelligent, with a bad attitude. A teacher must contest the hegemony of "the way things are" (McLaren 1992). If we do not question policies and practices, how can we ever become open-minded? Does questioning policies and practices constitute misbehavior? How do teachers and students understand what misbehavior is? (Berry 1992). According to Lewis (1992, 47) and Miller (1992, 155–57), "good behavior" is "replicating official knowledge." While teaching and learning do not necessarily have fixed boundaries (Britzman 1992; Steinberg 1992), teachers and students are immediately made aware when they are "bad."

> Surviving high school involves primarily remembering and regurgitating, plus mastering a few other polite behaviors. Showing up for class, not causing any trouble, and handing in something pretty much guarantees a passing grade.
>
> Because being nice is routinely rewarded academically, many students come to college expecting that if they behave themselves in class, they'll be fine. They arrive at college eager to fit in, to tell the professors whatever it is that they want to hear, to sit in class smiling and not causing any trouble. They expect that all will then be well. (Hinchey 1995, 39)

The syndicated columnist Thomas Sowell recently wrote of the shock and anger teachers display each time "I point out that innumerable studies have shown that students who are training to become schoolteachers have some of the poorest academic skills" (*Times Leader*, Wilkes-Barre, PA, January 16, 1996). Unfortunately, I cannot argue against that point; young people who aspire to perpetuate (and to be rewarded for) dualistic thinking only tend to hinder the education of future generations, not to help it.

IV.

Tell us what you want to hear, and we will tell you what we think. A long-existing problem in our schools, particularly in science classes, is the need for correctness. Piagetian conceptual change focuses on coming to consensus with the "accepted conception"; alternatives are misconceptions (Maloney 1994). Perhaps science educators need to realize that students' conceptions often reflect taking what is accepted out of context, thinking that a rule applies to all cases. Taking this into consideration, we should be more sensitive to these conceptions and refer to them as pseudoconceptions (Pushkin 1996).

> In modernist classrooms, we teach students that there is only one scientific method, only one way to write a lab report, only one way to formulate a hypothesis, and only one way to define scientific terms. If we think of the three stages of conceptual change: assimilation, accommodation, and equilibration, the message becomes loud and clear: *here is the correct way to look at it, accept it, and understand that your way is wrong.* If your interpretation is contrary to the book's, you are questioned, if not interrogated. If your interpretation comes from a journal or author that is "not mainstream," you are scolded, if not sanctioned. If you are taking time to contemplate things that others deem insignificant, then you are misguided. (Pushkin 1995a, 13)

The first response to a new paradigm is usually to find holes in the theory (i.e., where is the exception?). To offer students and teachers the freedom to chose their own methods of solving problems, to make them aware of options and of the value in alternatives, one might think that these poor souls were just sentenced to an eternity in purgatory. *Choices?! Please don't give me any . . . what if I make the wrong one?!* Perhaps they have a point. Galileo was excommunicated for his theories; Newton had to be prodded by Robert Hooke even to publish his laws of motion. Students must attend classes; teachers must teach them. Students and teachers alike are in quest for knowledge, as if it were *The Absolute Truth-after all, isn't this what we test on?* Unfortunately, once a new paradigm is learned and accepted, we often forget the previous ones as "old news." Students of science are often the worst students of the history in science; but an ignorance of the precursors for our current theories is a lack of respect for knowledge and its evolution. Then again, dualists do feed on factoids as

Dickens's peasants did on scrumptious morsels discarded by shops and bakeries.

> Does anything happen in the mind between the ages of 17 and 22 beyond a large intake of information, an enrichment of context? Is there any substance to the familiar claim that a liberal education means learning how to think? Is there during the college years any fundamental evolution of intellectual process comparable to the childhood stages described by Piaget or the levels of cognitive representation brought to light by Bruner and his associates? (R. W. White in foreword of Perry 1970, v)

> Insofar as the instruction asks students to enter into a single intentionality across multiple contexts, it serves developmentally to emphasize what might be called the continuity of socially derived criteria within the discontinuity of particular objective circumstances. It emphasizes, that is, the declarative knowledge base constraints on what must be done, while developing "cognitive flexibility." (Picard 1993, 27)

> Traditional representations of concepts mean different things to different learners (Perkins and Unger 1994); so do traditional presentations of concepts. Can we realistically expect students to accept concepts at face value simply because educators continue to teach with traditional methods? Can we realistically expect students to demonstrate an understanding of concepts simply because educators continue to assess learning by traditional means? (Pushkin, 1995a, 16)

> Paradigmatic shifts play an important role in how one views physical concepts and accepts laws of nature. From Aristotle to Newton, from Franklin to Rutherford, and from Brahe to Einstein, there are many episodes throughout history that indicate the painstakingly long time it takes for old ways of thinking to give way to newer, more plausible theories. (Pushkin 1995a, 20)

> In order to provide students opportunities to explore their views of concepts and gain insight into their mental models, appropriate learning experiences need to be part of the classroom culture throughout the introductory course. These learning experiences cannot be treated as "special events"; the resulting influence, if any, will be minimal and very short-lived. (Pushkin 1995a, 14)

During my "Physics and Society" course at Penn State, our class spent valuable time discussing the evolution of knowledge as atomic structure became more and more defined by the theories of Thomson, Rutherford, Bohr, and other physicists of the 1900s. One of my students, a senior about to graduate with her degree in developmental psychology, expressed her anger and frustrations with the class discussion. "I don't like the way you teach," she said, "because I can't learn from you this way." When I asked her what her learning style was, she proclaimed "This is how I learn: you write the facts on the board, I copy them in my notes, memorize them for the test, and get my A. All you're doing is wasting our time with a bunch of wrong information; you're not teaching us the right answers!"

I asked the student if Piaget meant anything to her. "Oh yeah, he's real important," she boasted, "he's on a lot of tests in my major." Here was someone about to receive her degree in a field of study, and yet she failed to see the significance of what she was being educated in. Whether I agree with Piagetian theory or not is irrelevant; I at least appreciate the theory for its significance with regard to other theories. A future psychologist who looks at the theory as no more than a choice for a test item is one who may never fully understand or appreciate what her profession is about. Is it no wonder that students view physics problems as isolated "plug-and-chug" exercises? If the classroom culture is one that presents knowledge as sterile trivia on a checklist, what right do educators have to complain about their students' lack of thinking skills? If one perpetuates this teaching practice, then s/he is indeed an accomplice in the "dumbing down" of learning.

> Consider the science educator, who during a discussion regarding students' conceptions of entropy states *there are students who still have an Aristotelian view of the world.* Translation: *If they do not understand Newtonian mechanics, how could these idiots possibly comprehend entropy?!* How do students' understanding of mechanics relate to their understanding of thermodynamics? Are these areas of

physics mutually dependent on each other? The inability to correctly label a force diagram hardly predicts one's understanding of a thermal process. Educators trapped in their modernity view learning as linear, a series circuit of concepts. Conceptual change is a convenient mode of behavior modification, a manipulative means of correcting *wrongness*. Heaven forbid if a student comprehends physics in a parallel manner. *The book starts with chapter one; mechanics is our first major topic. We will cover thermodynamics later, provided you have not been weeded out by then!* No wonder students might perceive general physics as an obstacle course, a mine field of endurance. Are undergraduates supposed to be obedient little stooges, blindly following Authority until a diploma is tossed their way? What will become of them in the job market? What kind of graduate students will they be? Do we program them as mindless robots to perpetuate a hallowed tradition, or do we expect more from them? (Pushkin 1995a, 173)

V.

There are physics faculty members who make efforts to help their students conceptualize physics before solving problems (Pushkin 1995b); sadly, the predominant Fordist culture in physics departments makes them the exception rather than the rule (Pushkin 1994). A number of studies (e.g., Chi et al., 1981 and 1989; Larkin 1981; Maloney 1994; McMillan and Swadener 1991) have shown that students who cannot conceptualize physical phenomena will have great difficulty solving physics problems. Although there is a growing interest in physics students' mental models or schemas (e.g., Pushkin 1995c; Redish 1994), traditional problem solving (or any single mode of assessment) will not provide sufficient information for science educators. To learn as much as we possibly can about our students' perceptions of learning, and their methods of learning, a wide array of learning experiences and assessment opportunities is necessary.

If any form of assessment is used too frequently, students can learn to respond automatically. Consequently the assessment might no longer measure quite what you want it to. Its validity lessens. People appreciate that this is so for well-known forms such as multiple choice tests. (White and Gunstone 1992, 180)

Yet, students need to be made aware of the purpose for thinking and learning. Students need to be constantly reinforced that taking chances and trying out new ideas is a good thing; passively sitting in a lecture hall and mimicking every step a professor or instructor employs while solving a problem is not necessarily a sign of learning. After all, forces interact differently for objects sliding down an incline than for being pushed up the incline. No educator can teach a student how to contextualize a problem by doing the problem simply for the class to watch on a chalkboard. Educators can, however, provide students opportunities to develop their personal schemas for different physical phenomena and their relevant contexts.

Learning means taking occasional risks in the presence of peers. Even if the outcome of risk taking is not what was anticipated, we can learn from it. This is how theories and laws evolved; this is how a greater understanding of concepts evolves as well. I recently watched *Third Rock from the Sun*. In this particular episode, the lead character, a college professor, was soliciting answers to define "Cleveland." One student was quite reluctant to offer an answer for fear of being wrong. The professor, attempting to put this student's mind at ease, informed him that he had nothing to lose by offering an answer since "the odds of you being wrong are staggering!" Reluctantly, the student offered "Cleveland is a feeling." The professor then proceeded to place this response into an algorithm that attempted to quantify one's feelings, looked at his final expression, and concluded "No, you're definitely wrong."

But there was some value to this student's answer. First, it helped the professor, an alien placed on Earth to research human life, gain an understanding that people do possess an abstract emotional attachment to concrete things (e.g., the certain pride we exude when we tell people the name of our hometowns). Second, it showed us that answers are worth testing, not simply dismissing. Last, and most important, this student's answer was solicited and welcomed (even begged); the student made a contribution to his learning community after all. As educators, we need to remind students that contributing and sharing is a good part of the learning culture—without this, learning lacks a culture.

Even if students' contributions are not what we hope for, we still need to respect their contributions, to appreciate them for both their strengths and limitations, and to help students grow from the experience. If we expect our students to be receptive to new ideas and alternative perspectives, we must be receptive too. We cannot expect students to stop thinking with blinders on if we do not. We cannot expect students to be educated thinkers if their teachers are trained and certified technicians, dispensing knowledge as if it were the headlights for a new car moving along the assembly line. How much faith can we have for students developing critical thinking skills when their teachers equate good secretarial skills with teaching excellence?

I once had a practicum student teacher who was afraid to be in the classroom with her students, never learned their names, demonstrated a mediocre command of her subject matter, and simply could not communicate her lessons. At the end of her five-week practicum experience, she received a grade that reflected potential, but a need for considerable growth as a classroom teacher. She was absolutely devastated by what she considered an unwarranted grade. Why did she feel this way? She never missed a day of school, was never late for meetings, and always had her assignments and lesson plans ready to hand in, prompt and grammatically correct. Yet, she failed to see a significant aspect of her experience. She was very competent in areas associated with an office worker, but these were hardly competency areas vital for successful classroom teaching. To her, education was not a learning phenomenon; it was a custodial process. To her, because she was not a troublemaker, she should be recognized and rewarded in accordance with excellence.

Higher education should be a place of higher order thinking. Yet, when students enter such an environment unprepared for this academic expectation, becoming an educated adult is hindered. If high school teachers deny their students the opportunity to grow intellectually, they are commiting a crime. Classroom teachers are vital for breaking the cycle of staying with the flock, coloring within the lines, and minding P's and Q's. If teachers do not learn to rebel, think for themselves, and make their own decisions, neither will their students.

> Perhaps the most critical point . . . comes at the moment where the student has indeed discovered how to think further, how to think relatively and contingently, and how to think about thinking. For here it is up to him in what crucial spirit he is to employ this discovery. (Perry 1970, 37)

REFERENCES

Berry, K. "Students Under Suspicion: Do Students Misbehave More Than They Used To?" In *Thirteen Questions: Reframing Education's Conversation*. J. L. Kincheloe and S. R. Steinberg, eds. New York: Peter Lang, 1992. 93–100.

Britzman, D. P. "Teachers Under Suspicion: Is It True That Teachers Aren't as Good as They Used To Be?" In *Thirteen Questions: Reframing Education's Conversation*. J. L. Kincheloe and S. R. Steinberg, eds. New York: Peter Lang, 1992. 73–80.

Chi, M. T. H., M. Bassok, M. W. Lewis, P. Reimann, and R. Glaser. "Self-Explanations: How Students Study and Use Examples in Learning to Solve Problems." *Cognitive Science*, 13(1989): 145–82.

———, P. J. Feltovich, and R. Glaser. "Categorization and Representation of Physics Problems by Experts and Novices." *Cognitive Science*, 5 (1981): 121–52.

Giroux, H. A. "Educational Visions: What Are Schools For and What Should We Be Doing in the Name of Education?" In *Thirteen Questions: Reframing Education's Conversation*. J. L. Kincheloe and S. R. Steinberg, eds. New York: Peter Lang, 1992. 277–84.

Greene, M. "Educational Visions: What Are Schools For and What Should We Be Doing in the Name of Education?" In *Thirteen Questions: Reframing Education's Conversation*. J. L. Kincheloe and S. R. Steinberg, eds. New York: Peter Lang, 1992. 285–93.

Hinchey, P. H. "The Human Cost of Teacher Education Reform." *Education Week*, 25, 9 (1995): 39.

Kincheloe, J. L. *Teachers as Researchers: Qualitative Inquiry As a Path To Empowerment*. London: Falmer Press, 1991.

———."Education Reform: What Have Been the Effects of the Attempts to Improve Education Over the Last Decade?" In *Thirteen Questions: Reframing Education's Conversation*. J. L. Kincheloe and S. R. Steinberg, eds. New York: Peter Lang, 1992. 227–32.

———. *Toward a Critical Politics of Teacher Thinking: Mapping the Postmodern*. Westport, CT: Bergin &Garvey, 1993.

Larkin, J. H. "Cognition of Learning Physics." *American Journal of Physics*, 49, (1981): 534–41.

Lewis, M. "Power and Education: Who Decides the Forms Schools Have Taken, and Who Should Decide?" In *Thirteen Questions: Reframing Education's Conversation*. J. L. Kincheloe and S. R. Steinberg, eds. New York: Peter Lang, 1992: 41–50.

Maloney, D. P. "Research on Problem Solving: Physics." In *Handbook of Research on Science Teaching and Learning*. D. L. Gabel, ed. New York: MacMillan, 1994. 327–54.

McLaren, P. "Education as a Political Issue: What's Missing In the Public Conversation About Education?" In *Thirteen Questions: Reframing Education's Conversation*. J. L. Kincheloe and S. R. Steinberg, eds. New York: Peter Lang, 1992. 249–62.

McMillan, C., and M. Swadener. "Novice Use of Qualitative versus Quantitative Problem Solving in Electrostatics." *Jornal of Research in Science Teaching*, 28 (1991): 661–70.

Miller, J. L. "Women and Education: In What Ways Does Gender Affect the Educational Process?" In *Thirteen Questions: Reframing Education's*

Conversation. J. L. Kincheloe and S. R. Steinberg, eds. New York: Peter Lang, 1992. 151–58.

Perkins, D. N., and C. Unger. "A New Look in Representations for Mathematics and Science Learning." *Instructional Science*, 22 (1994): 1–37.

Perry, W. G. *Forms of Intellectual and Ethical Development in the College Years, a Scheme.* New York: Holt, Rinehart, and Winston, 1970.

Picard, C. L. "Intentionality and Instructional Design: Revisiting Key Issues and Their Implications." *Educational Technology*, 33, 12 (1993): 23–8.

Pinar, W. F. "The Curriculum: What Are the Basics and What Are We Teaching Them?" In *Thirteen Questions: Reframing Education's Conversation.* J. L. Kincheloe and S. R. Steinberg, eds. New York: Peter Lang, 1992. 31–8.

———. *Autobiography, Politics, and Sexuality: Essays in Curriculum Theory 1972–1992.* New York: Peter Lang Publishing, 1994.

Pushkin, D. B. "Should the APS Get Involved With Education? Yes, But Look Before You Leap!" *American Journal of Physics*, 62, 969: 1994.

———. "The Influence of a Computer-Interfaced Calorimetry Demonstration on General Physics Students' Conceptual Views of Entropy and Their Metaphoric Explanations of the Second Law of Thermodynamics." Unpublished doctoral dissertation, Pennsylvania State University, 1995a.

———. "The AP Exam and the Introductory College Course." *Physics Teacher*, 33 (1995b): 532–35.

———. Answer #13— "A Central Organizing Principle for Statistical and Thermal Physics?" *American Journal of Physics*, submitted for publication, 1995c.

Pushkin, D. B. "A Comment on the Need to Use Scientific Terminology Appropriately in Conception Studies." *Journal of Research in Science Teaching*, 33 (1996): 223–24.

Redish, E. F. "Implications of Cognitive Studies for Teaching Physics." *American Journal of Physics*, 62 (1994): 796–803.

Steinberg, S. R. "Teachers Under Suspicion: Is it True that Teachers Aren't as Good as They Used to Be?" In *Thirteen Questions: Reframing Education's Conversation.* J. L. Kincheloe and S. R. Steinberg, eds. New York: Peter Lang, 1992. 67–72.

White, R., and R. Gunstone. *Problem Understanding.* London: Falmer Press, 1992.

XII

TEACHING/LEARNING MATHEMATICS IN SCHOOL[1]

Peter M. Appelbaum

You have choices in five realms for school mathematics: the first three take place in the context of the last two. To begin with, you must choose among strategies for teaching/learning, strategies for assessment, and strategies for connecting mathematics to other subjects. The decisions you make in these areas become points of reference for reflection and enhanced comfort in grappling with the decision-making process in your ongoing development as a teacher. They help you to understand your convictions regarding the last two realms of choice even as they enact these last two choices, which include: your strategy for defining the relationships among reflection, assessment, and evaluation; and your strategy for structuring activities that enable students to move within and among various positions vis-à-vis the subject matter of mathematics. This essay will discuss each of the above realms before offering some concluding questions for you to consider.

STRATEGIES FOR TEACHING/LEARNING

Train: Tell/show/drill/coach/practice

Models connect conceptual and procedural knowledge

Patterns

Problem solving

Problem posing

Let's start with the mathematics: What does it mean to "do" mathematics in your classroom? There are at least five different ways to think about this. Most of us have experienced only one of the five, the *Train/Show/Drill/Coach/Practice* method of teaching/ learning. The easiest way to understand what happens in this type of classroom is to think back to some of your own school mathematics experiences in which the teacher stood at the front of the room and showed the class how to get correct answers to assigned exercises. Because we have so much personal experience with this strategy, I won't dwell on it here. The important things to consider are those moments from your memory that "worked" using this system, and other moments that "failed" in some way. You should ask yourself how you might teach the same topic or skill "differently" so as to make such a class more consistent with your happy or successful memories, and as unlike any anxious, fearful, or anger-inducing memories as possible.

One complaint about the first strategy is that it often leads to students mindlessly applying incorrect procedures or algorithms in a confused muddle of incomprehension. Teachers have searched for ways to organize their classroom toward a goal of "meaningful learning." Each of the four remaining teaching/learning strategies I will discuss pursue this goal in different ways. Which will you choose? It depends on your personal desires and fears, and your own professional judgment.

The *Models Link Conceptual and Procedural Knowledge* approach emphasizes powerful distinctions in mathematics among conceptual, procedural, and factual knowledge. The argument here is that the reason the first strategy of teaching/learning fails is because it dwells on procedures for producing answers and the memorization of facts, ignoring the meaning, context, or purposes involved—the concepts. Concepts are "big ideas," not necessarily particular to mathematics, which cannot be learned in one lesson. They are relationships rather than things, learned over extended periods of time. Constructed by learners themselves out of multiple experiences, concepts are hard to define and a challenge to name, even as we might easily provide many illustrations or examples of particular cases of them. Themes, topics, subjects, and objectives are almost never concepts, so you won't find them listed in a teachers' manual. One of the important jobs for a teacher who chooses this approach is to decide on good concepts to drive lessons. We must look at the big ideas that cut across and underlie several themes, topics, subjects, or objectives. The ones that link in surprising ways are the interesting ones; these, in fact, often *could* be used creatively as themes for interdisciplinary units.

Here is a common example used by proponents of this second

strategy: Nkendra goes up to the board and confidently executes the following sums in second grade:

$$\begin{array}{c} 17 \\ +2 \\ \hline 19 \end{array} \quad \begin{array}{c} 15 \\ +3 \\ \hline 18 \end{array} \quad \begin{array}{c} 22 \\ +\ 5 \\ \hline 27 \end{array} \quad \begin{array}{c} 17 \\ +8 \\ \hline 115 \end{array} \quad \begin{array}{c} 15 \\ \times 9 \\ \hline 114 \end{array} \quad \begin{array}{c} 22 \\ +8 \\ \hline 210 \end{array}$$

You are the teacher. What do you think?

We don't really know *what* to think, unless we begin to apply some strategy of assessment, which we will get to later in this chapter. For now, we might think Nkendra has serious problems; but we may express these problems in different ways. Some of us might describe this student as missing the point completely: She needs to be taught how to "carry." Others of us might note something interesting: Whatever she is doing "works" for some cases. Indeed, Nkendra has very effectively learned a "procedure" for adding two-digit and one-digit numbers. In fact, we would not be at all surprised if she were capable of stating very articulate and detailed instructions or recipes for obtaining her answers. For example, "Add the numbers on the right, put that down. Now take the number on the left on top and put that down. You're done!" So in the past Nkendra has been a superb student. She learned what was taught: a procedure. What she may not have learned were *concepts*, such as place value, that would provide a meaningful context for a construction of number sense. Teachers who use base-ten blocks or other materials that give a physical *model* of the concept of place-value (the relationships among digits in a numeral) report that their students do, indeed develop a reasonable number sense, such that, if they added 17 and 8, and got 115, they might say, "That's peculiar—115 sounds too big . . ."

Working with tens and ones enables students to develop their *own* procedures for adding numbers. In this context, Nkendra might be asked to describe what she has done in terms of base-ten materials. 17 + 8 "means"

equals

in other words, exactly what she wrote on the board! One ten and fifteen ones. Could she come up with another way to say that? Students often write 115 as $\overline{|\,⑤}$, proceeding to combine the tens and concluding $(\overline{|+|})\,5$. Thus, a procedure linked with the concept, might, for Nkendra, result in something like this:

$$\begin{array}{ccccc}
\begin{array}{r}|5\\+9\\\hline\end{array} \rightarrow &
\begin{array}{r}|5\\+9\\\hline 1④\end{array} \rightarrow &
\begin{array}{r}|5\\+9\\\hline (1+1)4\end{array} \rightarrow &
\begin{array}{r}|5\\+9\\\hline 24\end{array} &
\begin{array}{r}|5\\+9\\\hline 1④\\(1+1)4\end{array}
\end{array}$$

Manipulative materials are thus intended, within this strategy, to provide a *model* that can link procedures and facts (such as 5+9=14, a "number fact") with students' ongoing conceptual development.

Another example of this strategy is seen in the way many teachers approach fractions in the elementary curriculum. While fractions have caused inestimable peril for hosts of students and adults, teachers who focus on underlying concepts have noted the relative joy and wonder their students experience with fractions. "Fractions" themselves are an exquisite example of a "big idea"; learned over *years* of experience with wholes and parts. Fractions are a family of overlapping notions about dividing a whole into "equal" parts. Concepts such as: The number of parts justifies a particular name. The "equality" of the parts needs elaboration over time through communication about these parts. And the understanding that a fraction is always a relationship between a particular thing that represents a "whole" in a particular case, and the equal parts of *that* whole, is yet another generalization from experiences with particular cases in varieties of contexts over time. All of these are generalizable "big ideas" that can be explored and discussed throughout a curriculum, providing a rich foundation of illustrative examples out of which a student might formulate a working comprehension of fractions. Within mathematics, teachers might use *models* of fractions, such as fractions strips, fraction circles, distance measured along masking tape on the floor of the room, or the weight of clumps of playdough. By challenging students to talk about dividing a whole into parts and then looking for as many different names for a part as possible, as many different names for one combination of parts, etc., teachers help their students form a conceptual understanding and a language for communicating that understanding. In the Train/Drill/Kill strategy, so many procedures build on so many others that students often can't remember which one to use at which time. The Models/Concepts strategy actually uses some conventionally "later" topics, such as equivalent fractions, and the addition and subtraction of fractions, to *introduce* the concept of fraction itself. In this way, the procedures for obtaining specific answers grow out of the ongoing development of the concept simultaneously with the construction of a language for describing that concept in particular meaningful instances.

The third strategy does not dwell on procedures, concepts *or* facts. Instead, the teacher embraces "patterns" as the essence and thrill of mathematics as an endeavor. This teacher would not want to know so much whether or not the students could get correct answers or whether or not the students could communicate understanding of concepts, but would want to see the students looking for, finding, and making patterns. Now, I don't mean that the teacher "teaches" students about patterns (that the teacher "teaches" students what a pattern is, and then tests them with probing questions to see if they can produce, reproduce, or identify a pattern). This strategy celebrates human beings as pattern beings— that people because they are people, see, make, and enjoy patterns. So the teacher can take advantage of that to provide experiences that enhance students' appreciation of the skill they bring with them to school, and through which they learn a lot of mathematics. We look for patterns everywhere in this classroom—do we see a pattern on the floor? On the wall? In the organization of time across the day/week/month? Can we play with a number pattern? Can we take a number pattern and make a representation of it with colors? with clapping sounds? with a dance?

A patterns strategy would want to establish the classroom as a patterns environment. For example, in literature we look for books that feature patterns, and when our students note them, we are joyous.[2] We ask for any other explanations for that pattern; we encourage looking for patterns as a way of reading a text and deriving meaning from it. We might introduce multiplication through the production of a picture with pattern blocks:

Zack's clothes

Repeated constructions of the "pattern" produces a corresponding "pattern" of repeated addition adults often know as multiplication. Further exploration of patterns of the individual colors/shapes of blocks used is also a discussion of associative and distributive laws of multiplication in the early stages of concept development about multiplication, yet it is not talked about in this way; instead, it is talked about as types of interesting or less interesting patterns.

In this classroom data collection and analysis become a search for patterns in the data. If we change categories for how we think of the data, do the patterns change? Is this what poll takers do? Carrying out our own surveys, we change our categories for people and see what patterns emerge.

The *Problem Solving* strategy for organizing one's classroom is like the Patterns strategy in that it assumes people come to school with a capacity for making meaning that the teacher can take advantage of and use as a context for learning/teaching mathematics; in this case we say that all people are problem solvers. We do not need to teach people how to solve problems, nor do we have to teach specific problem-solving techniques as a topic in our curriculum. Instead we immerse our students in problem-solving situations out of which they become more adept at using mathematics to solve problems. One version of the problem-solving teaching/learning strategy designs the classroom as a series of discussions of word problems. The teacher presents a situation and asks students to share strategies for answering the question; the teacher then encourages and applauds a multitude of different strategies for responding to the same problem. As students share strategies and compare how they are similar and different, they simultaneously "talk" mathematics and teach each other equivalent but variant ways to think about the mathematics involved in the situation posed.

Personally, I find word problems to be drill and practice in disguise. Most word problems in your textbook have been carefully skinned clean of the flesh and blood of real-life problem-solving contexts. Using them will only further emphasize for your students that mathematics is not really related to real life. Instead, these artificial constructions become "puzzles" that challenge the students to put together the pieces in the hope of stumbling onto the right "fit." In the fantasy classroom, we would ban all word problems in favor of some approach that turns them into real-life problem solving. Perhaps students could take real-life situations or classroom needs, and turn them into questions that they pose themselves as something they need to solve. Sometimes, these posed questions will resemble remarkably a type of word problem that we might find, and in order to solve them, the class might entertain variations on the posed question (in other words, a collection of word problems). Yet in this case, the classroom context would be significantly different, since the teacher and the students would have a genuine rather than an artificial purpose in mind for practicing on these problems.

204

As you try to move your classroom toward "genuine" problem solving, you could try two directions: (a) *real* real-life situations, or (b) games in which students make decisions. Constructing real-life situations requires a creative sense of the activities happening in your classroom and your community. Planning for a classroom pet, designing the arrangement of the furniture in the classroom space, planning a party, field trip, or book order, or planning a fund-raising project and then deciding on how to donate the profits to an appropriate charity all involve numerous categories of arithmetic, geometry, data collection, etc., and would resemble "authentic" problem solving in important ways. Steven Levy has had success with students building their own classroom furniture, as well as harvesting their own wheat, turning it into flour, and then marketing their own bread made from the flour in order to pay for next year's wheat to be sowed.[3]

Listening to students and noting particular community problems that they might be invested in is another route. One teacher overheard students complaining about the danger of being hit by a car on the way to school; the class studied the geometry of the intersection, the frequency of cars at certain times of the day, and so on, and made a presentation at a town council meeting in favor of a traffic light instead of a stop sign at the intersection. Another teacher noted that students were concerned with rumors regarding the potentially hazardous rating of the town's drinking water; an investigation led to more detailed information regarding the fluctuations of contaminants over the course of the year, and the effects of the weather on the level of toxic waste in the town's water, leading in turn to a major transformation in the community's water treatment program. Yet another teacher was tired of the students complaining that they were assigned to the hottest, smallest classroom in their school; the class began a study of classroom space per student, and convincingly argued that an exchange of types of desks would mean inequality of space allocation; the district moved the sixth grade into a middle school and rearranged the classrooms in the school. Other teachers have enjoyed watching students apprentice themselves to a local merchant or artisan in the community and report back in weekly after-school visits on the mathematics they have learned.

If you take on authentic problem solving, keep in mind that students need a forum in which to present their findings, or another means to impact in their community. One problematic aspect of this approach, noted by Stieg Mellin-Olsen,[4] is that students *can* inadvertently "learn" that they have *no* political power if they are ignored at a town council meeting or if their carefully researched recommendations are dismissed as cute kids' work. Teachers must prepare students for this possibility in class discussions, or must lobby parents and other community members to support the work of their students in these public fora. Letters home to parents explaining the project in terms of particular mathematics skill objectives can also do wonders in preventive work against doubting parents who are concerned about whether or not their children will be learning the "curriculum," and rally them into active support and participation in such projects. Scanning your district list of math objectives for the year, and checking off those that may potentially be "covered" through such problem-solving projects will pay off in the end and will also help you see how to channel and to cultivate mathematical discourse during the project itself.

Games can be problem-solving activities, too, if you choose and design them well. The important ingredient is student decisions based on the mathematics of the game. A contest to get correct answers will elicit virtually no problem solving and may deter students from thinking about the mathematics in favor of the answers. But a game in which a student's decision affects the outcome will require the student to think about how to make the decision well. A decent arithmetic game is *Cubo*, included in the *Real Math* Sampler of games that use number cubes.[5] Two or more players take turns rolling 4 cubes (two 0-5 cubes, two 5-10 cubes); using any combination of the 4 operations (addition, subtraction, multiplication, and division) on the numbers rolled (use the number on each cube once and only once), the player who can get 21 or closest to it is the winner of the round. Other ways to play the game include: making the goal other than 21; using a different combination of cubes (e.g., using more or fewer cubes; using additional cubes of 0-5 *tens*); choosing a set of numbers (0 to 10, 10 to 20, and so on) and trying to make all the "scores" in the set; having the group collaborate to find more than one combination that gets close to 21, and then reaching consensus on "the most interesting" combination. When students/players think about the combinations in this game, they need to decide how they will do it, how they will think about doing it, etc.; each aspect of strategy can be discussed as well as suggestions about patterns of combinations that are helpful in reaching the target of 21.

A good geometry game that forces students to develop language about properties and parts of shapes is the *Guess My Shape* game. In this one, a teacher or student makes a secret shape on a geoboard. The rest of the group asks yes-or-no questions about the shape, without using any shape names, until they are confident that they can reproduce the same shape on their own geoboard; in the competitive version, if you are "wrong" then you are out of the game until the next round, and the first person to display publicly the shape on his or her geoboard gets to lead the next round. In this game, players must decide which questions to ask in order to get good information about the shape they are figuring out. They also need to decide the point at which they are confident that they have the correct shape. Variations include: a *Battleship*-like approach in which pairs of players make shapes on a geoboard, and take turns asking each other questions—the first person to guess the other's shape wins; a collaborative approach in which at each stage in the questioning, the group tries to display as many shapes as possible that meet the criteria according to the questions answered so far, until only one possible shape is agreed upon by the group as matching the secret shape; and a logic-emphasis version in which the person answering the questions is allowed to lie once in the first five questions (but after five questions must truthfully say whether or not he or she has lied yet), and at most twice in the first ten questions (again being required to say after ten questions how many times he or she has lied).[6]

Unfortunately, most games in teachers' manuals are contests about getting the "right answer" and do not encourage reflection on the concepts or strategies for obtaining answers. So if you choose games you will have to adapt them in order to make them into experiences where students make decisions at key points. Often students themselves can be asked to design a better game with this in mind. The designing experience and subsequent "beta-testing" by class members can be a delightful "authentic problem solving" experience in its own right.

In the genuine problem solving above, students often confront situations in which the questions are not asked for them; they must figure out the questions themselves. Thus authentic problem solving supports the notion of a teaching/learning strategy that emphasizes problem *posing*; students develop ways to pose their own questions, and evaluate them for usefulness, interest, or elegance, among other criteria. In *Problem Posing* the students pose their own questions, out of which they learn mathematics—that is, out of which they continue to ask better and better questions. Again, this is a strategy thst takes advantage of what students bring with them to school: curiosity. Assuming that students have questions, the teacher wants to hear what they are. Experiences posing and then considering questions with the aim of identifying "better" or "more interesting" questions over time help students become highly skilled posers of problems. For example, Marion Walter once asked students, "What problems can you think of when faced with 2/3 + 1/5 ?" Usually when given such questions, students have either learned an algorithm for finding an "answer" or they make mistakes in performing some arithmetic manipulation of symbols. They are, in Walter's words, "usually not asked to think." Yet students Walter worked with suggested in response, "When in real life would you ever have to add these two fractions?" and "How many different ways can you add these?" Other questions include: "Which is bigger 2/3 or 1/5?" "Is the answer less or more than 1?" "By how much does 2/3 differ from 1?" "By how much does 1/5 differ from 1?" "What must be added to 2/3 + 1/5 to obtain a total of 1?"[7]

A "trick" for beginning problem-posing teachers developed by Stephen Brown and Marion Walter is the "what-if-not" technique:[8] You take something that you have been discussing and ask "what-if-not" about some aspect of it. In the above situation, Marion Walter noted that she could get the answer 2/15 by multiplying the numerators and denominators of 2/3 and 1/5. She had chosen 2/3 and 1/5 at random ... and was "lucky" ... This led her to say, what if we did NOT use the "right method" of adding fractions—what other fractions could one start with so that one could find the right answer by this "wrong" method? Another suggestion from Walter is, instead of learning how to construct a regular hexagon with straight edge and compass, ask, what if we constructed it some other way? Can we do it from a paper circle? from a rectangle? from a scrap of paper? from an equilateral triangle? Finally, Brown and Walter's famous what-if-not example[9] involves the picture version of the Pythagorean theorem. Faced with a picture of a right triangle with squares made

out of the sides, they ask, what if the shapes were not squares,

but semi-circles? what could you say about the area then? What if the shapes were equilateral triangles? Thus is the beginning of a powerful investigation

Problem Posing can be a successful change-of-pace oasis from other pedagogical styles. Consider scheduling a weekly "Math Talk" on Thursday or Friday afternoons.[10] One student poses a question that is interesting to explore but that is usually not asked in school. During the first few "Math Talks" the teacher helps the group learn how to interact with each other during a discussion led by a peer in which the few rules include "you are not allowed to raise your hand," "you may not interrupt anyone," and "you can disagree but you may not insult a person or make fun of an idea." Questions that typically come up in early grades often sound like: Where did numbers come from in the first place? What's bigger than infinity? Why are buildings made out of rectangles if triangles are the most rigid shape? Classrooms that encourage what-if-not questions will have to help the group save their variations on the original questions for later talks so that the one currently under consideration is not overlooked; even so, a group may reach a consensus that a refined or alternative question is a better one to pursue at the moment if the facilitating student accepts such a conversational direction. Videotaping or audiotaping the math talks can be both an assessment gold mine for the teacher and an enjoyable opportunity for students to review the discussion during free time in an area of the classroom. (Don't forget headphones if you think the sound will disturb other simultaneous projects!)

STRATEGIES FOR ASSESSMENT

Interview students test/obstacle course

Observe students working/record anecdotal evidence

Performance Tasks/rubric scoring

Journals/other Writing about mathematics

Student Self-Assessment (with or without peer assessment) Portfolios

Based on what you think it means to do mathematics in your classroom, you end up needing to reflect on how you will decide whether or not you are happy with how things are going, whether or not you think you need to change your teaching/learning strategy or improve on your enactment of a particular teaching/learning strategy, and what you think you ought to do next. In other words, you will perform a type of *assessment* through which you can reconsider your contentment with the teaching/learning that is happening in your classroom. If you believe in the *Train/Show/Drill/Coach/Practice* technique, then you will likely opt for a test to see if your students can get the correct answers frequently enough, thus displaying their ability to use the algorithms you have taught them to produce accurate results in the proper situations. But if you are focusing on the development of conceptual knowledge, a test will give you no more information than the symbols Nkendra wrote on the board: you will have little understanding of how the students are thinking about the mathematics. A desire to know more about students' thinking process suggests to teachers that they need to have students talk, write, or otherwise communicate *with* or *about* the mathematics. Consider interviewing students about a mathematical question. Here you would gain valuable insight into techniques by watching a lot of television talk

209

shows, and listening to a range of radio talk programs. Which questions generate detailed responses in the person being interviewed? Do you like Barbara Walters or Ricki Lake? Why? The point of an interview is to find out as much as possible about how the student(s) are constructing conceptual knowledge for themselves, and how they are connecting procedures for obtaining answers, and factual mathematics knowledge, through these concepts. Videotaping interviews can be helpful as you refine your interviewing skills. Tapes of interviews are often interesting to the students and they might be offered a chance to view them during a free-time period during the following week. Some teachers interview one student for about five to ten minutes every day, and in this manner get through their whole class a few times every year. Others interview in groups of three and observe the way the group members interact as they discuss the mathematics. Good questions to start things going after introducing an initial problem or mathematical situation include: How might you explain how you got your answer to your classmates if they had been absent from school last week? What if they didn't understand, could you explain it a different way? How might you teach this to someone in the grade before ours? What questions does this raise for you? Ask some what-if-not questions. Can you find a more interesting way to talk about this? In a group interview: What do your strategies have in common? How are they different? What do you think of that? Tell me more!

Teachers who use a fair amount of collaborative group work or manipulative materials find they can gather a great deal of anecdotal information simply by observing students as they walk around the room. Some like to carry a clipboard; others have an index card for each student, and jot down a few comments on five cards per day or week, collecting information on the whole class over a period of time. You might choose to focus on the strategies you identify students using on their own, the sorts of language choice they use in mathematical conversations with their peers, how well they work together in groups, which peer explanations seem to be more successful than the teacher's, or simply whether the students appear to be enjoying mathematics in school. Jean Moon and Linda Shulman note that documentation systems of this kind enable you to develop a picture of a student's work that is descriptive rather than normed (as in traditional tests); they point out that observational documentations translate the more complex assessment tasks you are doing in the classroom into data that can be used to report student growth over time, and that the development of a system for doing this will facilitate the gathering of information from tasks that are more open-ended and do not have a clearly defined objective.[11] Moon and Shulman suggest a "Problem Solving Record Sheet" for each student observed. The teacher records the activity, date, and descriptive information on the following: (1) Demonstration of confidence in the process of solving problems (volunteering, being enthusiastic with purpose, and communicating with others—talking to another group member about the mathematics, or talking and listening to the teacher); (2) Illustration, description, and modeling of a variety of problems (using objects, illustrating with graphs, drawing with pictures, and repeating the problem in his/her own words); (3) Verifying, interpreting, and justifying solutions strategies (explaining the problem solving process, seeing relationships between problem types and solution strategies, and checking the reasonableness of solutions in appropriate mathematical units); and (4) Constructing problems from everyday life with a variety of mathematics concepts (forming a mathematics problem and thinking about it, telling in his/her own words, forming a mathematics problem in a story, writing to others through illustrating with pictures, graphs and charts, and understanding how a problem can be solved or understanding the solutions strategy). Future instructional choices would respond to your observations. Additionally, you will collect a range of information to share with parents at conference times or as a supplement to periodic report cards.

Interviews and observational records expand our repertoire for reflecting on how our teaching/learning strategies are meeting our goals while documenting students' progress over time. Yet they are often criticized for drowning assessment in description to the detriment of careful evaluation of our pedagogical work. Sometimes it feels good to be able to register progress on a scale. In fact, many people will demand some sort of measurement of success from you; you may find that a version of quantitative evaluation might be a necessary component of your assessment process. One compromise teachers have comfortably adopted, and in many cases found efficacious, is the use of rubric scoring for open-ended performance tasks. A rubric scoring documentation system will help you maintain a holistic assessment approach as you assign a rating to indicate the level at which a student product meets predetermined performance standards, translate the more complex assessment tasks you are doing in your classroom into numerical data that can be used to report student growth over time, and manage information gathered from open-ended tasks.[12] Moon and Shulman suggest that an easy way to begin using holistic scoring is to sort papers into three piles: the papers that show the student understands and can communicate the mathematical reasoning involved; the papers that show a moderate understanding and ability to communicate; and those that appear inadequate in important ways. Then you could assign papers a 3, 2, or 1 rating respectively. If a large clump of papers ends up in the middle pile, you could sort that pile into two separate piles and assign ratings of 4, 3, 2, and 1. Or, you could extend the sorting of each of the three piles into two piles and assign numbers from 6 to 1. Once you do this, you should look over the papers in each category and try to identify what distinguishes each pile from the ones above and below, so that you could state a description of the difference in performance in terms of your performance standards or in terms of the conceptual, procedural, or factual goals of the mathematical activity. After a few times through this process, try planning a scoring rubric *before* the papers are sorted. Think of six categories in terms of the task and the expectations you have for your students: rewrite *these* general category descriptions (taken from the California Assessment Program[13]) in terms of the task: 6) Fully achieves the purpose of the task, while insightfully interpreting, extending beyond the task, or raising provocative questions; 5) Accomplishes the purpose of the task; 4) Substantially completes the purposes of the task; 3) Does not fully achieve the purposes of the task; needs elaboration; some strategies may be ineffectual or not appropriate; assumptions about the purposes may be flawed; 2) Important purposes of the task have not been achieved; work may need redirection; the approach may lead away from completion; 1) Purposes of the task not accomplished. Rubrics are best developed by a team of teachers; looking at students' papers together and talking about them in relation to each other can help you establish scoring criteria, and brings multiple perspectives to the scoring dilemmas as you develop relationships with other professionals. Clashing differences in cultural, racial and ethnic backgrounds challenge your ideas and force you to clarify your own thinking about mathematics and its potentialities. Once you get comfortable with rubric scoring or student papers you can consider moving on to rubrics for observation of students working on group tasks in class. Videotape students for a performance-based assessment portfolio.

Suppose, however, that you are looking for ways to assess your students' development in mathematics as an evolving literacy (reading, writing, listening and speaking mathematically), not in process as in an interview or group classwork, but after ideas have been thought through. You may wish to adopt techniques of writers' workshop approaches from language arts. Journal writing, for example, can be a superb vehicle for students to develop articulate mathematical concepts, and then, via various structures of peer and teacher feedback, to rewrite their journal entries in more public formats. Students enjoy publishing mathematical writing despite the complications of reproducing equations and diagrams on school computers. In the early eighties, Brown and Walter[14] suggested having groups of three to five students form editorial boards for mathematics journals. The board decides on a type of submission to advertise for (e.g., interesting descriptions of a solution to a problem, personal reflections on problem solving experiences, fiction, entertaining math puzzles or tricks, discussions of math in everyday life); students review the ads and create a submission. Editorial boards provide feedback to authors on how to improve their writing for the particular journal before accepting submissions for publication. Many teachers find open-ended structures for personal reflections to be useful as well.

Student analyses of classroom activity are interesting in the form of daily "Media Reports." Before a mathematical experience, choose several students to be the "media," or ask for volunteers. These students observe the class as roving reporters. Later that day, the media perform a television news program or publish a newspaper about the mathematics: news items, fashion reports, critiques of the class as if it were a film or music video, gossip columns, or satires are thanked for insightful or provocative commentary on the day's events.

The last two strategies for assessment allow even greater student input into the assessment process. For a portfolio, students should select items of their work that provide evidence of their growth in mathematics over a certain period. Journal entries, mathematical autobiographies, letters, or E-mail to the teacher or to mathematicians at universities, and reflective pieces are examples of written materials that are easily placed in a portfolio. But you will also want to stretch students to include items such as non-routine problems, revisions, and peer assessments.[15] A non-routine problem is a question made up by the student that demonstrates an understanding of the mathematics needed to solve the problem, or a significant effort toward solving the problem. Revisions include drafts of mathematics writing, work-in-progress, and final versions of work on complex questions; diagrams, graphs and charts, etc., should be included. Projects extend over a period of days or weeks, and tend to be most pedagogically effective when they result in a formal presentation or exhibition of the material in group or individual formats; feedback on the quality of presentation as entertainment and education for the classroom community is as crucial as feedback on the mathematics content. Peer assessment involves impressions from class members on a student's work, in relation to performance standards that have been established, or in terms of the student's contributions to others' learning. Encourage students officially with special forms, or informally, to obtain peer feedback on items chosen for their portfolios before they finalize the collection of sample work. Consider requiring an orientation guide to the portfolio, so that readers/viewers will be able to understand how to interpret the content. I also recommend that students be asked to write a conclusion that includes a brief statement regarding what they think is most important about the mathematics in the portfolio, their current questions, and tentative plans for how they expect to pursue these questions.

The form of portfolio conclusion I suggest is an example of a personal self-assessment. The best teachers guide students into processes of reflection on portfolios. For peer-feedback forms, or in conferences as students are assembling a portfolio over time, ask students why they selected a particular item, what they learned in doing a particular mathematics task that they did not know before, how their ideas changed as they revised a piece of writing, what parts of an activity they think they need practice on, as well as what skills they would like to feel more secure about. Once students begin to internalize these types of prompts, you may decide to stop using them or to introduce others. Another strategy, suggested by Moon and Shulman,[16] is to discuss a sample of student work from another class or school. You can ask your class why they think the student chose this item, and so on. When you begin to encourage such student reflection, however, keep in mind that your students may have never done this before, and are likely to have been "taught" not to trust their own opinions about their work, or to view a desire to improve as a symbol of failure; many students have been schooled into the notion that the teacher is the only legitimate judge of quality. It may take time before students adapt. In the meantime, collections of student work are readily admired by family members.

Students should persue other forms of student self-assessment as well. Search for ways to include student input into the design of the mathematics curriculum. A suggestion box can be a simple way to collect good ideas or complaints: Bring them back to the class for discussion. Student tallies of your interactions by gender or other criteria can help you achieve equity goals. Surveys can elicit feedback on particular issues. Keith Grove, a teacher in the Boston area, gives students a list of generalized evaluation criteria; the class then develops specific criteria that can be used for both self–assessment of work-in-progress and grading of final versions.[17]

Keith Grove's List of Criteria

Math:
Did you understand the question/problem/activity?
Did you express yourself clearly?
Did you summarize all that you learned about the question/problem/activity?
Did you answer all the questions?

Did you think about the question/problem/activity beyond what was asked?

Were you creative in your approach?

Presentation

Do you have an introduction that states what the paper is about?

Did you organize your paper into paragraphs?

Did you illustrate the paper adequately?

Did you avoid repeating yourself?

Is the paper neat and legible? Is it beautiful?

Were you creative in your presentation?

Note that most strategies of assessment are simultaneously a form of classroom activity and thus constitute a significant decision in teaching/learning strategy. Interviews, portfolio construction, observation of group problem solving, media presentations, and so on, require that the day-to-day allocation of time be appropriate. In most cases, what this means is that your teaching is at once both a form of assessment and instruction. Indeed this is the most efficient use of classroom time. A teaching/learning choice demands certain styles of assessment even as a particular assessment decision constitutes an implicit decision about what it means to be "doing mathematics" in your classroom. Susan Ohanian recently summarized the foundation of those classrooms she admired the most to be found in ten similar questions asked by the teachers in these classrooms:[18]

Fig. 12-B

Susan Ohanian's Ten Foundational Questions

1. Do my students see themselves as good mathematicians?
2. Do my students see mathematics as covering a wide range of topics?
3. Are my students developing a flexible repertoire of problem-solving strategies?
4. Are my students able to communicate their problem-solving strategies to others? Can they talk and write about how they solve math problems?
5. Are my students able to assess themselves? Are they able to develop and use criteria to evaluate their performance?
6. Do my students engage in mathematical thinking without a specific assignment? For example, if they have "free time," do they choose math?
7. Are my students developing the attitudes of independent and self-motivated thinkers and problem solvers?
8. Do my students welcome challenges in math? Are they able to focus

on math problems of increasing complexity for longer periods of time?

9. Do my students recognize the importance of math in the real world outside school?

10. Do my students use mathematics to solve problems outside math class?

CONNECTING TO OTHER SUBJECTS

Figure 13 highlights three approaches to connecting mathematics with other subjects.

Strategies for connecting math to other subjects

Start with a mathematical topic or project. Look for ways to extend subject areas by:

- applying the math to something in that subject
- using the math concept to thnk about that subject
- using something in that subject to illustrate the idea behind the math
- concept before learning the math concept

Start with a topic in another subject. Look for ways to link that subject with every possible math curriculum strand:

- measurement
- fractions and decimals
- geometry—two-dimensional
- geometry—three-dimensional
- probability
- data collection and analysis
- algebra: the notions of function and variable

Use a thematic/integrated approach to begin with.

- For every project, activity or investigation, identify the potencial to cover a conceptual, procedural, and factual goal in each of the curriculum strands.
- Scan your district or school curriculum goals for your grade or area in mathematics for objectives you need to integrate into this unit in order to make sure they are adequately explored this year.
- Use knowledge students BRING to school. School math is not naturally unrelated to the Math of Everyday Life!
- Use open-ended projects; periodically assess what curriculum objectives have been met.

For any of the three approaches, I find a thematic unit plan most effective in helping me structure the connections. My favorite version of thematic unit planning is elaborated in Baker, Stemple, and Stead's *How Big Is the Moon*[19]. We'll talk about planning a five-week unit. It is possible to adapt this as well to a one-week (five-day) unit in some contexts.

The idea is to think of the first week as introducing the theme. The second, third and fourth weeks together form the "middle" of the unit, during which two major things happen: (1) students work on individual and/or group projects; and (2) clinics are scheduled for direct instruction on specific topics or skills. The conclusion of the unit happens during the fifth week, which serves as a celebration of the knowledge gained through the previous four weeks; this last week is spent on applications of that knowledge to smaller project activities, puzzles, games, and other consolidation experiences.

Week One: Introduction

You need to plan the first day: how you will introduce the unit theme. Find an open-ended activity that can raise issues and questions and at the same time can serve as an assessment tool for you. After the activity ask the students: What do we know about this theme? What do we want to know? What do we need to learn in order to find out what we want to know? (Yes, this is a K-W-L activity). Break the students into groups to work on finding out those things they have identified as need-to-know; they find out and teach the class in an entertaining way for the last couple of days of the week.

What else do you need to plan? Think about equipment students might need for their initial investigations this week. Plan books for the classroom library. Arrange for permission and access to whatever is necessary (e.g., the library, and phone, a computer connection to the internet). Arrange for visitors you want to come in this week.

Weeks Two, Three, Four: Individual and Group Projects

You can't plan much for what the students will actually do this week, because it is up to them to think of a project . You will be conferencing with them as they come up with a topic or goal, do their research, and put together some sort of presentation or exhibit. What you CAN do is brainstorm potential projects students MIGHT choose for this unit: Based on their interests, what do you imagine they might think of? Might you suggest alternatives or gently steer them in a direction that would be more fruitful?

Brainstorming Projects: Use this planning time to help you think about how the unit will work for the curriculum. For each project you think of, list conceptual, procedural, and factual knowledge goals that the project can serve; think of connections across the curriculum for each project. Do this within the subject area or across subject areas as appropriate. Look through your district curriculum guide or textbook to find particular objectives that you can claim are being covered by this unit. Doing so will help you ensure you actually follow the curriculum. It will also help you think of possible clinics.

Brainstorming Potential Clinics: During these three weeks you should offer clinics of direct instruction as needed. One idea is to tape large sheets of newsprint on the wall. When you see a need for people to learn or practice a skill or concept, announce that you will offer a clinic if at least five people sign up. Having a minimum number lets people be good sports and sign up for help even though they don't want to admit they need it. They do it as a favor for someone else. Leave blank sheets for students to suggest their own clinic topics. As people sign up, THEN you can plan those lessons. For now, think about what lessons you might plan based on what you think about the unit and the possible topics it will raise. During the unit, you may want to announce that everyone should attend a clinic session because you want all students to practice something . . .

Materials Needed: Here, too, you'll want to prepare materials you think students might need, such as equipment, etc. Arrange for professionals (e.g., architects, bakers, masons, ad execs) to be called during this month. Think of permissions that will be needed, and so on.

During the first week of this middle part (week 2): students spend the week finding a project to pursue, starting it and rethinking it, until they are pretty sure that they have found a doable, reasonable project to research for the next week. You conference with individuals and groups as they plan. You decide how to organize the way people suggest projects to each other and form groups. You might offer a couple of clinics.

During the second week of this middle part (week 3): Students pursue their projects. You offer clinics. You plan possible informal assessments based on the goals you have for the unit.

The third week of this middle section (week 4): Students put together a presentation for the class or for the community. You plan how to organize the discussion so that students will care about each others' projects, and identify the connections across the projects.

Week Five: Archaeology of What Has Been Learned

Sometimes teachers love it when students are learning and they don't even know it. I think it is important for students to recognize that they HAVE indeed learned something, and that it can be called mathematics or science, or art, or something. This last week is a celebration of what has been learned, an archaeology of the unit activities to identify and to consolidate what has been learned. You plan projects, puzzles, and games that enable students to apply what has been learned through the thematic projects in the context of particular subject-specific activities. For example, a math game or puzzle is explored and analyzed, or an artist's work is studied in terms of the history and concepts of the unit. A report on a particular community issue could be prepared and presented to a town council meeting. This part of the unit is easy to plan: collect enjoyable games, puzzles, and activity ideas from teacher resource books or off the internet. Look for high quality performance assessment activities that might serve you in planning for the next unit or future topics that you can see students still need to work on.

Integrated Units

Ideally, the theme allows for integration across curriculum strands or subject areas. You want to find a fairly general topic to pursue. The approaches in figure 14 suggest various possibilities.

RELATIONS AMONG ASSESSMENT, REFLECTION, EVALUATION

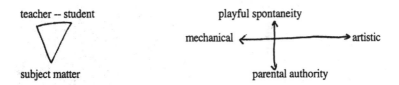

Now as you consider one of the above strategies, recalling Peter Elbow's notion that teaching is the "embracement of contraries" (that efforts to move in one direction with one strategy are likely to result in less efficacious movements in other areas), I want to suggest that it is helpful in making these decisions to think about their ramifications and implications in two areas: first, you need to examine how your decisions enact particular relationships among assessment, reflection, and evaluation; and second, the position of the learners vis-à-vis the subject matter is affected. Let's begin with a discussion of the relationship among assessment, reflection, and evaluation. What is your image of yourself as a

Figure 14

Five-Week Thematic Unit Plan

1	2	3	4	5
Introduction	*Individual*	*and Group*	*Projects*	*Archaeology*
	Formulation of Project	Data Collection & Research	Presentation / Exhibition	Subject for Subject's Sake
Introductory open-ended activity K-W-L for initial week	Potential Project Ideas: Brainstorm ahead of time. Identify Conceptual, Procedural, and factual knowledge goals	Assessment Strategies: journal, conference forms, peer feedback	Format of Discussion: connections across projects	Celebration of content learned through unit::
		Potential Clinic Topics: Use district curr guide or textbook to determine possible lessons		Collection of Activities: Projects, Puzzles, Games
Material Needed: books, equipment, phone, visitors, trip forms, etc.	Materials Needed: books, equipment, phone, visitors, trip forms, etc.			

teacher? Is your reflection on your work primarily in terms of a critique of yourself, or do you dwell instead on your students' abilities to figure out what you want from them? Are you mainly a facilitator of their learning and thus do you need to reflect on how you must transform your own identity to perform your best work for the students, or are you primarily a judge or patriarchal parent who studies students from above and manipulates them and the material to maximize the attainment of objectives? Would you prefer to think of yourself as a hostess at a dinner party, who invites people to enjoy themselves, prepares delicious things to consume (perhaps keeping in mind the guests' preferences, expectations, allergies, etc.), and facilitates conversations toward the goal of creating personal relationships among her guests? Or perhaps a midwife, who confronts not only the joy of creation but the pain and fear that must accompany it; and how the act of creation transforms the creator and requires an assumption of new responsibilities? The technical training and social communication skills are different for each image. Someone hoping to become good at one or the other of these roles would pursue varied paths of preparation. Yet a midwife might be an excellent hostess in another context of her life, and vice versa. At times, she may feed information and at other times she may coach individuals in the creation of their own knowledge. Joseph Fischer and Anne Kiefer have created categories of teacher images based on case study interviews;[20] I find them helpful in examining the power relationships among myself and my students, and thus useful in forming the decisions that I make regarding reflection, assessment and evaluation.

Fischer and Kiefer's first collection of images clarifies the teacher's place in the classroom. These images are helpful in analyzing your beliefs about the triangle of relationships among the teacher, student, and subject matter. The teacher who views himself as an "interpreter" understands teaching as fundamentally an act of interpretation. To act well is to interpret a situation demanding action and to interpret a correct strategy for that action; to be experienced is to have become a good interpreter. A teacher who sees herself as a "presence" has a clear and vivid focus about what she does, and seems to have a comfortable sense of her own personality, point of view, and style. Having sifted through the multitude of potential images that they might hold for themselves, teachers who are "presences" in the room are unique and enjoy taking advantage of their own idiosyncratic background and life experiences in exerting their character on the life of the classroom. Many teachers, however, identify a major reason for becoming a teacher in their desire to share knowledge, and to pass on to a new generation the joys of learning. Such scholars or experts may be broadly classified as "elders"; as mentors or models, elders have experienced the traditions, treasure the continuities of life, are aware of life changes over time and the cultural values they hold dear, and impart not only accumulated knowledge but a moral dimension of life as well.

Other images identified by Fischer and Kiefer can help you examine your relationship with your students, especially in light of the power dynamics, authority constructed, and the relationship between evaluation and assessment of students. In these images, the subject matter is a mediating factor in the ongoing development of teacher-student interactions. The teacher as "child" likes to work with children, feels young because they do, enjoys the sense of wonder that children possess, and experiences a sense of adventure along with the students—he is in awe of his own teaching. The teacher as "advocate" was always disappointed with his own teachers and enacts a mission to be the teacher that children deserve; this teacher helps children to resist the pressures of insensitive adults or other children, exerting extra effort to see that the rights of children are protected, and that children's feelings are respected—she affirms children. The teacher as "therapist" provides emotional support for his students. This teacher understands that children cannot learn until important emotional and social problems have been dealt with; he also seeks to appreciate the ways that students elicit emotions from the teacher to better understand his own feelings toward his students. The teacher as "parent" may be nurturing, caring, giving, and guiding, or controlling, dominating, abandoning, rejecting or abusing. The teacher as "animator" sees motivation as intrinsic, originating within the students; the teacher, a catalyst, activates the potential for growth and then watches it happen, or takes the students' ideas and makes things happen as a drama unfolds. The teacher as "companion" sees the classroom as mutually benefiting both teacher and student. Like the teacher-child, the companion shares mathematics with the students, and together they learn as they share views of the mathematics discussed. Finally, the teacher as "storyteller" provides a story *about* the mathematics—the actual content of the units or lessons is filler for a conceptual message about mathematics itself, what it is, does, and creates as a character in the "story of life."[21]

> Another set of teacher images, discussed by Sara Efron and Pamela Bolotin Joseph,[22] further illustrates the nature of the teacher-student relationship, and the structure more or less needed for classroom management. Efron and Joseph identify two continua: one stretches between the artistic and mechanical teacher; the other

ranges from the teacher authority wielded by the "parent" image, with the adult as the all-knower and the student as a child needing adult guidance and control, and the playfulness, spontaneity and excitement of working with young people. "Artistic" teachers include the "light breeze" (touching the student, maybe bending a little bit this way or that—sometimes it's a warm breeze when it's cool outside, sometimes it's a cool and refreshing breeze when the students are excited), the "director of a play," the "actor," the "orchestra conductor," the "juggler," and the "gardener." The artistic teacher generates movement, excitement, and sensitivity. She touches the students but does not shape or transform them. Contrasting images stress the teacher as forcefully molding and shaping students to allow the students' talents to reveal themselves: the "potter," for example, has a stronger sense of her own power.

Some teachers see themselves as an "engine" (everything is well taken care of, everything works the way it is supposed to work, there is a set rhythm and reason to why things work the way they do). Others see themselves as a "manager" or "leader." The "dentist" teacher (tell them to brush brush brush, try to fill in the cavities . . .) also sees the student as a well-cared-for machine and her role as caring for and maintaining the machine. These teachers emphasize the authority end of the second continuum. They might be contrasted with the teacher who sees herself as a "learner" (my students know I don't know everything—I'm proud of it), "guide," "mother," or "helper." The teacher who describes herself as an "iron butterfly"—strong but with the sensitivity to flit from flower to flower and draw out what is needed in it, yet very organized and structured and strong—is grappling with the tensions along the continuum. Likewise, the potter is not so much an "artistic" metaphor as a figure of strength and guidance.

One way to use the teacher images is to examine your own classroom and teaching within the context of each one. Instead of picking the one that sounds best to you ideally, use every metaphor to describe your own teaching. This can help you think about how your future decisions will differ from your past decisions. Particular attention to the power dynamic between yourself and your students will very possibly challenge you to be more consonant with your ideals and your vision of yourself as a teacher. Consider also trying to look at yourself from the perspective of your students: Would they use a different image than you? Why? What student actions force you unwillingly to slip into a different mode of behavior and change from one image to another without warning? For each image, identify for yourself what that teacher image suggests for reflection on your own work, assessment of your curriculum and pedagogy, and of your students, and for evaluation of students.

POSITIONS VIS-`A-VIS THE SUBJECT MATTER

Students as Mathematicians—(does what mathematicians does)

Students as Citizen-Mathematicians—(can make informed decisions about math in newspaper, on TV, knows about the math of the lottery and gambling, uses math in empowering ways to participate in the "community")

Students as Objects of Mathematics—(manipulated and interpreted through mathematics, student becomes the paramecium under the microscope, studies the hidden math in everyday life like scantrons and price-fixing)

As you examine the images that provide the most satisfaction in understanding the relationships among you, the students, and the subject matter, you will also begin to reflect on the particular relationship between the students and the subject matter in terms, once more, of what it means to "do" mathematics in your classroom. Matthew Weinstein is especially helpful in his characterization of three potential positions that a student might be expected to take with respect to the mathematics knowledge.[23] A common image of the student is the "mini-mathematician." In this position toward mathematics, students do what mathematicians do: They explore abstractions and occasionally apply them to contexts in which they attempt to use mathematical relationships to model something found in the world. Students are like apprentice mathematicians; as they develop, they become more and more like professional mathematicians in the way they think, act, and perceive the world. One example of this approach to teaching is found in the Van Hiele levels paradigm for development in geometry;[24] students are analyzed in terms of what level they are at in geometric thinking and communication, ranging from shape name identification to the ability to make conjectures about abstract contingencies on multiple geometries. A critic might skeptically cry out that all forms of geometry are appropriate but in particular contexts—for example, we would not shout Euclidean axioms in a floor tile store, or even ask for samples of tiles in terms of angles and sides of shapes, yet we may want to discuss parts of shapes and compare commonalities across shapes if we were architects or

CAD designers. Despite such potential criticism, however, the mathematician-in-waiting is a popular approach which emphasizes the creativity of the student and the potential of every student to become an out-of-work Ph.D. in math. More positive interpretations of this approach see the student as a genuine creator of knowledge, and therefore honestly understanding it and using it, and bearing responsibility for its use in society.[25]

A second position for the student vis-à-vis the subject matter is that of the "citizen-mathematician." Here the student is understood as needing to become a member of a democratic society in which mathematical forms of communication and rhetoric have a major role. A community member needs to be able to read the newspaper, or to decide how to vote on the local school millage issue. A person should be able to make an informed contribution to discussions about the placement of a toxic waste dump in a nearby town, and therefore needs to be able to comprehend the implications of the units and measurements of predicted radiation seepage and so on. Being a competent consumer and a prepared worker requires certain levels of numeracy and mathematical reasoning ability. A critical perspective on society would demand even more strongly that students be cognizant of the increasing "invisibility" of mathematics as the rapid technologicization of society "demathematizes" our actions to the point of noncomprehension, as in scantrons at the supermarket, credit-line databases, and worker-proofed workplace environments (e.g., McDonald's cash registers). Students developing this relationship with mathematics might interrogate the rhetoric of military requests for modernization of its weapons, or the recent healthcare and insurance debates in the United States.[26]

A third position that students might take, and this is the one that has been most seriously ignored in schools and thus the one that we must desperately work towards cultivating, helps the students to take on a position as "object" of the mathematics. Weinstein suggests science lab reports from the perspective of the bacterium under the microscope. We should do no less in mathematics: Students should be learning about and thinking about the ways in which they are turned into objects of study through and by mathematics, examining issues that range from the quantitative categorization of themselves with innumerable tests of IQ, California Achievement test performance, state standards mandated tests, and teacher-designed quantifications, to social security numbers and market-researchers' databases on regionalized and economic class-based scales. Action figures marketing campaigns and *American Girl Magazine* ploys to perpetuate a consumer-based identity, and the town's decisions about allocation of funds to various grade levels of the schools, or across enrichment options such as arts, sports, and intercollegiate academic contests, share a rhetoric of persuasion couched in mathematical jargon and mathematized notions of logical sequence or proof. Architectural spaces—homes, schools, religious facilities, street designs and green areas—as well as measurement of time across the day or week enculturate the student as an object of mathematical concepts and techniques, and might form the basis of a wide range of explorations and projects.

TEACHING/LEARNING MATHEMATICS IN SCHOOL

Teaching school mathematics is a joyous responsibility. Every action becomes the result of an explicit or implicit decision regarding your own personal negotiation among reflection, assessment, and evaluation, and the politics of education that you create in the positioning of learners (students and/or teacher) relative to the discipline of mathematics. Nevertheless, another layer of complication—perhaps the most paramount—remains: as Maxine Greene once said, unlike an artist, scholar, or scientist, a teacher cannot withdraw to a studio or laboratory and still remain a practitioner.[27] You work with students, colleagues, school board members, parents, and others, whenever and wherever you pursue your fundamental project. In fact you do not work alone. Indeed, you cannot and certainly should not avoid or ignore what is going on beyond your classroom doors, "the great social structures."

> There is always a sense in which [you] must mediate between those structures and the young people [you hope] to liberate for reflection and choice. [You] must initiate them in certain patterns of thinking and acting; [you] must enable them to recognize and choose among the options presented to them. [You] must sensitize them to inhumanity, vulgarity, and hypocrisy; [you] must help them seek equivalents for violence and for war. And, at some level, [you] must enable them to comprehend their society's professed ideals: freedom, equality, regard for the individual. These are all fundamental to the democratic credo; they distinguish and dignify the democratic way of life. But they are norms, conceptions of what ought to be; and they must be created anew with each generation, by each person choosing to live a principled or norm-regarding life, if they are to become viable ideals that summon human beings to moral action in the world they know.[28]

As Greene wrote, "The teacher's responsibilities become more and more complex; and [s/he] is required every day to reinterpret, to make his [or her] own sense of modern life."[29] It is only in the way you imagine such an interpretive response in terms of the decisions you make that you can begin to embark on the project of teaching mathematics. I cannot tell you which strategies work better than others, and in fact no one strategy *is* better than any other in meeting the vision that Maxine Greene sets before us. I have come to believe that any particular teacher might use any combination. What distinguishes the "good" teacher from the "stupendous" teacher is that the stupendous teacher is able to articulate in terms of her or his immediate conception of a democratic classroom life *how* the strategies she or he has chosen fit together as part of the larger life project of becoming a teacher. Where one hopes to be, as an ideal, in two years, five years, is the direction of movement and change for the moment. Strategies today may work to help you make decisions next year that you never imagined possible. The crucial component is that you raise the questions for yourself, that you determine a working sense of how you want to *choose*, and in doing so, become—for that moment—a teacher of mathematics.

NOTES

1. I would like to thank Rochelle G. Kaplan, Mildred Dougherty, and Marjorie Goldstein for their careful critiques of an earlier draft of this paper.
2. A good example is *The Doorbell Rang*, by Pat Hutchins (NY: Mulberry, 1986). A reading of this story about more and more people arriving and sharing cookies is also a potential discussion of a number pattern joke: the pattern looks like skip counting by two's, but turns out to be factors of twelve. Extensions into other possible numbers of cookies and patterns jokes based on them lead into a host of arithmetic and number fact topics.
3. Levy, Steven, *Starting From Scratch*. Portsmouth, NH: Heinemann, 1996.
4. Mellin-Olsen, Stieg. *The Politics of Mathematics Education*. Dordrecht, Holland: D. Reidel, 1987.
5. Willoughby, Stephen, Carl Bereiter, Peter Hilton, and Joseph Rubinstein. *Open Court Real Math*. Chicago: Open Court Publishing Company, 1981.
6. The format of this game is based on Fred Goodman's version of "Twenty Questions."
7. Walter, Marion. *Curriculum Topics Through Problem Posing, in Talking Mathematics: Supporting Children's Voices*. Rebecca Corwin, ed., with

Judith Storeygard and Sabra Price. Portsmouth, NH: Heinemann, 1996. 141–47.

8. Brown, Stephen I., and Marion Walter. *The Art of Problem Posing*. Philadelphia: The Franklin Institute Press, 1983. Brown & Walter, eds. *Problem Posing: Reflections and Applications*. Hillsdale, NJ: Erlbaum, 1993.

9. Brown & Walter, *The Art of Problem Posing*.

10. This idea is adapted from a marvelous book, *Talking Their Way Into Science*, by Karen Gallas, NY: Teachers College Press, 1994. Gallas uses "Science Talks;" we could certainly try Math Talks! On a related note, National Public Radio's Talk of the Nation is Science Friday on every Friday, and many weeks features a mathematics topic; this is a nice adult-oriented discussion on interesting topics that you would enjoy on your drive home from work.

11. Moon, Jean, and Linda Shulman. *Finding the Connections: Linking Assessment, Instruction, and Curriculum in Elementary Mathematics*. Portsmouth, NH: Heinemann, 1995.

12. Moon and Shulman: 56.

13. And reproduced in the Moon and Shulman book: 57.

14. *The Art of Problem Posing*.

15. Moon and Shulman: 99.

16. Moon and Shulman: 102.

17. See also Wah, Anita, and Grove, Keith. *Algebra: Themes, Concepts, Tools*. Creative Publications.

18. Ohanian, Susan. *Garbage Pizza, Patchwork Quilts, and Math Magic: Stories about Teachers Who Love to Teach and Children Who Love to Learn*. NY: Freeman, 1992. 55–6.

19. Baker, Dave, Cheryl Stemple, and Tony Stead. *How Big is the Moon? Whole Maths in Action*. Portsmouth, NH: Heinemann, 1990.

20. Fischer, Joseph, and Anne Kiefer. *Constructing and Discovering Images of Your Teaching. In Images of Schoolteachers in Twentieth-Century America: Paragons, Polarities, Complexities*. Pamela Bolotin Joseph and Gail E Burnaford, eds. NY: St. Martin's Press, 1994. 29–53.

21. See also Kieran Egan. *Teaching as Storytelling: An Alternative Approach to Teaching and Curriculum in the Elementary School*. Chicago: University of Chicago Press, 1989; and *Narrative in Teaching, Learning, and Research*, edited by Hunter McEwan and Kieran Egan. NY: Teachers College Press, 1995.

22. Efron, Sara, and Pamela Bolotin Joseph. *Reflections in a Mirror: Teacher-Generated Metaphors from Self and Others. In Images of Schoolteachers in Twentieth-Century America: Paragons, Polarities, Complexities*. Pamela Bolotin Joseph and Gail E. Burnaford, eds. NY: St. Martin's Press, 1994. 54–77.

23. Adapted from: Weinstein, Matthew (1996) "Towards a Cultural and Critical Science Education." Paper presented at the annual meeting of the

American Educational Research Association. New York, NY, April. Weinstein describes such positions for science education. I want to adapt them for mathematics education with minor adjustments.

24. Van Hiele, Pierre. *Structure and Insight: A Theory of Mathematics Education.* Orlando, FL: Academic Press, 1986.

25. For a classic in this vein, try Hans Freudenthal's *Weeding and Sowing.* Dordrecht, Netherlands: D. Reidel, 1983, and for an inspirational discussion, see Stephen Brown's *Ye Shall be Known By Your Generations*, in *For the Learning of Mathematics* 1 (3), March 1981. 27-36.

26. For especially good resources on this perspective, see Stieg Mellin-Olsen's classic, *The Politics of Mathematics Education.* and Ole Skovsmose's *Towards a Philosophy of Critical Mathematics Education.* Dordrecht, Netherlands: Kluwer Academic Press, 1994. See also Marilyn Frankenstein's *Rethinking Mathematics.* London: Free Association Books, 1989, and Peter Appelbaum's *Popular Culture, Educational Discourse, and Mathematics.* Albany, NY: SUNY Press, 1995.

27. Greene, Maxine. *Teacher as Stranger: Educational Philosophy for the Modern Age.* Belmont, CA: Wadsworth, 1973.

28. Greene: 290.

29. Adapted from: Weinstein, Matthew (1996) "Towards a Cultural and Critical Science Education."

XIII

SURFING AND GETTING WIRED IN A FIFTH GRADE CLASSROOM:
CRITICAL PEDAGOGICAL METHODS AND TECHNO-CULTURE

John A. Weaver and Karen Grindall

Consensus has become an outmoded and suspect value. But justice as a value is neither outmoded nor suspect. We must thus arrive at an idea and practice of justice that is not linked to that of consensus. A recognition of the heteromorphous nature of language games is a first step in that direction...The second step is the principle that any consensus on the rules defining a game...must be local...and subject to eventual cancellation. The orientation then favors a multiplicity of finite meta-arguments. (Lyotard 1991, 66)

These encounters are about relationships between bodies and personae/selves/subjects, and the multiplicities of connections between them. They are about negotiating realities, and the conjunctions of social spaces and activities bound together by webs of physical and ideological force. They map out a field of discourse for which they act as experiential demarcations: Many persons in a single body (multiple personality). Many persons outside a single body (personae within cyberspace in its many forms and attendant technologies of communications). (Stone 1996, 86)

The electronic media is perhaps the greatest site of pedagogical production that exists—you could say it is a form of perpetual pedagogy. In addition to understanding literacies applicable to print culture, students need to recognize how their identities are formed and their "mattering maps" produced through an engagement with electronic and other types of media so that they will be able to engage in alternative ways of symbolizing the self and gain a significant purchase on the construction of their own identities and the direction of their desiring. (McLaren, 1995, 21-2)

In this chapter we want to highlight some critical methodological approaches for the incorporation of technology into the elementary classroom. We want to discuss our experiences of surfing the net and getting wired to inspire teachers to nurture the "multiplicity of finite meta-arguments" that Lyotard highlights. We do not want to promote a false notion of consensus of teaching that erases difference and ignores alternatives. Rather, we wish to foster the development of multiple personalities within all students in order to encourage them to see life as a process of negotiations and creations rather than as linear steps towards a universal and final goal. Finally, we join Peter McLaren in his charge to utilize technology as a tool to promote what we refer to as a critical techno-mania. We wish to utilize technology as a form of power to interrogate society and to provide students with the means to define themselves and to contest those who wish to define them.

In what follows, we will outline what we mean by a critical techno-mania and then proceed to describe through narratives, critical dialogues, and classroom exercises mediated or provoked by some form of technology how we try to construct a classroom based on critical techno-mania. We do not intend these descriptions to serve as a blueprint to promote technology in the classroom or to nurture the development of techno-cultures in other classrooms. We reject ideas of replication. Just as the internet promotes the creation of thousands of conversations that are always becoming and constantly dependent on historically situated knowledge, so does any methodological approach to learning in the elementary classroom. But, we believe teachers can glean from our experiences some insights that will summon their creativity and imagination to construct a classroom that promotes the development of a critical perspective within their students and themselves. Before we get into these issues, we wish to begin with an excursion into the ways in which technology has been envisioned in the classroom and society to this point in time. For reasons of space, we will break these visions into two groups: techno-maniacs and techno-phobes. These are not our terms but we graciously co-opt them to Carol Stabile, *Feminism and the Technological Fix* (1995). From these visions we will build our vision of a critical techno-mania classroom where a multiplicity of voices, multiple personalities, and critical insights are nurtured within our students and ourselves.

TECHNO-MANIACS AND THE POST-FORDIST WORLD

For centuries now we have lived with technological change and "innovation." Modernists like Jeremy Bentham co-opted the power of technology to construct the panopticon and to increase the efficiency of surveillance; Adam Smith praised the spirit of technological advancements to construct a world free from poverty and social inequality; and Andrew Carnegie worshipped the brutality of technology as workers were declared obsolete and displaced in the name of ruthless competition, progress, and profits. These techno-maniacs envisioned a world that never came. Instead, as postmodernists and critical modernists remind us, technology fueled the ovens in Auschwitz with an efficient means to eliminate Jews, homosexuals, gypsies, and political dissidents, provided the United States with "smart bombs" and other high-tech war toys that protect "our" soldiers while obliterating others, and created a comfortable lifestyle for select fragments of the world population while the world confronts an environmental crisis and millions work to survive as wages stagnate and welfare safety nets crumble.

In spite of these experiences, techno-maniacs who worship the power of technology to change the world persist. These prophets, however, are different from their predecessors. They envision an improved world, but they drop any utopian notion technology might bring. In a way, they view technology as the means to increase profits and productivity while containing wages and the power of the working poor and un(der)employed. Technology for contemporary techno-maniacs is the new credo of a post-Fordist world. They have taken Lyotard's advice and accepted consensus as outmoded. Yet they erase and ignore the "heteromorphous" and "multiplicity of " possibilities created in a postmodern world. As McLaren (1995) notes this post-Fordist techno-mania "can stand naked in its unholy splendor; it can make no claims to be just and fair; it can now survive thrillingly without artifice or camouflage" (2).

We can find this post-Fordist philosophy of techno-maniacs embedded in the political, economic, cultural and educational realms. For these techno-maniacs solidarity, collective movements, and political action are out and decentralization and unbridled capitalism is in. Alvin Toffler, the often cited techno-psychic of Newt Gingrich and Al Gore, captures the way techno-mania has shaped economics. Toffler (1980) sees computers saving the environment (i.e., lower energy costs and reduction of pollution), reducing the work week, and rescuing the family as work shifts from the office to the home. For Toffler *The Jetsons* are not a cartoonish futuristic family but the techno-maniac's symbol of those living in the plush worlds of "Cyberia" free of all the cultural headaches urban decay, racism, sexism, and homophobia bring to society (Rushkoff 1994)

Mondo 2000, that hip new wave on-line magazine, shares much of the vision of Toffler. They envision a world in which on-line interaction and software development is completely unregulated. Regulation represents stagnation and unwanted barriers to their pleasure and advancement towards a world where bodies are optional and social problems non-existent. Like their print medium rival, *Wired*, *Mondo 2000* differs from Toffler, however, in that they are progressives on most issues outside the boundaries of economics. The founders of *Mondo 2000*, *R. U. Sirius* and *Queen Mu*, are outspoken critics of reactionary politics, confronting homophobia, racism, and sexism when it manifests itself in public discourse. Nevertheless, in spite of progressive window dressings clearly *Mondo 2000* will discard its social agenda before it forfeits its economic independence. As Vivian Sobchack (1993) points out, Mondo 2000 embodies the ambiguity of technomania. It seeks to reclaim "the sixties' countercultural 'guerrilla' political action," yet staunchly defends a "privileged, selfish, consumer-oriented" romanticism of a world in which information and the technology that mediates the flow of this information is pure (574).

The creator of Channel One, Chris Whittle has become the conduit for techno-mania in education. Whittle sees technology as the savior for schools that are controlled by corrupt unions, incompetent teachers, inefficient administrators, and suffocating bureaucracies. Technology will increase the interest of students in geography, world politics, and history. According to Whittle's formula, schools only need the equipment "donated" by his company, some fast-paced segments covering current events, cool talking heads, and, a few innocent commercials designed to fund Whittle's projects and maybe to sell a few M & M's here and some Clearasil there. And before we know it the power of technology will transform our students into information cyborgs: half-teenager and half-computer data banks accumulating crucial knowledge of current events and making the world safe for entrepreneurial capitalism.

Whittle certainly is not the only one promising a new world through the incorporation of technology into your classroom. Other educators are promising new jobs that are high skill and high pay and geared towards a rapidly changing economy in which flexibility could be the difference between enjoying the pleasures of a consumer culture and repeating over and over "Hi. Welcome to McDonald's. Can

I take your order?" Ray Marshall and Marc Tucker (1992) note that "most educators reject the idea that schools exist in part to prepare people for work . . . but this has to change" (180). We need the efficient utilization of technology to meet the needs of business and to create a "smart" and "world class" work force. Our political leaders, too, are touting the need to restructure our schools in order to meet the demands of a high-tech economy, global competition, and a shrinking world. Today's students must be ready for the future world of cyberspace, politicians proclaim. But, the world is not ready for these types of students. Monty Neill (1995) points out that although techno-maniacs envision a world of great opportunity for those industrious students who are prepared, the business world is unilaterally imposing austerity measures on workers. "First, continual lowering of wages is already a fact," Neill reminds us, "and not likely to turn around; second, most new hires are not likely to be doing high-skill work" (182).

TECHNO-PHOBES AND ALIENATION

While techno-maniacs make promises of a world unlikely to emerge, techno-phobes warn of a world of enslavement, disempowerment, and Foucauldian surveillance brought about by technology. Such a stance against technology can be traced at least as far back as the late eighteenth century (the Luddites in England). There are extreme examples of contemporary Luddites like the accused Unabomber, Ted Kaczynski, who use violence to halt the onslaught of technology into our lives. But, most contemporary techno-phobes reject such desperate measures. Instead, most contemporary techno-phobes are concerned with the ways in which new technologies such as computers and data banks are used to increase surveillance of our interactions through the internet or our transactions at ATM machines, widen social inequalities such as who has access to information, enhance the reach of multinational corporations into our lives through telemarketing and the selling of information about our habits, concerns, and interests, and further pacify the "masses" into accepting their lot in life and deferring their democratic rights to those in power. We are sympathetic to these perspectives, however, we find them one-dimensional. As we will note in our section on critical techno-mania, we reject any notion that sees the effects of technology as fixed. Part of creating techno–cultures in the classroom is to see it as a fluid process capable of producing empowerment and/or enslavement.

In spite of this disagreement, we believe techno-phobes set off some warning flags in their analysis of technology in contemporary society that all teachers ought to be aware of. For instance, Herbert Schiller (1996) has written extensively on what he sees as a growing information inequality. For Schiller the intense distrust of the public sphere since the Reagan years has brought forth not only a belief in the ability of the private sector to solve problems, but also a crisis of democracy. As technology expands and a society based on information, bytes, and cyberspace emerges, Schiller contends questions of access are becoming more important yet are largely ignored. What is emerging is a society of information haves and have nots.

The implications for schooling from Schiller's perspective are obvious. Students who have access will be at a greater advantage than those who do not. Those schools wired to the internet and connected to the world will be able to create students who will not only know how to access the information needed to solve problems but they will also be at a distinct advantage over other students in gaining access to the "good" jobs and "prestigious" universities. Their opportunities will not be built on hard work but privilege and easier work gained from information inequality. We are concerned about these trends but we do not share Schiller's view that technology is the culprit behind this growing inequality. Access to technology will not guarantee opportunities, especially if teachers continue to use computers as new toys that can produce "cool" graphics to support the same old stale rote memorization exercises. Instead, students who are creative and imaginative in constructing meaning out of the infinite amount of information they will have access to, (and their wealthy parents) will invent opportunities. We believe teachers are the key to produce such an environment. We must promote a critical pedagogy that exposes students to the possibilities of technology while making them aware of the potential inequalities technology can promote.

Another techno-phobe who sees technology as a source of a growing social inequality is Monty Neill. As mentioned above, Neill questions whether technology in the schools will promote social equality when workers are forced to accept low wage jobs. The call to promote "higher order thinking" within the schools, Neill claims, is a myth that erases the reality of the current capitalist economic order in which "following orders, not questioning, being on time, and submitting one's personality to the dictates" of businesses is the way (188). Schools and businesses do not want students who are critical thinkers since "it might get out of control, leading students to 'unrealistic expectations'" (189). Neill argues that technology is utilized to reinforce the capitalist system and to develop "a more sophisticated system for sorting students" (190). For Neill, "only egalitarian, collective working class power can assure that any particular technology will be used for its benefit—if it should be used at all" (193). We share Neill's concerns, yet at the same time we find his analysis reductive and simplistic. We recognize the potential for using technology to dumb students down, sort them into low-wage jobs, and disempower them. However, this trend is not as deterministic as Neill contends. While businesses are making alarming and rigorous attempts to turn schools into their own personal job training facilities, other contradictory and ambiguous forces are resisting such actions. There are teachers questioning the motives of these businesses, students who are gaining on-line access to discussions that expose the motives of businesses to forge the future of students into dead-end careers, and techno-cultures within the schools in which students use the internet to drop out of the classroom where they are learning to be "good" workers to enter alternative worlds that reject the initiatives of businesses to colonialize their minds. Neill's techno-phobic approach to technology erases these counter-currents.

Neill's worldview cannot see what Sadie Plant envisions. For Plant, technology redefines domination:

> In human hands, and as a historical tool, control has been exercised merely as domination, and manifests only in its centralized and vertical forms. Domination is a version of control . . .even self-control is conceived by man as the achievement of domination. Only with the cybernetic system does self-control no longer entail being placed beneath or under something: there is no "self" to control man, machine, or any other system: instead, both man and machine become elements of a cybernetic system which is itself a system of control and communication. (1995, 54)

Hierarchies are questioned, even shattered in cyberspace as power is dispersed. Suffering from techno-phobia Neill can spot current economic, political, and cultural contradictions in our society, but he cannot see how technology has mutated these contradictions. As teachers we must nurture a critical awareness within our students of the contradictions technology brings into the classroom, but, at the same time, we must provide them space to invent themselves and the knowledge they value through computer hacking and on-line surfing.

Within critical theory there is a tradition of techno-phobia. For the first and second generation of critical theorists technology further alienated the individual from the Enlightened goal of perfect autonomy from any form of enslavement. Machines, like the bourgeois ruling class, exploited the "masses" further perpetuating a society that prevented the achievement of the modernist goals of freedom, liberty, and equality. Herbert Marcuse (1964), for instance, viewed "technology as form of social control and domination" (58). Technology in Marcuse's eyes like other repressive forces worked in modernist society to reduce humanity to what he referred to as "one-dimensional man." Technology controlled and dominated lives by chaining humanity to it. Citing Gilbert Simondon, Marcuse believed that "the machine is a slave which serves to make other slaves" (159). The result was the stifling of alternative world visions and the reification through science and technology of a world built on exploitation.

Jürgen Habermas took up Marcuse's tenets of control and of domination in the late sixties. For Habermas, the exploitation of individuals resulted from the reduction of science from an endeavor of potential liberation to one that was welded to technology and a rationality based on production. "With the advent of large-scale industrial research," Habermas pointed out, "science, technology, and industrial utilization were fused into a system. Since then, industrial research has been linked up with research under government contract, which primarily promotes scientific and technical progress in the military sector" (104). This alliance between political, military, and economic powers and technological innovation was justified by a "technocratic consciousness" that distrusted any human interaction and communication not controlled by "purposive-rational action" (117). As a result, Habermas painted a dystopic vision of the future in which technology would bring about "pervasive techniques for surveillance, monitoring and control . . . new and more reliable 'educational' and propaganda techniques affecting human behavior . . . other genetic control or influence over the basic constitution of an individual" (117). For Marcuse and for Habermas, the autonomous subject was not problematized. As Mark Poster suggests, first and second generation critical theorists "saw no alternative to the modernist subject: either that subject existed or it was 'dissolved' leaving no subject at all" (1995, 10). Hybrids that transcended and blurred this dichotomy did not exist in their worldview; therefore, technology, and its ability to reconfigure the subject, was seen primarily as a tool that threatened the emancipatory agenda of the Enlightenment.

We do not reject outright Marcuse's and Habermas's technophobia. We are concerned with the growing use of surveillance technology to monitor the interactions of groups and individuals particularly in the schools, of the use of data banks to extract information about individuals, and of the lack of any critical self-reflection of the potential developments associated with gene splicing and replication. But, the use of technology whether in the classroom or in society is more complex than Marcuse or Habermas recognized. Surveillance technology, as computer hackers who monitor and disrupt the interactions of TRW (the biggest surveillance company in the world) know, can be used to resist domination, and the transformation of the body into cyborgs not only blurs our modernist boundaries of human and machine but also enhances our lives through hearing aids, pacemakers, and prosthetic limbs.

CRITICAL TECHNO-MANIA

We find a critical techno-mania fruitful in developing critical pedagogical methods in the classroom. Critical techno-mania is concerned with technology's potential to enhance the processes of empowerment emerging from dialogues between students and teachers. Our critical techno-mania is not driven by a reductionist phobia that technology inevitably leads to domination, erasure, and silencing. Nor is it based in a utopian or naive vision that creates its own form of domination and erasure. We see the potential of technology as always already a contested issue, working across contradictory terrain as students' and teachers' own histories shape their relationships with others. Because these histories and contradictions cannot be erased, we are driven by a passion to utilize technology in a manner that nurtures critical dialogues that decenter our notions of power, that recognizes difference as a linchpin for emancipatory conversations, that (re–) constitutes the subject in a manner which allows students and teachers to define themselves and that challenges those who attempt to use technology as a means to control.

Following the work of Mark Poster (1995), critical techno-mania envisions the new technologies such as virtual reality, the internet, and other modes of information as a part of the postmodern movement(s) that promotes "play and discovery, instituting a new level of imagination" (31). We agree that these revolutionary modes of information create a new form of interactivity that form "virtual communities" and create conversations in which "the many are talking to the many" in "symmetrical relations" (36–38). But, where Poster imagines the formation of "virtual communities" in which "people connect with strangers without much of the social baggage that divides and alienates," critical techno-mania sees technology as potentially enhancing the inequalities and discriminatory practices that divide and alienate in the "real" world (35). As Anne Balsamo (1993) insists, no matter what new opportunities technology brings, we must realize "these technologies are already determined in advance by the economic/social/cultural system within which they are developed and deployed" (125).

In terms of the classroom and critical pedagogical methods, teachers must rethink their approaches to children. In the world of techno-cultures, we must ask how we can promote play and discovery that permits the nurturing of multiple personalities unique to a postmodern world, yet never lose sight that these personalities are constituted within a world infested with racism, sexism, social class discrimination, and homophobia. We believe a critical techno-mania promotes a stance that accomplishes these goals. That is, we can harness the power of technology to constitute re-configured selves in students and in teachers without adopting a techno-mania that erases any form of discrimination as if they were only historical categories irrelevant to our contemporary world. As critical techno-maniacs we see technology as having an undetermined potential that must be defined by those specific historical and personal forces that shape each classroom.

Critical techno-mania does not lose sight of the privilege technology brings to the classroom. In a world where information is disconnected from meaning, and power no longer implies wealth but access, we are aware that as students and as teachers we are privileged (Hayles 1990). Just as it is privileged to be a cyborg with a prosthetic limb, breast implants, or pacemaker, to be wired is privilege. The internet affords opportunities to explore worlds, to create networks, to converse with others, and to gain access to information other students do not share. In this sense, technology will only enhance the disparity between the haves and have nots. As critical techno-maniacs we believe, however, it is important to expose students to cyberworlds because to deny access when it is available further enhances the disparity between the world of cyber-privilege and the disconnected.

Gaining access for students also means that technology is not just another toy that makes the lessons of the day cooler. To utilize computers for rote memorization, for controlling students during "free" time, or for preparing them for the latest standardized test only denies students access to the world cyberspaces opens up to them. It creates a world of "lo-teks" William Gibson describes in his short story *Johnny Mnemonic*: Students who use technology but do not have the access and power to influence the flow of information or the decision-making processes of how the information will be used and what it will mean. Surfing and getting wired must be used in a way that disrupts the modernist world of Tylerian rationale, Hunter techniques, and prescripted lesson plans. While a wired classroom places into doubt modernist methods, a postmodern world thrives in this type of classroom. Noise is crucial, chaos necessary, collaboration and dialogue inevitable, and "leaving" the classroom unavoidable. Critical techno-mania only asks that this postmodern world and the wired classrooms that are its tenants live by the principles of self-reflection, anti-foundationalism, and anti-essentialism. Without these principles, *Mondo 2000* becomes the norm, and disparities are accepted with a new Darwinian philosophy suited for the cyber-age.

We see critical techno-mania also as a way to promote hybrid identities. It is in the construction of hybrid identities that students and teachers create opportunities to challenge forms of domination. Donna Haraway has had a profound influence on our notion of a critical techno-mania. Following her lead, we see the metaphoric cyborg as a tool needed to challenge those who attempt to fix the identities of students and teachers, to station students and teachers in cemented social roles, and to monitor the actions of students and teachers in order to discipline and manipulate. The cyborg promotes an oppositional existence "committed to partiality, irony, intimacy, and perversity . . . wary of holism, but needy for connection" (Haraway 1991, 151). The cyborg's need for connection is sustained by interfaces mediated through computers, while identities are re-constituted by "stories, retold stories, versions that reverse and displace the hierarchical dualisms of naturalized identities" (Haraway 1991, 175). In critical techno-mania, students and teachers are not given a voice by a mandated curriculum or by the enlightened authority of the teacher. Instead, ambiguity, contradiction, and uncertainty are the spaces that nurture meaning. The acceptance of partiality in the classroom means teachers will have to recognize that students can and do construct their own identities and invent their own voices sometimes contradict the schooling process. Teachers must construct a critical pedagogy that always already admits students construct their identities. It is the task of the teachers to construct a classroom that permits the further development of these identities, knowing full well that if it is not happening in the classroom it will take place in another realm.

A CRITICAL TECHNO-MANIA CLASSROOM: NARRATIVES AND
CRITICAL

Dialogues

In the following discussion, we outline some critical pedagogical methods we utilized to promote the development of cyborg identities through play and discovery and critical dialogues on technology, schooling, and society. We want to focus on three activities that have nurtured the development of techno-cultures within the classroom. Each of these activities reconfigure the classroom. In fact, much of what will be discussed has taken place outside the classroom in a metaphoric and realistic sense. After all when we surf the net we leave the classroom. The teacher is no longer the lecturer or controller. S/he at best becomes a fellow traveler leaving bodies behind, traveling to worlds different from that of our modernist classrooms, and reaching goals that cannot be established the night before in a lesson plan. We physically left the classroom as well either going to the school's computer lab or travelling throughout the area to various sights. Like Haraway's cyborg our experiences in creating techno–cultures are filled with ambiguity and contradiction. There are moments when our students re-invent identities, and times when we reverted back to the comforts of modernist teaching, obsessing over control, monitoring behavior, and prescribing answers.

During these activities we were embarking on techno-journeys in which the exercises not only transformed us but the experience in itself did as well. We were reinventing ourselves through the narratives and dialogues we actively partook in. There are no authentic voices or pure identities in these techno-journeys, only contradictions and fragments. Our experiences as teachers constantly merged with the experiences of the students forming a new mutated culture. As students were constructing their stories, we became a part of them as we edited, probed, and provoked. As teachers, we were changed by the stories our students told. For me (Weaver), playing the role of university professor, was constantly questioned as arbiter of all that is worthy of knowing. Techno-culture does not ask what one's title is; rather it asks how do you create a different world with access to cyberspace; how do you make meaning out of the information flooding your mind through the internet.

HOLLYWOOD HIGH AND THE BLURRING OF IDENTITIES

The first techno-journey we want to discuss is about (re)creating one's identity through the stories one writes and re–writes. This journey takes us into the world of *Hollywood High*. *Hollywood High* is a CD- ROM interactive storytelling program designed for elementary schoolchildren. In essense, *Hollywood High* is an elementary form of a hypertext. What George Landow points out in regard to hypetexts, is also true for Hollywood and the effects it has on the children and teachers. "The great and defining power of digital technology lies in its capacity to store information and then provide countless virtual versions of it to readers, who then can manipulate, copy, and comment upon it without changing the material seen by others" (1994, 11). Hypertexts such as the ones children create in *Hollywood High* fundamentally change the classroom. Teachers become "'coaches' who help students in their searching" (30); students' identities are blurred as the role of the reader merges with author as "readers choose their own paths through a set of possibilities" (33); and classrooms become diverse as one true interpretation is impossible and information is "reconfigured according to the needs of different people rather than being preconfigured to meet certain but not other needs" (27-8).

In *Hollywood High*, children are required to create their story from constructing their own setting, choosing the characters, determining the length of the story, inventing their own structure, and creating the identities of their own characters. *Hollywood High* is different from other interactive programs in regards to the number of options made available to the children. They can choose from thirteen characters including a narrator, thirty-six settings, and multiple character profiles that include voices, names, roles, emotions, and hobbies. Not only do these options require children to create their own dialogues but to construct the identity of the characters as well.

The following excerpts are taken from my (Weaver) notes on conversations students had as they were creating their stories about *Hollywood High*.

Scene 1
Student 1: *You can't have a nerdy female voice for that character; it's a he.*
Student 2: *I can give it any voice I want.*
Weaver: *How do you know it is a male? Does the character look like you or me?*
Students: *No.*

Student 1: *No, it doesn't but I thought it was a male character so a nerdy female voice wouldn't fit.*
Grindall: *Time's up, let someone else use the program.*

The time constraints on using the program are part of the techno-struggle over access to information in a techno–economy in which scarcity is the accepted norm. What Andrew Ross (1994) observes about the current discourse over environmental issues is also true for technology in the classroom, "most people tend to accept that 'limits,' whether they are socially imposed or socially chosen, are a necessary feature of any . . . reorganization of social life" (263–4). But, whereas time limits were placed on the students, they were questioning limits as they were morphing the characters they were creating and giving female voices to assumed male characters.

Scene 2

Two students create a story about the extinction of dinosaurs. They create two characters that join the dinosaurs and witness their extinction. One is a mellow male hippie while the other is a male who sings all the time.

Student 1: *How many minutes?*
Grindall: *Seven.*
Student 1: *You got to be kidding.*
Student 1: *OK,* (getting back to writing their story) *the dinosaurs become extinct from a big explosion.*
Student 2: *No, they died from a cloud of dust.*
Weaver: *Could it have been both?*
Student 2: *No, I doubt it.*
Weaver: *Do we really know? Besides the issue is how will you create a story.*
Student 1: *Why don't we make our characters experience what we believe happened.*
Weaver: *Do you mean create two stories?*
Student 1: *Yes.*
Weaver: *Good idea, this way you leave it open as to how they actually died. You let the reader decide.*

Sometimes stories do not have endings. *Hollywood High* does not impose a modernist story structure of a beginning, middle, and end. The children were given the latitude to question this notion of fixed narrative structures as *Hollywood High* provided them the opportunity to leave their story without an end, only questions and the possibility of returning to their story at a later date.

Scene 3

University student: *What do we have to do?*

Student: *We have to create a story about the Underground Railroad. I want to show you this program called Hollywood. You can create your own characters, give them voices, and make your own scenes.*

University student: *OK. Show me how it works.*

Students: *Let's have some people who escaped slavery through the Underground Railroad on a talk show* (clicks the mouse and the set is a radio studio).

University student: *What will we have them talk about?*

Student: *They can talk about their experiences as slaves and escaping.*

University student: *Let's give them voices and then create a story line.*

Student: *The people who escaped should have rough voices because of all they just went through. We should also have someone who speaks out against slavery on the talk show.*

In each of these scenes, technology became a medium to renegotiate identities. Restraints such as time and specific assignment (Underground Railroad) were placed on the children, but the *Hollywood High* program allowed them the opportunity to negotiate these limitations. They were able to construct their own stories in which time blurred as figures of the past blended with characters created in the present. The children were able to leave their stories open-ended rather than try to reach a forced consensus in which only one possible story line was acceptable and an ending required. More importantly, they were able to morph identities. They turned males and females into hybrids, forming new identities that transcend the world of modernist dichotomies and assumed fixed roles in society. Through this process their identities were changed. No longer were they stationed into fixed categories such as male and female, past or present. They could move in between them, constructing new markers that better captured the complexity, ambiguity, and contradictions of life.

RAP'N AND MIX'N: TECHNO-CULTURE AND MUSIC

Another project we worked on with children was the effect of music on history and the history of music. We wanted the children to understand how the words and style of music captured many of the feelings of the time period in which they were written, including the protest songs of the 1960s and 1970s and rap music of the 1980s and 1990s. With the help of CD-ROM's on the history of music, students were required to create their own interactive program on the history of any type of music and any musician they selected. They were also required to compose their own songs. In order to enhance their experience with the history of music we journeyed to the Cleveland Rock n' Roll Hall of Fame.

Many of the children focused their attention on the role of rap in the history of music. In this sense, we as teachers did not initiate their interest in technology, instead we only nurtured an interest that was already there. Rap is a techno-culture that the children brought to the school. Cultural commentators interested in rap as a techno-culture note how the music creates a cyborg as the rap artist mixes a new beat through the interaction with the turntable and synthesizers the same way that a hacker interacts with the computer keyboard (Lupton 1993). Its blurring of the lines between machine and humans in part gives rap its unique sound and beat. These children were no different from the early rappers like Grand Master Flash and Africa Bambata. They created their own rap songs as they sang into the microphones built into the computers and played back and remade their songs as they listened to their recordings on the speakers in the computers.

As one particular group of children huddle around the computer to mix their rap, I (Weaver) ask them what rap is all about. One girl says it is rhythm and the rest say "yeah." I ask: Is there a message in rap? Most of them say not really. Rap is about a feeling not a message, they reply. One African-American child, however, begins to speak up and says yes there is a message in rap. She is normally quiet, but rap, like poetry, interests her and offers her an opportunity to express herself. Rap to her speaks about the experiences of urban youth in particular. It addresses the poverty urban youth experience along with the open peddling of drugs and the common occurrence of violence. She is not an essentialist though and understands that suburban youth like rap too. By this time, an Asian-American student intervenes and agrees that rap has a message, and she likes it too. She notes as well that her mother is not too thrilled with rap, but she (confusing R & B with rap) is going to ask her to buy her the latest Boyz II Men anyway.

Prior to this conversation, I read Jonathan Scott's thoughts on rap. Scott (1996) suggests that "something interesting and complicated is going on, and one will find very few answers by looking to categories like 'oppositional' and 'counter-hegemonic.' Hip-hop is hegemonic and refuses to be treated as a minority culture—as disadvantaged and excluded" (170). So I asked this group whether rap is unfair to women. They asked, "What do you mean?" I said does rap treat women in a way that is disrespectful. They replied "yeah but only a few." They reminded me that there were plenty of female rap groups like Salt 'n' Pepa and TLC. It was these groups they admired, talked about in class, listened to, and tried to mimic as they were rap'n and mix'n into the computer mike.

The rap'n and mix'n the children do and the conversation we have afterwards demonstrates how technology can be a tool to create critical pedagogical methods. Access to technology permitted these children the opportunity to develop their own talents and to create their own songs that speak to their experiences whether they are just feelings or deeper social problems that adults seem uninterested in addressing. Like *Hollywood High*, rap blurs the lines of identity. Not only is rap about taking from and adding to previous forms of music, thereby creating a hybrid, it also is about mix'n ethnicities. The Asian-American girl who liked rap was also experiencing a cultural clash with her mother who was not particularly enamored with rap and possibly saw it as a threat to their identity as Asians. The African-American girl knew that suburban children enjoyed rap as well and that their consumption changed the meaning of rap. They also knew that rap was hegemonic, capable of providing an outlet for urban youth, but also potentially a conduit to promote sexism. In the world of techno-culture, essences are challenged and hybrids are the norm. Critical pedagogical methods have to take into consideration this fundamental change that technology brings to the classroom.

One way in which we tried to meet this challenge was through a visit to the Cleveland Rock n' Roll Hall of Fame. The teachers and volunteers were each assigned a small group of children to escort throughout the Hall of Fame. The children were asked to find three musicians they were familiar and unfamiliar with and how their music affected the everyday lives of people.

The children in my (Weaver) group were first struck by a display entitled "Video Killed the Radio Star" (from an early 80s hit). It was a multimedia presentation in which fragments of video clips flash across the scenes of numerous television sets. The children were mesmerized by the lure of video images. As they were watching the video screens they did not see all the inanimate artifacts that were on display charting the development of Rock n' Roll. Video not only has killed the Radio Star but it also has changed the way we understand the past. Technology has constructed a historical consciousness based in/on/through video in which time and space are compressed, and the past becomes a compilation of fragments constructed by those who have access to and control of the images. At the same time the children were negotiating these images taking in those that appealed to them while constructing their own historical consciousness. From this interaction with fragmented images, the children were able to answer the question of how music affected the everyday lives of people by reflecting on their own lives as their own historical consciousness of music was being constructed by a barrage of images from one exhibit.

Technology and a critical techno-maniac approach we believe was the key to their experiences, and enhanced their learning about the history of music. Technology promoted noise, interactive learning, multiple perspectives, and critical self-reflection. Compare this experience with another trip these children took to the Akron Art Museum. Instead of being bombarded by images they had to interpret, they were struck by a constant stream of commands of what not to do. As we entered the museum and stared at *Diepoltz* by Stella the students were asked by the guide, "What do you like about this painting?" The students reply: "The different colors, the different textures, different shapes." The guide then asked what the students thought it was. She paused for a few seconds and then said "The painter was fascinated with race tracks and this is what it is." We then move on as a group to Chuck Clute's *Linda* and the guide asks "Is it a painting or a photo?" She structures their world of possible interpretations of art into an orderly, linear, dichotomous world in which they are given two choices, one of which is true. As we continue the tour, we are constantly reminded of where we are and that we do not belong here. We are followed by other guides who are there just to watch us, making sure we do not touch the art. After a while, we do not need guides to remind us, we control ourselves or, we remind the students to keep their hands in their pockets and to stay away from the art. Interaction with the painting is not encouraged, noise is a hindrance, identities are clearly marked.

ENVIRONMENTAL STUDIES AND THE INTERNET

Finally, there is the environmental project the class works on in the spring. As a class, we went to the Cuyahoga Environmental Education Center for four days. The children spend this time outdoors learning about various issues concerning the environment. They break up into small groups as they go on night hikes to listen to the sounds of life in the forest, discuss the origins and evolution of rivers, and debate the problems facing the environment. They also continue other themes they covered throughout the year. For instance, they connect their work on music by singing and discussing the lyrics of a local environmentalist folk singer who sings about the recent history of the Cuyahoga River.

Out of these exercises grew some conversations that we think reflect critical pedagogical methods. One of the days the group I (Weaver) was with explored the stream. The university student who was their guide asked the children to find a unique rock because they were going to tell stories about their rock. As we walked back to a grassy area it was time to tell our stories. One student said "My rock is a gun and if anyone messes with me I will have to shoot them." I asked him why he would have to shoot anyone. He replied "Because they were messing with me that's why!" I said to the rest of the students. This story reminds us that we may be in peaceful surroundings now, but there are always problems we have to deal with sooner or later. We will all have to decide when we leave this center how we are going to deal with the violence that plagues our environment back home.

During the last day of our stay at the center, we focus the children on their own communities. I (Grindall) asked the students what could they do in their community to improve the environment. They immediately focused on the school.

Grindall: *Does it bother you the way the school is now, does it send messages?*
Students: *Yes.*
Grindall: *Now, we are not trying to scapegoat here. Richard* (the janitor) *works hard. What can we do to improve the school, sort of leave a legacy?*
Students: *We can clean up the playground, remove the rubber chips around the playground, and plant some flowers at the school.*
Grindall: *How are we going to pay for these improvements?*
Student 1: *We can sell blowpops and pop.*
Grindall: *What can you do to improve the environment at your house?*
Student 2: *I can fix some of the wooden posts at my house.*
Student 3: *We can recycle more.*

Had we ended the conversation here, the children would have left the environmental center thinking that selling blowpops and pop for a good cause would solve our environmental problems. They would have learned that consumer environmentalism was the answer rather than community and global activism. However, as soon as the children return to the school our critical techno-mania began to play an instrumental role in assuring that the experiences they had at the center are connected to the wider world. They interfaced with the Environmental Center for children in Braslavia in order to share concerns with the destruction and preservation of rivers throughout the world. Via the internet the children created their own environmental organization as they learned about other environmental problems beyond their local community, and how to act collectively to assure that the destruction of rivers will not continue. They became techno-activists developing a critical sense of environmental issues, and voicing their concerns about problems throughout the world without leaving the classroom. Being wired gave them access to issues they would not normally be made aware of, and it served as a conduit for action. The internet transformed these students from future encyclopedia salespersons who began by selling blowpops into individuals who began to think of problems as global issues.

SOME BEGINNING THOUGHTS ON TECHNO-CULTURES AND CRITICAL PEDAGOGICAL METHODS

We decided that we would not leave our story by synthesizing our thoughts in a traditional conclusion. Instead we want to end with some beginnings. As we walk through the postmodern cyber-era of schooling, our methods have to shift to meet the needs of the posthuman generation. The identities of our children are dramatically shifting as virtual reality, internet interactions, and computer hacking become more prevalent in our classrooms. Children can no longer be conveniently classified as male and female, nor can we structure our lessons around gendered expectations. Now, as they interface with others across the world and connect with a computer keyboard, children are invited into worlds where they become cyborgs and social problems do not disappear, they just mutate. How do we educate children in these new environments? What methods do we create so that we can capture the shifting identities of ourselves and of our students, and, at the same time, critically examine the ways in which these new identities re-align power blocs and challenge or reinforce the status quo? These are some of the challenges that teachers face in the futuristic world we call the postmodern classroom of today. There is no master plan, only clues that, as teachers, we have to learn to interpret and read. From these clues we will have to develop methods that change as fast as our identities and the techno-cultures around us do.

REFERENCES

Balsamo, A. "The Virtual Body in Cyberspace." *Journal of Research in Technology and Philosophy*, 13(1993):119–39.

Habermas, J. *Toward a Rational Society: Student Protest, and Politics.* Boston: Beacon, 1970.

Haraway, D. *Simians, Cyborgs, and Women: The Reinvention of Nature.*

Routledge: New York, 1991.

Hayles, K. *Chaos Bound: Orderly Disorder in Contemporary Literature and Science*. Ithaca: Cornell, 1990.

Landow, G. *Hyper/Text/Theory*. Baltimore: Johns Hopkins University Press, 1994.

Lupton, D. "The Embodied Computer/User." In *Cyberspace, Cyberbodies, Cyberpunk: Cultures of Technological Embodiment*, eds., M. Featherstone and R. Burrows, London: SAGE, 1995: 97–112.

Lyotard, J-F. *The Postmodern Condition: A Report on Knowledge*. Minneapolis: Minnesota, 1991.

Marcuse, H. *One-Dimensional Man*. Boston: Beacon, 1964.

Marshall, R., and M. Tucker. "Building a Smarter Work Force." In *Education 95/96*, F. Schultz, ed. Guilford, CT: Dushkin, 1995. 177–81.

McLaren, P. *Critical Pedagogy and Predatory Culture: Oppositional Politics in a Postmodern Era*. New York: Routledge, 1995.

Neill, M. "Computers, Thinking, and Schools in the New World Economic Order." In *Resisting the Virtual Life: The Culture and Politics of Information*, J. Brooks and I. Boal, eds. San Francisco: City Lights, 1995. 181–94.

Plant, S. "The Future Looms: Weaving Women and Cybernetics." In *Cyberspace, Cyberbodies, Cyberpunk: Cultures of Technological Embodiment*, M. Featherstone and R. Burrows, eds. London: SAGE, 1995. 45–64.

Poster, M. *The Second Media Age*. Cambridge: Polity, 1995.

Ross, A. *The Chicago Gangster Theory of Life: Nature's Debt to Society*. New York: Verso, 1994.

Rushkoff, D. *Cyberia*. San Francisco: Harper, 1994.

Schiller, H. *Information Inequality: The Deepening Social Crisis in America*. New York: Routledge, 1996.

Scott, J. "Critical Aesthetics on the Down Low." *The Minnesota Review*, 43 and 44 (1995):164–71.

Sobchack, V. "New Age Mutant Ninja Hackers: Reading Mondo 2000." *The South Atlantic Quarterly*, 92:4 (1993): 569–85.

Stabile, C. *Feminism and The Technological Fix*. London: Manchester, 1995.

Stone, A. *The War of Desire and Technology at the Close of the Mechanical Age*. Cambridge: MIT, 1996.

Toffler, A. *The Third Wave*. New York: Morrow, 1980.

XIV

TEACHERS AND ADMINISTRATORS:
A VISION OF PROPHETIC PRACTICE
Patrick Slattery and Rebecca McElfresh Spehler

INTRODUCTION

We are two educators and school administrators who believe that education is a human endeavor that must be passionate and prophetic. We believe that if educators are to make any difference in a world filled with injustice, indifference, despair, and environmental degradation, then we must take an approach to schooling different from the traditional philosophies and practices that have dominated education in America. We must become fully engaged in a soulful life as expressed and communicated autobiographically. In other words, the foundation of the educational process for members of the learning community is characterized by an openness to the wonder of the universe, a willingness to take risks, a commitment to life-long learning, an excitement about the discovery and construction of new ideas, an activist stance in the realm of the sociopolitical milieu of the local and global community, and an examination of the inner life. We believe that this vision will help those preparing to become teachers to work effectively with administrators and to have a meaningful and consequential impact upon the learning communities in which they participate.

As administrators and university professors, our life experiences and our professional responsibilities in schools and classrooms have shaped this vision. I (Patrick Slattery) began my career as a high school English and mathematics teacher. After several years of intense and personally satisfying experiences that involved rigorous academic teaching, creative activity planning, and rewarding interactions with students, I decided to study school administration. Assuming that I could alleviate many of the problems that I faced as a classroom teacher, I embarked on a seven year odyssey into the realm of K-12 school administration. Frustrated by the bureaucracy, political posturing, budget constraints, apathy, and a myriad of social problems, I left the schools to study curriculum theory at Louisiana State University. For the past several years I have taught curriculum studies, hoping to share both my positive and negative experiences with university students so that they will be better equipped to understand the nature of K-12 schooling and to help improve our current schooling crises. In addition to my university teaching, I have always remained connected to K-12 schooling through my three school-age children and my association with local school districts in staff development programs. I am committed to a quality educational experience for all children. In order for this vision to become a reality, educators, support personnel, and parents must work together to reconceptualize curriculum and schooling. In this essay I hope to contribute to a conversation that will help you to become an active participant in this process so that you can effectively work with administrators to bring about a renewed vision.

I (Rebecca Spehler) have served as classroom teacher, district program coordinator, elementary principal, and adjunct university professor. Although the specifics of my professional vision have evolved through the years, the spirit of this call upon my life to inspire and to evoke human growth has remained constant. My ability to influence students, parents, colleagues, and administrators has been directly related to my willingness to share the stories of my own growth process. Of primary importance, then, has been the commitment to remain constant in the quest for growth as an individual and as a member of families, learning communities, and the larger global community.

We realize that as preservice education students, you have many thoughts and feelings about your classroom, your students, and your teaching styles. Some of you may have even developed a broader vision of the impact you wish to have on the social, political, economic, and religious dimensions of our society. Others of you may have been working for years developing a rich inner life—possibly including autobiographical reflection, journal writing, spiritual renewal, dream analysis, or vision quests—which have contributed to your sense of the importance of the relational aspects of the teaching and learning process. Included here would be your concern for the physical, emotional, and psychological well-being of students, colleagues, the environment, and yourself. We affirm this process that you have begun; indeed, we are on this same journey. In order to inspire other human beings, to create meaningful learning environments, and to establish healthy community relations, we have discovered that it is essential that the growth of the inner life and concern for broader social visions remain foregrounded in our work as educators. Working with administrators, students, parents, and colleagues will certainly be challenging—and sometimes frustrating. You will find, from time to time, that your vision will conflict with the expectations of building administrators and/or district leaders. Yet, the development of the traits we described above will serve you well in your work as a teacher. Why? Because these are essential dimensions of being human; for a teacher is not a machine but a human being touching the lives of students and colleagues in the learning environment.

UNDERSTANDING THE CONTEXT

If we are to allow our vision to impact our students within the context of the school community, we must learn to distinguish the framework through which the administrator views the local school community. As we observe and internalize environmental cues—such as spoken language, body gestures, physical surroundings—it is possible to give meaning to the context of the particular school community in which we work. As you develop this understanding, it may become possible to communicate your vision in terms that will increase the likelihood of acceptance on the part of your building administrator.

As a first year teacher, I (Rebecca) had a well-developed sense of my personal vision as an educator. When I met with my building administrator for the first time, I was eagerly anticipating an environment in which my vision would thrive and continue to grow. However, at our first meeting, I was handed a set of teacher manuals tied neatly with a string and labeled "grade four." This single event, more than any other, created an awareness that my personal vision might conflict with the established expectations of my new administrator.

Among other textbook manuals, this set included a basal reading series complete with a typical workbook emphasizing isolated reading skills. Since my vision involved creating a classroom where making meaning was not only encouraged, but honored, I struggled with the lack of depth and of opportunity for incorporating the imagination in the district basal reading series. I wanted to create an environment that would encourage students to connect learning to their lives. In other words, learning is not a matter of transmitting information from the set of manuals to a group of receptive students, but it is a transformative process of coming to understand ourselves, our environment, our culture, and our world. This transformation occurs as an interactive process between the learner and the whole environment. Contemporary educational literature sometimes describes this vision as constructivism (Brooks and Brooks 1993; Henderson 1995).

Since I was determined to find a way to allow my own vision to thrive, I set about the task of determining the specifics of the orientation to my principal's educational process. To do this, I believed, would give me valuable information about the kind of language I needed to use to communicate effectively with her. This examination led me to understand that she expected a very directive approach to instruction that would ensure coverage of all required objectives over the course of the year and that growth would be quantifiable through standardized testing.

Knowing full well on an intuitive level that engaging the imagination of my students was primary in the development of life-long readers, I set out to create a plan for the year that would do just that, as well as meet the accountability demands of my administrator. This plan involved the use of trade book literature arranged in thematic units. These themes were selected because they were deep, broad-based, and would invite student initiated inquiry. Through the course of the next several years, these units evolved to incorporate student interests, not only in the area of language arts, but in other subject areas as well.

Because I was able to communicate my ideas to my administrator within the context of her vision, and yet not sacrifice my own, I gained her trust as a first year teacher. As a result of this initial trust-building experience, I was able to continue this process so that my classroom practice would express my vision, which often deviated from traditional classroom practice.

At the end of four years in this building, I transferred to another in the district to accept an assignment as the teacher for an intermediate level classroom for high ability students. The expectations for my teaching in this context were highly consistent with my own vision, and I was able to experience a great deal more freedom to express this vision within my classroom. Yet, I will always value the experience of my first years of teaching for what I learned about the importance of understanding the context of another's vision. This example illustrates the value of acting upon the intuitive sense so often attributed to a feminine sense of knowing and understanding the world (Belenky et al., 1986).

UNDERSTANDING THE POLITICAL REALITY

Despite our commitment to affirm our intuitive sensibilities for implementing our vision of a just, compassionate, caring, and academically challenging learning environment in our classrooms, the political climate of the schools is often overwhelming and discourages even our most sincere efforts. Many teachers have shared with us their frustration with bureaucratic regulations, economic constraints, political maneuvering, and the like. Many teachers find themselves in a position where they do not believe they have the power to challenge the political system. Some are concerned about keeping their job, others are fearful that they will not receive tenure, many worry about family finances, a few are place bound and unable to relocate, and social pressure or peer pressure inhibit some from challenging the politically powerful. For all of these reasons—and others—many teachers find it almost impossible to challenge the prevailing political or administrative practices. Political pressures will often seem insurmountable to beginning teachers. Our experience, however also tells us that young teachers do have the drive, energy, and commitment that allows them to see possibilities that veterans often overlook.

As a young teacher I (Patrick) found myself in such a circumstance in my first year of teaching. As with all beginning teachers I was thrilled to have been hired and willing to do almost anything to succeed. I even accepted—without complaint—a request by my new principal to teach one period of a subject outside of my areas of certification. Thus, in addition to my secondary English and math classes (my major and minor), I was assigned one section of eighth grade speech. It was late July when I received my schedule and textbooks, so I began planning furiously. A veteran teacher saw me on campus arranging my classroom and asked about my schedule. She offered her consolation when she heard that I had been assigned the speech class. She informed me that this was the "class from hell" that had driven away three teachers the previous year, and all of the tenured staff had refused to teach this class. The next day I learned from the principal that two boys in the class were on probation for drug distribution on campus, and that I was expected to join in the effort to catch these boys doing something wrong so that there would be enough evidence for an expulsion hearing. Everyone at the school wanted these two hoodlums to be removed, and it was now my job to support this effort.

I was uncomfortable with this assignment. I had always been taught to value the worth and dignity of each human being regardless of his or her race, gender, socioeconomic status, religion, and the like. I had volunteered in a state penitentiary while in college, and I had come to realize that all human beings had the potential to contribute to society and grow. I was especially appalled that eighth grade students would be judged and condemned before the school year began. I was determined to reach all of my students, even the two on probation.

After a few days in my new classroom, I started to doubt my positive vision of the innate goodness of human beings. The "class from hell" was much worse that I could have imagined—like the students depicted in Michelle Pfeiffer's first class in the movie *Dangerous Minds*. I tried every learning method and teaching strategy I could remember from my teacher education classes. Nothing worked. The students were belligerent, lazy, obstinate, and surly. I was not covering the chapters in the speech book as required in the curriculum guide—even though I was always reading a chapter ahead so that I could learn the material before the students. This did not matter; the students would not read or present speeches. I longed for help and suggestions, but I was afraid to ask my principal or colleagues for advice out of fear of appearing to be a failure at my new job. I labored in vain waiting for the year to end—and it was only October!

One day quite unexpectedly help arrived from an unlikely source— my two students on probation. As I was introducing a unit on duet acting, I asked for two volunteers to role play a scene from "The Tortoise and the Hare" in the textbook. Rich and Tyronne, who were not only on probation, but also instigators who dominated the entire class, blurted out a challenge: "We'll do some acting if you let us do a drug bust in Harlem." My whole career as a teacher flashed before my eyes. Time froze. What was I to say? The curriculum guide clearly required that we only use approved texts; recent controversies in the district about violence, sex, and drugs in literary selections had forced the reassignment of the curriculum director. The principal had clearly warned me that these two students were to be forced to conform to all school rules. The racial tension in this Southern community was explosive; Rick, a white student, and Tyronne, a black student, were clearly at the forefront of racial antagonism on campus. And now they were volunteering to create a racially charged drug scene with Rick acting the part of a white cop and Tyronne acting the part of a black drug dealer.

I asked myself a hundred questions in the seconds between Rick and Tyronne's offer and my response. What if they were deceiving me and only intended to disrupt the class and to embarrass me? What

258

if someone found out that I allowed my student to perform a drug bust scene? Could my students really learn about duet acting from such a stunt? What if the class exploded in race riots? What if the principal came into my room? I was petrified at the thought of letting Rick and Tyronne take over my classroom. Yet, I figured that they were already in charge anyway, so what the heck. I looked them in the eye, and to their shock, I said, "Yes, let's do it!"

Rick and Tyronne performed a somewhat awkward, yet very realistic drug bust scene. They knew the language, the law, and the logistics! The class applauded enthusiastically. I was delighted, nervous, and shocked all at the same time. Other students began to volunteer to perform duet acting scenes that were of interest to them. For the next week I coached my students in techniques for improving their improvisational skits. When the time arrived for Rick and Tyronne to present their final performance, the class sat in hushed anticipation. The performance was flawless and dramatic. In fact, it was so realistic, that the principal, who happened to be walking down the hall, rushed into my classroom and grabbed Rick and Tyronne by the collar and shoved them against the blackboard saying, "This is the final straw. You are both out of here!" As the principal turned with the boys to exit he saw me sitting in stunned silence in the back of the room. "This is a duet acting scene, sir," I said with awkward hesitation. The principal turned bright red, let go of the boys, and stormed out of the room. A few moments later the class erupted in applause. Not only were Rick and Tyronne good actors, they had won a moral victory over the dreaded principal. While the class from hell had won a battle, I was afraid that I had lost the war.

Interestingly, a letter came in the mail the next week from the local university advertising a junior high speech tournament. I had another bright idea. I asked my class if they would like to do their duet acting skits at a speech tournament. They gagged. "Not with all of those speech nerds," they protested. Again Rick and Tyronne intervened. When they said yes, then the entire class wanted to attend. Not only did we attend the speech tournament, but Rick and Tyronne won the first place trophy for duet acting. It was now November, and I was not only enjoying my first year of teaching but I actually looked forward to being with my "class from hell." Little did I know that all of my efforts were about to be undermined.

It was the custom in this school to announce all student awards and accomplishments on Monday morning. Trophies were presented in the office and displayed in the front window. I was thrilled to bring Rick and Tyronne's trophies to the office before announcements. My "class from hell" was anxiously awaiting their first public recognition in the school community, not only because of their pride in their work, but also, I believe, as a way of proving their dignity to the principal and staff that had labeled them for years. When I brought the trophies to the principal, he confiscated them and said, "Students on probation are not allowed to receive awards." I was shocked. When I returned to my classroom and explained the situation to my students, they were furious. While they never blamed me personally for the lack of recognition, they quickly returned to their old behaviors. Despite my best efforts, the class was never the same again.

In this case, administrative rules and regulations prevented learning from flourishing. As a young teacher I wanted to make a difference in the lives of my students. I also wanted them to learn to become public speakers. I saw a glimmer of success. However, I was not able to overcome the conflicts between my vision and administrative philosophy. In an effort to balance my intuitive sense of injustice in this case and my desire to keep my job, I waited until the end of the school year and went to a local trophy house and bought two new trophies for Rick and Tyronne. I told them that they had been outstanding speech students, and I encouraged them to develop their talents in the future. I still believe that I made a difference in the lives of the students in the "class from hell" despite the conflict with the administrative philosophy of the school. You, too, will have to constantly find ways to implement your vision within a school system whose rules, regulations, or philosophies are in conflict with your own intuitions and beliefs. This story from my first year of teaching is a metaphor for my entire career.

PROLEPTIC VISION

The two stories above illustrate the lived experience of teachers as they work with administrators in schools. Sometimes visions are shared, sometimes compromises are easily negotiated, and sometimes conflicting visions remain unresolvable. You will find yourself in all of these situations throughout your career. But, in order to maximize the opportunity for you to implement your philosophy and to have a greater impact on the lives of your students, we believe that it is essential to develop a proleptic vision.

William Faulkner wrote, "There is no such thing really as was, because the past is" (1942, 288). Faulkner was trying to explain that historical events continue to have an impact on present generations. The experiences of "the good old days" are never really over. The impact of childhood memories continues to influence our behavior and attitudes today. In schools we often teach history and literature as depositories of ancient texts, dates, and ideas to be memorized, or information to be repeated on standardized tests. We challenge this concept of teaching and learning. We are committed to the idea that texts, historical information, and literary selections are living artifacts that can and should be reinterpreted, reexperienced, and reinvigorated continuously. For example, every time we listen to a musical selection, watch a movie, or read a book, we get new insights into the meaning of the selection, film, or book as well as new insights into our selves. You know this to be true. Do you ever enjoy watching a movie several times? Do you ever get new feelings or insights when you hear a song over time? Words, dates, scientific data, stories, and songs are living artifacts that require a participant in the experience to give them meaning. (Note that this is similar to the constructivist philosophy that we introduced above.)

Pablo Picasso believed strongly in the power of the participant to create meaning:

> A picture is not thought out and settled beforehand. While it is being done it changes as one's thoughts change. And when it is finished it still goes on changing according to the state of mind of whoever is looking at it. A picture lives a life like a natural enough, as the picture lives only through the man who is looking at it (1971, 268).

As we understand Picasso, a painting from the past continues to inspire new ideas and interpretations over time. If this were not the case, why would people continue to research any topic? There is always something new to discover and construct.

We agree with emerging postmodern scholarship that contends that the world has reached a point where we must be open to a multiplicity of interpretations and understandings. There are a variety of ways of looking at the world. Our differences do not need to separate and to divide us. Rather, the goal of education should be to affirm the beauty and richness of many cultures, religions, artistic styles, and philosophies. The philosopher Robert Bellah, in *Beyond Belief*, explained it this way:

> We may be seeing the beginning of the reintegration of our culture, a new possibility of the unity of consciousness. If so, it will not be on the basis of any new orthodoxy, either religious or scientific. Such a new integration will be based on the rejection of all univocal understandings of reality , or

> all identifications of one conception of reality with reality itself. It will recognize the multiplicity of the human spirit, and the necessity to translate constantly between different scientific and imaginative vocabularies. It will recognize the human proclivity to fall comfortably into some single eral interpretation of the world and therefore the necessity to be continuously open to rebirth in a new heaven and new earth. It will recognize that in both scientific and religious culture all we have finally are symbols, but that there is an enormous difference between the dead letter and the living word. (cited in Tarnas 1991, 415)

We agree with Bellah that there is a difference between inert information—dead letters—and imaginative thinking—the living word. It is in the realm of imagination and living that persons find hope, and the sense of hope only arises when the past is experienced as an integral part of the present moment. With Faulkner, Picasso, Bellah, and so many other contemporary artists, authors, and philosophers, we insist on a constructivist approach to life. In education this means creating classroom environments where students and teachers are alive with creative ideas, imaginative interpretations, and a passion for understanding. This is the first step in the development of proleptic hope.

The second step in the process involves the future. Just as the past is not inert and irrelevant data about ancient texts, science, ideas, so too the future is not predetermined and remote. The future, while not yet complete, is already present in the choices that we make today. John Dewey (1938) observed: "The ideal of using the present simply to get ready for the future contradicts itself. Hence the central problem of an education based on experience is to select the kind of present experiences that live fruitfully and creatively in subsequent experiences" (28).

In our classrooms this means that we will have to stop saying things like, "You will need this algebra one day in the future," or "you are the future of America." Students today are the past, present, and future of the world all at once. Empowerment of students—indeed of all citizens—means legitimizing their unique contribution to the global community in the present moment. This empowerment is what we mean by proleptic hope. Students and teachers armed with a renewed sense of their possibilities will be able to exercise their imaginative, intuitive, and transformative powers in the educational process. It is only with such renewal that our vision of a just, caring, and ecologically sustainable global community is possible. Therefore, a sense of proleptic hope is the essential ingredient in our proposal for educational reform. If we develop this sense of proleptic hope, then we believe that you will be equipped to work effectively with administrators—albeit with struggle and frustration at times, especially when these leaders lack such a vision themselves. We challenge teachers to develop a sense of hope, not only for the sake of your students, but also for their own personal growth.

REFERENCES

Belenky, M. F., B. M. Clinchy, N. R. Goldberger, and J. M. Tarule. *Women's Ways of Knowing: The Development of Self, Voice, and Mind.* New York: Basic Books, 1986.

Brooks, J. G., and Brooks, M. G. *In Search of Understanding: The Case for the Constructivist Classrooms.* Alexandria, VA: ASCD Press, 1993.

Dewey, J. *Experience and Education.* New York: MacMillan, 1938.

Faulkner, W. "The Bear." In *The Portable Faulkner.* Crowley, ed. New York: Viking Press, 1942. 225-363.

Griffin, D. R. *The Reenchantment of Science: Postmodern proposals.* Albany, NY: SUNY Press, 1988.

Henderson, J., and R. D. Hawthone. *Transformative Curriculum Leadership.* New York: MacMillan, 1995.

Jung, C. G. *Synchronicity: An Acausal Connecting Principle.* New York: Bollingen Foundation, 1960.

Kliebard, H. *Forging the American Curriculum: Essays in Curriculum History and Theory.* New York: Routledge and Kegan Paul, 1992.

Moore, T. *The Reenchantment of Everyday Life.* New York: Harper Collins, 1996.

Morrison, T. "Unspeakable Things Unspoken: The Afro-American Presence in American Literature." *Michigan Quarterly.* Winter, 1989. 1–34.

Picasso, P. "Conversations." In *Theories of Modern Art: A Source Book of Artists and Critics.* H. B. Chipps, ed., Berkeley and Los Angeles: University of California Press, 1971. 268.

Pinar, W. F., and M. R. Grumet. *Towards a Poor Curriculum.* Dubuque, IA: Kendall / Hunt, 1976.

Sergiovanni, T. J., and R. J. Starratt. *Supervision: Human perspectives.* New York: McGraw-Hill, 1988.

Serres, M. *Hermes: Literature, Science, Philosophy.* Baltimore: Johns Hopkins University Press, 1982.

Tarnas, R. *The Passion of the Western Mind: Understanding the Ideas That Have Shaped Our World View.* New York: Crown, 1991.

Notes on Editors and Contributors

Joe L. Kincheloe teaches Pedagogy and Cultural Studies at Penn State University. **Shirley R. Steinberg** teaches Educational Foundations and Curriculum at Adelphi University. They are the authors and editors of many books and articles on critical pedagogy and cultural studies.

Joshua Anijar is a student at Glendor Senior High School, Glendora, California.

Karen Anijar teaches at California State Polytechnic University.

Peter M. Applebaum teaches at William Patterson University.

Kathleen S. Berry teaches at the University of New Brunswick, Fredrickton.

Timothy A. Dohrer is finishing his doctorate at Penn State University.

Dennis E. Fehr teaches at Texas Tech University.

Ronald Gonzales teaches in the Pomona School District, Pomona, California.

Ivor F. Goodson teaches at the University of East Anglica, England.

Karen Grindall teaches at the University of Akron.

Lana Krievis teaches in the Covina Valley School District, Covina, California.

Ann Watts Pailliotet teaches at Whitman College.

David B. Pushkin teaches at Montclair State University.

Marge Scardina teaches in the Dade County Public Schools, Miami, Florida.

Ladi Semali teaches at Penn State University.

Lourdes Diaz Soto teaches at Penn State University.

Patrick Slattery teaches at Ashland University.

Rebecca McElfresh Spehler is a doctoral student at Ashland University.

John A. Weaver teaches at the University of Akron.

Nina Zaragoza teaches at Florida International University.

INDEX